World Religions
and
their Beliefs System

World Religions and their Beliefs System

Dr Shiv Shanker Tiwary

MD Publications Pvt Ltd
New Delhi
www.mdppl.com

Published by :

MD Publications Pvt Ltd
"MD House", 11, Darya Ganj,
New Delhi - 110 002
Phone : +91-11-41563325 (Customer Service)
+91-11-41562846 (Editorial)
E-mail (orders): order@mdppl.com
Website: www.mdppl.com

ISBN: 978-81-7533-229-4

Published and Printed by Mr. Pranav Gupta on behalf of **MD Publications Pvt Ltd** at Times Press, New Delhi.

PREFACE

A number of modern scholars of religion have commented on the difficulty of defining what religion is. Over the centuries, influential thinkers have offered their own definitions, with greater or lesser degrees of assurance, but virtually all of these definitions have been found wanting by the majority of scholars. In some cases the definitions are too narrow, defining religion in terms of the speaker's religious beliefs or those of his or her culture and tending to exclude the religious beliefs of other cultures. In other cases the definitions are so vague and inclusive that they do not sufficiently delimit religion from other areas of human thought such as psychology, law, economics, physics, etc.

Religion originates in an attempt to represent and order beliefs, feelings, imaginings and actions that arise in response to direct experience of the sacred and the spiritual. As this attempt expands in its formulation and elaboration, it becomes a process that creates meaning for itself on a sustaining basis, in terms of both its originating experiences and its own continuing responses.

The people of ancient cultures, in their perpetual struggle to explain their existence and the world around them, developed complex religious ideologies that were based most often in mythology. The majority of the religious belief systems of the ancient world were polytheistic, with specific environmental events such as rain and wind believed to be the result of the current will or mood of an individual god or goddess.

The gods and goddesses that were believed to be

responsible for various aspects of the human experience differed among the civilizations of the ancient world. The importances of the mythological gods were determined by their place in an intricate hierarchical order, usually based upon the influence of the individual deities upon the daily lives of ancient peoples. Individual deities were often depicted as having human characteristics both physically and emotionally and were believed to exercise great influence over almost every aspect of ancient life.

I am very grateful to Mr. Pranav Gupta, Director of MD Publications Pvt Ltd, New Delhi, for his kind cooperation and support for this book.

Dr Shiv Shanker Tiwary

CONTENTS

1

World Religions
An Introduction

Many say the etymology of religion lies with the Latin word religare, which means "to tie, to bind." This seems to be favored on the assumption that it helps explain the power religion has. The Oxford English Dictionary points out, though, that the etymology of the word is doubtful. Earlier writers like Cicero connected the term with relegere, which means "to read over again" (perhaps to emphasize the ritualistic nature of religions?). Some argue that religion doesn't really exist — there is only culture. Jonathan Z. Smith writes in Imagining Religion:

"...while there is a staggering amount of data, phenomena, of human experiences and expressions that might be characterized in one culture or another, by one criterion or another, as religion — there is no data for religion. Religion is solely the creation of the scholar's study. It is created for the scholar's analytic purposes by his imaginative acts of comparison and generalization. Religion has no existence apart from the academy."

It is true that many societies do not draw a clear line between their culture and what scholars would call "religion." This does not mean that religion doesn't exist, but it is worth keeping in mind that even when we think we have a handle on what religion is, we might be fooling ourselves. Definitions of religion tend to suffer from one of two problems: they are either too narrow and exclude many belief systems which most agree are religious, or they are too vague and ambiguous, suggesting that just about any and everything is a religion.

A good example of a narrow definition is the common attempt to define "religion" as "belief in God," effectively excluding polytheistic religions and atheistic religions while including theists who have no religious belief system. A good example of a vague definition is the tendency to define religion as "worldview" — but how can every worldview qualifies as a religion?

Some have argued that religion isn't hard to define and the plethora of conflicting definitions is evidence of how easy it really is. The problem lies in finding a definition that is empirically useful and empirically testable. So far, the best definition of religion I have seen is in The Encyclopedia of Philosophy.

It lists traits of religions rather than declaring religion to be one thing or another, arguing that the more markers present in a belief system, the more "religious like" it is:

- Belief in supernatural beings (gods).
- A distinction between sacred and profane objects.
- Ritual acts focused on sacred objects.
- A moral code believed to be sanctioned by the gods.
- Characteristically religious feelings (awe, sense of mystery, sense of guilt, adoration), which tend to be aroused in the presence of sacred objects and during the practice of ritual, and which are connected in idea with the gods.
- Prayer and other forms of communication with gods.
- A world view or a general picture of the world as a whole and the place of the individual therein. This picture contains some specification of an overall purpose or point of the world and an indication of how the individual fits into it.
- A more or less total organization of one's life based on the world view.

- A social group bound together by the above.

This definition captures much of what religion is across diverse cultures. It includes sociological, psychological, and historical factors and allows for broader gray areas in the concept of religion. It's not without flaws, though. The first marker, for example, is about "supernatural beings" and gives "gods" as an example, but thereafter only gods are mentioned. Even the concept of "supernatural beings" is a bit too specific; Mircea Eliade defined religion in reference to a focus on "the sacred" and that is a good replacement for "supernatural beings" because not every religion revolves around the supernatural.

This is the definition of religion used here. It describes religious systems but not non-religious systems. It encompasses the features common in belief systems generally acknowledged as religions without focusing on specific characteristics unique to just a few.

World Religions

From the earliest known evidence of human religion by Homo Sapiens Neanderthalensis around 100,000 years ago to the present day, religion continues to be a very influential aspect of human lives. Today, there are numerous challenges and problems faced by humans from every possible background, location and social class. Every day people must face issues of health, safety and mortality. It is because of these daily challenges that religion continues to exist. Religion is the universal tool for explaining things which we do not understand through the context the known physical world.

Although there are countless religions, each different from the other, they all serve the same purpose. Each answers questions which all humans seem to be programmed to ask: Why are we here? What happens when I die? How shall I live my life? Religion helps us to transmit our values from one generation to another, and influences the way we interact with the natural environment. It teaches us how to see ourselves in light of the universe and gives purpose and meaning to life.

The following pages serve as a brief introduction to several world religions. They are intended to to whet your appetite for further study and to help you understand those around you better. With our global society, it is likely that in your lifetime you will meet people from every corner of the planet. Understanding the religious beliefs of these people is one of the many steps which mankind must take in order to someday prosper together in peace.

Thoughts on Religions and on Belief Systems

1. How much the various secular belief systems have in common with religious belief systems.
2. How important aspects other than beliefs are to the systems.

Examples of Belief Systems

It seems like we encounter quite a number of secular belief systems, such as:

1. The Oil Drum and our message.
2. Contemporary economic theory (several different flavours).
3. He who dies with the most toys wins.
4. Beautiful bodies are everything.
5. Technology will solve all problems.
6. Anthropogenic global warming (AGW).
7. Beliefs of a political party.
8. Permaculture can save the world.

Role of a God

A god is anything that one attaches supreme importance to. Money can be a god. In fact, in "contemporary economic theory" and in "he who dies with the most toys wins," money becomes a god. In "technology will solve all problems," science becomes a god. In "beautiful bodies are everything," perfect bodies become a god. I don't think that a belief system necessarily has to have a god, although it will have some articles of faith. On The Oil Drum, it is an article of faith that geological limits are of supreme importance in determining the future flow of oil. When someone (like me) suggests that this may be trumped by the indirect influence of the financial system, this is viewed as a form of heresy by some. Anthropogenic global warming has as its central belief, the belief that man caused recent changes in climate. There are different flavors of this belief system, depending on whether one believes that one can change the course of events, and if so, what needs to be done.

Writings or Stories Underlying the Belief System

The Oil Drum has its series of posts. There are also related writings by people at the various ASPO organizations, and by people like Matt Simmons. Not all of these writings would be viewed as being equally true by Oil Drum readers; some are even contradictory. The Oil Drum belief system is constantly being refined and added to. Each of the other belief systems, as well as the religions, has its own set of stories or writings, generally by several authors. Not all are viewed equally true or important. In the "He who dies with the most toys wins" belief system, additional chapters are added each week in slick magazines advertising the things that a person must have to impress others. With enough repetition, those who adhere to a belief system consider the belief system's major points to be true and important.

Filter for Viewing what Happens in the World

The world is a mysterious place. Since ancient times, people have been putting together stories to try to explain their understanding of how the world operates and what it truly important. In many ways, each of these (and other) belief systems provides a way of viewing the world and determining what is truly important to our existence. To some extent, these belief systems also provide a view as to what future outcome is likely. This outcome may vary depending on what actions we take (reduce carbon dioxide emissions; increase fuel efficiency; initiate free trade; fund enough scientific research; perform the right rituals).

The belief systems also provide sayings and understandings that filter how we view the world. "The Lord is my Shepherd, I shall not be in want," can be viewed in many ways. It can be taken to mean that there is a God who will stop AGW and will stop any problem with oil supply (as well as any other problem). I personally don't consider this be a valid interpretation, since clearly the world is full of problems, and so far, no being has intervened to stop them, even for the very religious. The Lord is my shepherd statement can also be taken as a way of viewing the world: there is no need for concern about tomorrow, because we each have the resources we need to face the challenges ahead. We need not waste our energy on worry.

View of How we Treat Others

Religions probably excel in this area, with lots of sayings like, "Love your neighbor as yourself," "Honor your father and mother," and "Do unto others as you would have them do unto you." Modern economic theory gives another view of how we treat each other. Whatever provides the most profits is "best." If this can be done by reducing the wages of workers, so be it. Even at The Oil Drum, we have both a written and an unwritten code of how we treat each other. There is a precedent for civil discussions, and everyone knows that Leanan (or someone else) will delete their posts, if they start behaving in too abusive a manner.

Circle of Friendships

Each group has its own organizations, where one gets together with other like-minded people. If one is concerned about AGW, one can joint the local Sierra Club, and work together with like-mined individuals. If one believes a beautiful body is all important, there are gyms and health food stores that one can become associated with. In a business community, one is likely to encounter a huge number of people believing contemporary economic theory. If a person raises doubts about its truth, one risks ostracism from the group.

The Oil Drum has its own online circle of friendships. Staff members particularly communicate frequently with each other. We also have quite a number of regular commenter, whom all of us look forward to hearing from. It is this circle of friendships that is part of the reason that adopting new belief systems is difficult. If all of our friends believe one way, it is difficult to change our belief system.

Reconciling Different Belief Systems

Each of us is likely to end up adopting at least some parts of different belief systems. Sometimes there are conflicts–what is important to one, is not necessarily as important to another. The friendship groups may be different. The way of acting may be different. Probably the first step in reconciling belief systems is stopping to realize that there are a multitude of different belief systems "out there". One could quite easily come to the belief that He who dies with the most toys wins is such a statement of truth, that one need not even question it. It isn't a religion, is it? So what is there to question?

At the same time, it is easy to disregard religions, because they seem to be carryovers from a pre-scientific era. We all know the world most likely wasn't created in seven days, and that "be fruitful and multiply" doesn't make sense is a day of modern medical treatment and overpopulation But the unlimited growth preached by economists doesn't make any more sense, and it was developed much more recently.

Each of us needs to make our own choices regarding belief systems and religions. I am probably one of the few religious folks on The Oil Drum staff–not necessarily because I believe that the church's teachings are "true" in a scientific sense. I come from the liberal end of religious belief–the Bible (and religious books of other religions) have worthwhile things we can learn, especially with respect to how we treat others and how we view the world. The collection of writings is not literally true. It is more a collection of stories that have been passed down through the ages that we can learn from.

In the next few years, it is likely that some form of relocalisation will be needed. In the USA, churches may be good centers for this type of activity, because many people are already members of a church, and have many friends there.

(In Europe, I would expect the situation to be different.) This reason, apart from any other, might be a reason why some Oil Drum members might want to join a church (or other local religious group), even if a person doesn't agree with all of the beliefs. I personally would have difficulty with the more conservative religious groups, because I would have difficulty with many of their teachings. But even these groups have value for their members, providing a network of friendships and shared values.

Belief Systems

Religion, apparently banished from the world by reason, now threatens us with a global war. We can throw up our hands in horror, or we can throw them up in prayer; but it might be more useful to try and understand why this has happened, and what are the features of religion that make it so strong and so resilient, even in technologically advanced countries. To do this, we need science humble enough to recognise that the first and biggest problem is that religion does not exist. There is no more a thing called religion that can be studied than there is a thing called life. In particular, there is no definition that will encompass religion and exclude everything that is not religion. The chief reason why people can never say that religion is "really" anything else is that it isn't, really, anything to start with.

There is another reason: the most popular atheist myths about religion are just demonstrably false. There is the theory that religion is a device for giving us what we cannot have, whether it be freedom from death, or other forms of existential anxiety: that it is, essentially, a giant apparatus of wish-fulfillment. Yet plenty of religion has existed without belief in the afterlife, and certainly without any belief in any afterlife that would be better than what we have now. There is no afterlife in the Old Testament and no one could regard the Greek afterlife - as a twittering grey shade, yearning for blood to drink - as anything other than a horrible fate which would come to everyone, irrespective of their merits.

Such a view depends on an extraordinarily narrow and parochial view of what religions are: monotheistic, literate, with priests and leaders, and, best of all, sacrifices. This looks very like a 19th-century Protestant's idea of Roman Catholicism. It doesn't look like any of the religions or spiritual practices of the hunter-gatherer tribes from which we evolved; and, while I suppose that the Pope might feel that human history was all a dress rehearsal for the emergence of the Vatican, it seems an odd claim for atheists to make.

There's a theory that seems to get away from this and finds the lowest common denominator of religion in spiritual impulses, which can in turn be regarded as something that goes on in the brain, perhaps a malfunction in a temporal lobe, so that the beatific vision could be induced by a man with a kind of hairdressers' helmet hooked up to an MRI machine in a lab in Montreal. The simple observation that disproves this is that almost all religious revivals start in devout societies where people have kept their faith without any spiritual experiences, while night shelters of any large city are full of people who talk to God all the time, out loud, and hear his voice answering very clearly.

Some arguments are more sophisticated. The French anthropologist Pascal Boyer thinks that the problem of explaining religious belief is essentially the problem of explaining superstition. If we knew why people believe in things that aren't there, we would have solved it. Boyer started his career as an anthropologist among the Fang of Cameroon. Among other things, they believe that any man of exceptional power or vigour has an invisible organ in his stomach, the evur, which can, when necessary, leave his body and fly by night to suck the blood of rivals. He had been trained in Cambridge by Jack Goody, an anthropologist who believed in human nature.

He thought that the ways that cultures persist must reflect the ways that our minds work. It is a very curious feature of religions that they tend to stay stable: the same stories are passed down for generations pretty much unchanged. So what is it that makes some stories easier to tell, and transmit to your children, than others? Among the Fang, he came to believe that myths, like language, flourish because of the way that our minds have evolved. No one has to explain all the features of a religious belief for it to spread and be repeated, any more than children need written and explicit grammars to speak grammatically. In fact, in some respects the anthropologists' codifications of mythology are just as misleading a guide to the ways that people actually believe as a travellers' phrase book is to the way that we actually speak.

But there is a huge difference, in Boyer's account, between the brain structures involved in language and those that determine which myths are memorable. The language areas have, presumably, been selected because they are good at language. You can talk about genes "for" language; but there aren't any genes "for" the experience of God. The features of our brains that determine which religions make intuitive sense need not have been selected at all. Superstition, and spiritual experience, could be simply side effects of the ways that our minds work towards more important ends.

However, it is not just agency that we naturally ascribe to gods or spirits. They don't just do things. We also believe that they have ideas and beliefs about the world, and this is a generalisation of a faculty that social animals need. They need to assume that the animals around them have minds and purposes as well as appetites. In particular, if we are to be successful users of language we have to be able to estimate what other people know about the world, and what they don't know. Otherwise, we can neither sympathise nor lie successfully. We can't even tell when other people are lying to us.

The most important of these is the tendency to see purpose in the world. This operates far below the level of conscious apprehension. If we see something moving, we think it's alive. It's obvious that this is going to be highly developed in all animals, since; in general, it is the bits of the world which are alive that they need to pay attention to if they want to eat or to avoid being eaten.

Just as obviously, we see a lot more life than there really is in the world: that is why even the crudest video games immediately make sense. It is probably not a coincidence that so many visions come from the desert places. The sheer blank lifelessness of the surroundings may well provoke us into seeing pure agency where there is nothing.

The ability to understand the workings of other's minds seems quite fundamental to any belief in Gods or spirits. To this extent, any novelist has to have the equipment of a theologian. He must be able to know what his characters are thinking; but also what each character knows and believes about the other characters' motives and, finally, what the reader believes about it all. This is three or four layers of understanding: not just that other people have ideas about the world, but they have ideas about each other's view of the world. In War and Peace, when the vile Hélène is tricking Pierre Bezukhov into marriage, we readers have to know many things to understand what's going on: we have to know that she knows some of what she's doing, that her mother knows more but conceals this from her daughter, that Pierre knows less, that his friends know more but feel they can't tell him - and Tolstoy himself must have understood our understandings of all this, and manipulated them, without showing any strain at all. Without that very sophisticated theory of mind the plot makes no sense. It lacks, as we say, realism.

What relevance has War and Peace to the Fang belief in mobile, invisible organs of the stomach? The answer is that supernatural beings, even supernatural organs, also have a theory of mind: they have beliefs about what we believe. This is not to say that they know everything, nor even that they can't be fooled: Jehovah, walking in the Garden of Eden in the first version of the Genesis story, is a good example of a supernatural agent whom Adam could hope to fool. But all divinities have ways of finding out the sort of information that gives then an edge: the stuff we would like to conceal. In Boyer's theory, the divinities we believe in are better poker players than we are.

There's some perverse evidence for this in the fact that the Gods of believers are not omniscient in the way that the God of philosophers is, and interesting experiments have been conducted to prove this. For instance, if you ask whether God knows if you steal a bar of chocolate from a refrigerator in an empty room, of course He does. But does He know whether the chocolate bar was on the left or the right of the shelf? Here people hesitate a long time. Logically, the questions seem quite equivalent: if God sees you lifting the chocolate bar, then he sees where on the shelf you lifted it from. But if omniscience is about detecting guilt and not about detecting facts, then the details of the crime don't matter. And this is what children's intuitions tend to show.

Believers in religion frequently argue that morality proceeds from religious belief: Boyer points out those moral sentiments perfectly well exist and flourish in societies that have more or less abandoned religion, such as those of Scandinavia. "Moral intuitions don't come out of moral codes. They develop very early in children, who understand that moral questions are about cooperation, and about constructing coalitions. Even four-year-olds have a good grasp of the distinction between moral rules and social convention. The difference is that a social convention is not violated if there was no explicit convention, but moral rules can be broken even if no one told you not to break them. Four-year-olds have the intuition that there are circumstances in which it is wrong to do certain things even when they have not explicitly been stated."

It may be that people are naturally moral; it may be that they are naturally supernaturalists. But there need be no relation of cause and effect. The faculties that make supernatural belief natural may well have been shaped for other purposes, just as my nose was not shaped to rest my spectacles on. Yet, without a nose on which to rest my spectacles, I would have hard time writing. Supernaturalism, once established, might have arisen as an accident, yet still have effects, in combinations with other things, which are themselves evolutionarily significant, and which would tend to fix it in the population.

Others have tried to rescue the idea of religion by claiming that it describes group behaviour. This can be done with some subtlety. The theoretical biologist David Sloan Wilson argues that religious behaviour persists because it links human beings into coherent and successful groups which can then evolve in competition with other groups. It is certainly the case that societies tend to understand their own ordering in religious terms, rather than looking squarely at the power relations involved. If you want to enforce absolute rules of behaviour, which will always be followed, these need some kind of irrational force that overrides simple reason and Wilson analyses a number of religious rules in terms of their social effects, from a hunter-gatherer tribe in the Malaysian rain forest, which ensures that food is always shared out on egalitarian principles, to the written constitution of Calvin's Geneva, which established a set of tremendously effective totalitarian theocracies.

These, too, had a measurable effect on the survival of the group. In purely demographic terms, the Puritan emigration of English Calvinists to New England was phenomenally successful: the 21,000 English settlers who arrived between 1629 and 1640 had produced 16 million descendants by 1988 and this can't be understood without reference to their religious beliefs. It was their understanding of the Bible which led them to emigrate, and which later determined their practice of universal marriage and their horror of contraception. The Bible, too, justified their slaughter of the existing population.

It is an important part of Wilson's argument that he's concerned with the effects of religious emotion and not how it feels. To take an analogy from sex, it's obvious that the biological purpose of lust is to make babies. We have the emotion because babies are its ultimate result. But the immediate desire is not for babies at all, and in many societies the most powerful argument against sexual intercourse is precisely the thought that babies might come of it. So it may be that the sacred has a biological purpose because one of its effects is to hold groups together. But that wouldn't mean that we want group coherence, consciously or unconsciously. What people want is a common experience of the sacred, which explains why God remains a more popular object of veneration than the United Nations.

Yet even when the theory is this large, there doesn't seem to be anything distinctively religious about it, or else football fans would be religious - they too are driven by an irrational common purpose that binds them together and leads them towards self-sacrifice; few religious mortifications could be worse than the discomfort and boredom of watching a football match and then listening to people talking about it afterwards. But Nick Hornby and the late Pope John Paul II are not equally religious, even if both of them were, or are, depending on whether the Pope is right, football fans.

One might try to combine these two theories of religion into a single whole, arguing that religious belief should appear to science like a complex number which cannot exist without two parts that we call real and imaginary. Science, when it studies religion must take into account both its sociological functions and its psychological ones; and to understand how these two work together on each other. Any particular religion must be specified with reference to both. This is true but I don't think it goes far enough. The range of human societies and their effects on the psychologies of their members is just too great for there to be any single form of social organisation, and thus any single thing called religion, which is found in all of them. Technological revolutions, like agriculture, and writing, fundamentally change the nature of religious beliefs. So does trade.

The shaman drinking reindeer piss to bring back a vision for his tribe is not performing the same functions as a Jesuit missionary at the court of a Chinese emperor in the 16th century. They aren't doing different versions of religion. They are doing entirely different things. Neither is more or less religious than the other. Not to believe in religion is in some ways a more radical step than not believing in God, but it might get us out of rather more difficulties; and it still lets even atheists say, with a clear conscience, Merry Christmas.

2

Religions

A Case Against Belief

In the current and quite popular assessment of religion, there is one thing conspicuously missing: religion itself. It has long been a fashion, and even more so now, to frame arguments against religion in largely scientific language. From that perspective critics are right to expose the inherent falsehood of much that believers claim to be true. The popular argument states that those who do believe in God, or Allah, have fallen "under a spell" worked on them by clever but fraudulent thinkers. Or that religious belief was once useful to the evolution of human culture but is now an impediment to mature societal advance. What is more, believers are not just wrong; they are also dangerous. Here, too, critics have abundant material to target. So-called true believers—those so convinced of the rectitude of their convictions they are eager to die, or to kill, for them—have brought once inconceivable havoc to the human community.

Even a cursory glance at the present conflicts across the globe, executed in the name of religion, seems to justify a twist on the traditional Islamic exclamation, asserting that God is not good. For all of their righteous passion, however, what these critics are attacking is not religion, but a hasty caricature of it. Religion has presented itself in so broad an array of disconnected and unique manifestations across the span of human history that no generalization can conceivably apply to the full variety of its expression. Although the critics in question are for the most part accomplished students of both science and modern society, their interest in the subject of religion seems to have been exhausted by a few initial glances at the actions of several selected groups of avid believers. This is a misfortune. Considering the extent of the chaos attributable to it, a reflective and religiously literate critique of belief is a necessity.

Offering a religious case against belief obviously implies that religion is not strictly a matter of belief. It may come as a surprise that a thoughtful survey of the history of religion provides scant evidence for an extended overlap of the two. Quite simply, being a believer does not in itself make one religious; being religious does not require that one be a believer. This improbable distinction has been hidden by the tenacious notion that religion is chiefly a collection of beliefs. By this account, Hindus have a certain catalogue of assertions to which one must assent in order to take the name for oneself, Jews another. This leads to the absurd perception that one could, for example, come to a full understanding of what it means to be a Jew by carefully listing everything Jews are thought to "believe."

But if a religion is not strictly a matter of believing, what is it? Although Islam and Christianity have been close neighbors for a full fourteen centuries, it is unthinkable that Muslims might occasionally mistake themselves for Christians. There is something in each tradition that definitively sets it off from the other. But what? It might seem reasonable at this point to consult Christians to learn what their religion is at its core, and then turn to Muslims with the same request. After the first few inquiries, we would discover that there is little agreement within Christianity and within Islam as to how the core of each faith is to be articulated. Indeed, this is such an open question that both traditions largely consist in the struggle over what it means to be a Muslim or a Christian.

At the center of each, in other words, is a mystery they

cannot fully comprehend; neither can they cease attempting to comprehend it. They may give this mystery the name "God" or "Brahman" or "Tao," but when we ask for more complete clarification, agreement among them scatters. How then can we say what the Christian religion is when Christians themselves have never been able to do so? Yes, an inclusive definition of religion is out of reach, but to acknowledge that is not to terminate meaningful discussion of the issue. Instead, we must integrate the factor of unknowability into each of our conceptions of religion. This can have a strong effect on our thinking in general: reflecting on the remarkable way the great religions seem to develop an awareness of the unknown keen enough to hold its most ardent followers in a state of wonder, we may begin to acquire the art of seeing the unknown everywhere, especially at the heart of our most emphatic certainties.

This is not just to develop a new intellectual talent, but to enter into a new mode of being, a "higher ignorance." Through higher ignorance, an open-ended dialogue becomes possible. It is the goal of this book to reach beyond the phenomenon of belief not merely to defend the religions but to discover how higher ignorance can inform our most ordinary experience. Far from being a critical failure of religion, valued in this way higher ignorance is the beginning of wisdom.

Religious Case Against Belief

In one respect, it is not a mistake to associate religion with belief. Mystery is difficult to live with, and for some even terrifying. It can often be of great comfort to hide our unknowing behind the veil of a well-articulated belief system. For this reason, the historic religions seem to be a particularly fertile source for absolutisms. But when "true" believers claim that their convictions have been validated by a given religion, they are patently unaware that in doing so they have just rejected it. The certainties that led Christians to the Crusades or Hindus to the universal imposition of a caste system, or Muslims to truck bombs all constitute a repression of the tradition they claim as their own. What is more that the belief systems or ideologies that originate elsewhere—Nazism, Maoism, Serbian nationalism, American triumphalism—present themselves as the equivalent of religion, often taking on its presumed trappings: Nazi ritual, Mao's Little Red Book, the demarcation of sacred soil, the mission of democracy to enlighten a corrupted world.

This should be enough to indicate that the act of belief is highly complicated and richly nuanced behavior. That it consists of an avowed commitment to a set of truth-claims is the least part of it. On closer analysis in the following chapters, we will find that, among other features, belief thrives on conflict, depends on the clarity and restricting power of its surrounding boundaries, has a one-dimensional understanding of authority, possesses a kind of a temporality that denies any possibility of an open history, and builds on a severe form of self-rejection. These are characteristics of belief rarely cited in the general discussion. They appear in sharp profile only when we consider their inherent hostility to religion.

In sum, to counterpoise religion and belief is to make possible a deeper insight into both. Given the violence that originates in the absolutism of belief systems, it is urgent that we come to a more incisive grasp of what is at stake. It is proper to hold belief systems to the most stringent canons of knowledge in all its forms. In the process, however, we must take care not to pitch knowledge against religion, as though one is the violation of the other, for in truth they are in essential harmony. The challenge is not to make religion intelligible but to use knowledge religiously. Aristotle wrote that knowledge begins in wonder. By thoughtfully assessing the unmatched vitality of the great religions, we can begin to see that knowledge also ends in wonder.

Belief Systems

Looking back over the history of the monotheistic religions, one could make a pretty good case for the argument that:

1. They are systems of control used to manipulate groups of people within societies;
2. They are systems of control used to provoke hatred between peoples who worship different aspects of the overall monotheistic theology;
3. They discourage independent thought and critical thinking;
4. They encourage ritualistic behaviour the real meaning of which has been lost and is not understood by the practitioner;
5. They have taken whatever germ of spiritual truth they may have had initially and crushed it;
6. Their impact on human life is overwhelmingly negative.

The foundation of the monotheistic religions are the books of the Jews, works that are claimed to be the word of God himself, but which were more likely to have been artfully cobbled together from various sources during the exile in Babylon to give a common history to disparate tribes. No archaeological work has ever uncovered anything in the way of remains of the supposed Temple of Solomon, nor does it show Jerusalem of the Davidic epoch to be anything more than a "typical hill country village" during the period ascribed to David. You can be certain that both Jewish and Christian archaeologists have been spending years looking for such hard evidence because so much is riding on the find, but they have found nothing to confirm the glorious tales of David and Solomon as told in the Bible.

If the historical veracity of the great kingdom of David goes down the drain, the rest of the Bible goes with it. But the Temple is not the only historical problem. The story of Moses and the slavery of the Jews in Egypt appear to have been a rewriting of events that occurred during the time of Akhenaton, perhaps mixed with the history of an exodus from Egypt that occurred much earlier. The curious result of accepting the Bible as history is that it is then used to date Egyptian dynasties, usually by Christians from Europe who had a vested interest in making Egyptian history fit the

"Biblical record". As result of this, the dating of the reign of Akhenaton is several hundred years after it is most likely that he lived. Events of Akhenaton's rule appear to us to match the period of the eruption of Thera on the island of Santorini which has been dated to 1628 BC. For more information on these topics, we refer you to The Secret History of the World by Laura Knight-Jadczyk.

The Old Testament is not history, it is fantasy. What about the history of Jesus? Was there an historical figure from Nazareth who was crucified by the Romans, whose story is accurately recounted in the Gospels? No.

Textual analysis of the gospels shows us that they were put together at different times and for different audiences. They were based upon an earlier document, known as *Q*, that collected the sayings of a Cynic-like teacher. The earliest documents mention nothing of the crucifixion, nothing of the life of the man behind the teachings. That story, in other words, "the historical Jesus", was put together much, much later, and there exists no historical evidence from the period that would independently confirm the gospel stories. All we have to go on are the religious texts of Christianity itself, which as we have seen from the Jewish texts, are being promoted by people with a vested interest in the outcome of the debate.

Islam claims to be a further development of the same tradition. Yet if the historical basis for the first two has been shown to be invalid, then the religion of the sons and daughters of Ishmael is also deprived of its foundations. All three appeal to a divine source, a source that cannot be put into question by mere mortals. Their authority rests upon this divine source and the belief that the texts are literally "the word of God". The literal believers of the Word of God, be it the Judaic, the Christian, or the Islamic, are put into a corner because modern archaeological and textual research have removed the foundations of their belief systems, and we know what happens when someone is backed into a corner and is given no way out. They will fight to the death to preserve themselves. And since each version of monotheism invalidates its predecessor, they must fight each other as well as that modern demon, secular society.

There is something about our root systems of belief, and this extends beyond religion to the modern, rational forms of belief such as humanism, or certain forms of belief in science or even democracy, that they seem to us both self-evident and unquestionable. To question the basis of our beliefs is to put ourselves as individuals into question because we identify so strongly with them. A fervent evangelical Christian could no more put this system of ideas and beliefs into question than could the Pope, the settlers in the occupied territories killing Palestinians to steal their land, an imam in a Moslem country, or Richard Dawkins at his desk at Oxford.

However, we see that these beliefs are constantly under attack because the mere existence of another system claiming the same status as final arbiter of behaviour, custom, and thought, and therefore, of identity, is a threat. There can only be one absolutist position, one place at the top of the pyramid, one boss. Therefore, the true believer must draw around himself a line in the sand that circumscribes Truth, within which stand the faithful, and outside of which are found the pagan, the heathen, the non-believer. Here we find a second level of identification, a negative form of "all that I am not" whereby one takes all attributes of "good" and "holy" for oneself and assigns the opposite attributes to the Other, to those outside of the circle. Having done this calculation, it is then very easy for the believer to be manipulated into believing that the other is less-than-human. Such demonisation is necessary during periods of conflict and war. When the two sides have thoroughly demonised the opponent, they will stop at nothing, no humiliation, no form of torture or brutality, because inflicting such punishment is a way to reinforce one's own special ness.

This process is repeated by each and every member of any absolutist belief structure, which means just about every person on the face of the planet. No wonder things are such a mess. In the seventeenth and eighteenth centuries with the rise of rationalism in the West, the religious structure began to be replaced by the scientific mindset which displaced the Earth from the centre of the universe, posited the existence of other worlds in the Cosmos, and proposed that mankind, rather than being created in the physical image of God, was the result of a long process of evolution from simpler forms of life. The Word of God as transcribed in the Bible was put into question. Identification with national structures became more and more pronounced, so that one's nationality took precedence over one's common religious affiliations in many Western countries.

To reconcile the religious and the national, politicians would claim that God was on their side. Many Jews continue to place their tribal or religious affiliation before their national identity, while among the Arabs; there is still a strong pan-Arab sentiment that is closely tied in with Islam. Against the modern way of structuring the world arose the first forms of modern Christian fundamentalism, an attempt to return to the old days of certainty and unquestionable rules, coupled with the fervent belief that no matter the trials and tribulations in the here and now, there was a better world awaiting in the hereafter for those who maintained their faith in the face of their earthly suffering.

In Arab countries, the existence of corrupt, secular states that were beholden to Western interests laid the groundwork for the rise of calls to a return to traditional Islam, or the return to Islamic law, the Sharia. Here, religious, national, and pan-Arabic structures all come into play because with globalisation, Western customs are imposed, in this case, with appeals to the divinity of "the market", and traditional ways of life, which may only be tangentially linked with Islam, are lost.

This interweaving of different levels heightens the tensions. The ruthless use of force on the part of Israel, the United States, and their allies in imposing the belief structures of "the market", Judaism, or Christianity on the Arab and

Muslim people calls forth a resistance. This reaction is normal and quite mechanical.

Newton described it in his third law of dynamics: for every action, there is an equal and opposite reaction. When one body exerts a force on another, the second body exerts on the first a force of equal magnitude in the opposite direction. We should therefore not be surprised that there is a reaction on the part of Muslims to the modern Crusade launched by Bush and his neocon friends. As this reaction is easily predictable, the next step is for the aggressor to seek to control it. We know that American intelligence agencies were in Afghanistan while the Russians were there, supporting the Islamic "freedom fighters". This was, of course, before these same people became "terrorists" after the Russians were expelled. There are sites that offer evidence that British intelligence has long been connected with the Muslim Brotherhood in Egypt. None of this should be surprising.

It simply makes sense from a strategic point of view for the occupier to infiltrate and seek to manipulate the resistance. While we may appear to have moved away from our initial discussion on religion, it should be clear that religion is a powerful motivator because it appeals to absolutes. Things are always all or nothing. One is saved or one is not. One is a believer, or one is an infidel. It is a zero-sum game where only one player can win, and every gain for one player means a loss for another player.

Clearly, the only way out of this impasse is to get rid of such belief structures altogether, but as they are so tightly bound with our ideas of who we are, as they are the foundations of all we think and believe, the work of rooting them out can only take place one individual at a time. Such work cannot be imposed on anyone because it would then become nothing more than the replacement of one structure by another, based upon an appeal to the authority of the one with the power to impose it. Rooting out belief structures must be done by each of us, at our own speed, motivated by an internal drive to be free. Only then can we put our basic assumptions into question. A group of like-minded individuals is also necessary because we often are blind to the deepest of our beliefs. They are so "self-evident" that we don't see them. But, here again, the group is not there to impose its point of view.

It exists to help us free ourselves and find the answers for ourselves, or to be able to admit where there is not enough data in hand to come to a response and so the answer must be held in abeyance. Such a liberatory structure is more a method than a system of answers because any answer has the potential to be revised when new data arrives. Furthermore, the more we learn, the more we learn how to learn so the method itself is open to constant improvement. In short, nothing is fixed except the direction we wish to move. When we start, we may not even know enough to have more than an intuition of what the destination is like. We do not have the knowledge to judge it or to know it in detail beforehand.

But of one thing we can be certain from observation: the monotheistic religions are traps. Judaism, Christianity, and Islam are walls we erect within us to keep us apart and above others on the ladder of power. Whatever spiritual truths they hold come from a far older tradition, one that encouraged people to see the world objectively and free from the type of all-encompassing explanatory and belief structures these religions have become. It is likely that these religions arose in opposition to this older tradition, as means of coopting it and turning its deeper, spiritual truths into a tool for power in the material world. The first step to the spiritual life is the renunciation all forms of belief systems, and that includes religion.

Major World Religions

Major world religions have been distinguished from minor religions using a variety of methods, though any such division naturally reflects a particular bias, since many adherents of a religion are likely to consider their own faith "major". Two methods are mentioned in this article, number of adherents and the definitions used by classical scholars of religions.

Defined by Population

One way to define a major religion is by the number of current adherents. Population numbers by religion are computed by combination of census reports and population surveys (in countries where religion data is not collected in census, for example USA or France), but results can vary widely depending on the way questions are phrased, the definitions of religion used, and the bias of the agencies or organizations conducting the survey. Informal or unorganized religions are especially difficult to count.

This listing does not draw distinctions between organized religion, which has a single belief code and religious hierarchies, and informal religions, such as Chinese traditional religions, which are a mix of different folk religious ideas.

1. Christianity 2.1 billion
   - Roman Catholicism: 1.1 billion
   - Protestantism: 350 million
   - Eastern Orthodoxy: 240 million
   - Anglican: 84 million
   - Oriental Orthodoxy, Assyrians, and other Christians: 350 million
2. Islam 1.3 billion
   - Sunnism: 940 million
   - Shi'ism 170 million
   - Sufi, Ibadiyyah, Ahmadiyyah, Druze and other Muslims
3. Secular/Irreligious/Agnostic/Atheist 1.1 billion
4. Hinduism 900 million
5. Chinese traditional religion 394 million
   - Not a single organized religion, includes elements

of Taoism, Chinese folk religion, and traditional nonscriptural religious observance.

6. Buddhism 376 million
    - Mahayana: 185 million
    - Theravada: 124 million
7. Primal indigenous 300 million
    - Not a single organized religion, includes a wide range of primarily Asian traditional or tribal religions, including Shamanism and Paganism.
8. African traditional and diasporic 100 million
    - Not a single organized religion, this includes traditional African beliefs such as Yoruba as well as diasporic beliefs such as Santeria (which itself draws from Catholicism) and Vodoun.
9. Sikhism 23 million
10. Juche 19 million
    - Not considered a religion by adherents, who view it as secular and anti-revisionist. Juche is the political ideology of the Workers Party of Korea, the ruling party of the DPRK; some have argued it constitutes a religion due to its Great Leader Worship characteristics. The number is approximately the entire population of the country.
11. Spiritism 15 million
    - Not a single organized religion, includes a variety of beliefs including some forms of Umbanda.
12. Judaism 14 million
13. Bahá'í Faith 7 million
14. Jainism 4.2 million
15. Shinto 4 million
16. Cao Dai 4 million
17. Zoroastrianism 2.6 million
18. Tenrikyo 2 million
19. Neopaganism 1 million

20. Unitarian Universalism 800,000
21. Rastafari movement 600,000
22. Scientology 500,000

Organized Religions by Population Ranking

The Christian Science Monitor used a separate standard, examining only organized religions. The newspaper listed the following in 1998 as the "Top 10 Organized Religions in the World" based on descending level of population:

1. Christianity
2. Islam
3. Hinduism
4. Buddhism
5. Sikhism
6. Judaism
7. Bahá'í Faith
8. Confucianism
9. Jainism
10. Shintoism

Historic Classic View

Major religions have also been identified based on their perceived importance, whether theological or temporal. This sorting has been generally been the preserve of Western, Christian scholars, so lists of classic major religions betray this bias. Early Christian scholars, the earliest known classifiers of major religions, recognized only three religions: Christianity, Judaism, and Paganism (which they considered to encompass every other religion). Views evolved during the enlightenment, however, and, by the 19th century, Western scholars considered the five major religions to be Judaism, Christianity, Islam, Hinduism, and Buddhism. As the exposure of Westerners to other religions increased, five other religions were added to the original five: Confucianism, Taoism, Jainism, Shinto and Zoroastrianism. Later, the Bahá'í Faith was added to this list, resulting in eleven classic religions:

- Bahá'í Faith
- Buddhism
- Christianity
- Confucianism
- Hinduism
- Islam
- Jainism
- Judaism
- Shinto
- Taoism
- Zoroastrianism

Modern Western definitions of major religion come from the classical definition, often expanding on "Christianity," and omitting Jainism and Zoroastrianism. An example is this list found in the New York Public Library Student Reference:

- Bahá'í Faith
- Buddhism
- Catholicism
- Confucianism
- Hinduism
- Islam
- Judaism
- Orthodox Eastern Church
- Protestantism
- Shinto
- Taoism

Hinduism

Hinduism is the predominant religion of the Indian subcontinent. Hinduism is often referred to as Sanâtana Dharma, a Sanskrit phrase meaning "the eternal law", by its adherents. Hindu beliefs vary widely, with concepts of God and/or gods ranging from panentheism, pantheism, monotheism, polytheism, and atheism with Vishnu and Shiva being the most popular deities. Other notable characteristics include a belief in reincarnation and karma, as well as personal duty, or dharma. Among its roots is the historical Vedic religion of Iron Age India, and as such Hinduism is often stated to be the "oldest religious tradition" or "oldest living major tradition." It is formed of diverse traditions and types and has no single founder.

Hinduism is the world's third largest religion after Christianity and Islam, with approximately a billion adherents, of whom about 905 million live in India. Other countries with large Hindu populations can be found across southern Asia. Hinduism's vast body of scriptures are divided into Shruti ("revealed") and Smriti ("remembered"). These scriptures discuss theology, philosophy and mythology, and provide information on the practice of dharma (religious living). Among these texts, the Vedas and the Upanishads are the foremost in authority, importance and antiquity. Other major scriptures include the Tantras, the Agama, the Puranas and the epics *Mahabharata* and *Ramayana*. The *Bhagavad Gita,* a treatise from the *Mahabharata,* spoken by Krishna, is sometimes called a summary of the spiritual teachings of the Vedas.

Hinduism is unique among the world religions in that it has no founder or date of origin. While most major religions derive from new ideas taught by a charismatic leader, Hinduism is simply the religion of the people of India, which has gradually developed over four thousand years. The origins and authors of its sacred texts are largely unknown. Although today's Hinduism differs significantly from earlier forms of Indian religion, Hinduism's roots date back as far as 2000 BC, making it one of the oldest surviving religions. Because of its great age, the early history of Hinduism is unclear. The most ancient writings have yet to be deciphered, so for the earliest periods scholars must rely on educated guesses based on archaeology and the study of contemporary texts.

In the last few decades, the history of India's religion has also become a matter of political controversy. The history of any nation (or individual) is an important part of its self-identity, and this is especially true of India, which so recently gained independence after centuries of colonial rule. The controversy over India's history centers on the origin of the Aryan culture.

The Term Hinduism

The English term Hinduism was coined by British writers in the first decades of the 19th century and became familiar as a designator of religious ideas and practices distinctive to India with the publication of books such as *Hinduism* (1877) by Sir Monier Monier-Williams, the notable Oxford scholar and author of an influential Sanskrit dictionary. Initially it was an outsiders' term, building on centuries-old usages of the word *Hindu*. Early travelers to the Indus valley, beginning with the Greeks and Persians, spoke of its inhabitants as "Hindu" (Greek: *'indoi*), and, in the 16th century, residents of India themselves began very slowly to employ the term to distinguish themselves from the Turks.

Gradually the distinction became primarily religious rather than ethnic, geographic, or cultural. Since the late 19th century, Hindus have reacted to the term *Hinduism* in several ways.

Some have rejected it in favour of indigenous formulations. Those preferring *Veda* or *Vedic religion* want to embrace an ancient textual core and the tradition of Brahman learning that preserved and interpreted it. Those preferring *sanatana dharma* ("eternal law") emphasize a broader tradition of belief and practice (such as worship through images, dietary codes, and the veneration of the cow) that is not necessarily mediated by Brahmans (members of the highest social class who are usually priests).

Still others, perhaps the majority, have simply accepted the term *Hinduism* or its analogues, especially *Hindu dharma* (Hindu moral and religious law), in various Indic languages. Since the early 20th century, textbooks on Hinduism have been written by Hindus themselves, often under the rubric of *sanatana dharma*. These efforts at selfexplanation have been intended to set Hinduism on a par with other religious traditions and to teach it systematically to Hindu youths. They add a new layer to an elaborate tradition of explaining practice and doctrine that dates to the 1st millennium BCE.

The roots of this tradition can be traced back much farther—textually, to the schools of commentary and debate preserved in epic and Vedic writings from the 2nd millennium BCE; and visually, through artistic representations of yakshas (luminous spirits associated with specific locales and natural phenomena) and nagas (cobralike divinities), which were worshipped from about 400 BCE. The roots of the tradition are also sometimes traced back to the female terracotta figurines found ubiquitously in excavations of sites associated with the Indus valley civilization (3rd–2nd millennium BCE) and sometimes interpreted as goddesses. In recognition of this ancient tradition of selfexplanation, present-day Hindus often assert that theirs is the world's oldest religion.

General Nature of Hinduism

More strikingly than any other major religious community, Hindus accept—and indeed celebrate—the organic, multileveled, and sometimes internally inconsistent nature of their tradition. This expansiveness is made possible by the widely shared Hindu view that truth or reality cannot be encapsulated in any creedal formulation, a perspective expressed in the Hindu prayer "May good thoughts come to us from all sides." Thus, Hinduism maintains that truth must be sought in multiple sources, not dogmatically proclaimed.

Anyone's view of the truth—even that of a *guru* regarded as possessing superior authority—is fundamentally conditioned by the specifics of time, age, gender, state of consciousness, social and geographic location, and stage of attainment. These multiple perspectives enhance a broad view of religious truth rather than diminish it; hence, there is a strong tendency for contemporary Hindus to affirm that tolerance is the foremost religious virtue. On the other hand, even cosmopolitan Hindus living in a global environment recognize and value the fact that their religion has developed in the specific context of the Indian subcontinent. Such a tension between universalist and particularist impulses has long animated the Hindu tradition. When Hindus speak of their religious identity as *sanatana dharma*, a formulation made popular late in the 19th century, they emphasize its continuous, seemingly eternal (*sanatana*) existence and the fact that it describes a web of customs, obligations, traditions, and ideals (*dharma*) that far exceeds the Western tendency to think of religion primarily as a system of beliefs. A common way in which English-speaking Hindus often distance themselves from that frame of mind is to insist that Hinduism is not a religion but a way of life.

It has been pointed out by Dr. Arnold J. Toynbee, in A Study of History, that the principal civilisations of the world lay different degrees of emphasis on specific lines of activity. Hellenic civilisation, for instance, displays a manifest tendency towards a prominently aesthetic outlook on life as a whole. Indian civilisation, on the other hand, shows an equally manifest tendency towards a predominantly religious outlook. Dr. Toynbee's remark sums up what has been observed by many other scholars. Indeed, the study of Hinduism has to be, in a large measure, a study of the general Hindu outlook on life.

Receptivity and all-comprehensiveness, it has been aptly stated, are the main characteristics of Hinduism. Since it has had no difficulty in bringing diverse faiths within its ever-widening fold, it has something to offer to almost all minds. Monier-Williams in his notable work Brahmanism and Hinduism dwelt on this aspect about a hundred years ago. The strength of Hinduism, he emphasized, lies in its infinite adaptability to the infinite diversity of human character and human tendencies.

It has its highly spiritual and abstract side suited to the philosopher; its practical and concrete side congenial to the man of the world; its aesthetic and ceremonial side attuned to the man of the poetic feeling and imagination; and its quiescent contemplative aspect that has its appeal for the man of peace and the lover of seclusion. The Hindus, according to him, were Spinozists more than 2,000 years before the advent of Spinoza, Darwinians many centuries before Darwin and Evolutionists many centuries before the doctrine of Evolution was accepted by scientists of the present age. No civilisation anywhere in the world, with the probable exception of China, has been as continuous as that of India. While the civilisations of Egypt, Babylon and Assyria have disappeared, in India the ideas emanating from the Vedic times continue to be a living force.

European scholars of Sanskrit like Sir William Jones noted similarities in the languages, terminology and substances of Indian scriptures with those of Greece and Rome. Even a superficial study convinced them that, while the language of the Vedas is a great critical instrument in the construction of the science of philology, the Vedic hymns constitute a compilation of most Indo-European myths in their primitive form. Max Muller went so far as to say that the Vedas are the real theogony of the Aryan races, Homer and Hesiod having given a distorted picture of the original image.

The excavations at Harappa and Mohenjo-daro and those in Saurashtra have disclosed the existence of a highly evolved culture long before the Aryan immigration, perhaps dating back to 3000 B.C. or later. Among the remains discovered are three-faced prototypes of Siva seated in a yogic posture, representations of the Linga, and a horned goddess associated with the pipal tree.

These symbols, evolved by a very ancient civilisation, were assimilated by the Aryan immigrants in slow stages-their earliest literary work, the.Rig Veda, almost overlooks these aspects. The Vedic Aryans, it has been suggested, partly assimilated and partly destroyed the earlier culture.

Vedic Aryans and Zoroastrianism

It seems clear from the hymns of the Rig Veda and the Persian Gathas and Avesta that the Vedic Aryans and the

Zoroastrians had a common origin. The languages in which Zoroaster preached and the Rsis sang their hymns are almost identical, and Vedic meters are re-produced in the Avesta. Evidently, the two groups of Aryans separated after a violent quarrel, so that several deities of one group - Indra or Jindra, Sarva and Nasatya - were transformed in the other into evil spirits. It is, however, to be noticed that Mitra, Aryama, Vayu and Vrtraghna are divine in both the systems. A period of unity was probably followed by civil war, as envisaged in the fight between Asuras and Devas.

The Vedic Aryans were warlike, while the Avesta reflects an abhorrence of war. In the period when the ancestors of the Iranians and the Hindus had lived together, Asura had been a term of honour; and the Zoroastrian Ahura Mazda was Asura Mahat, the great Asura. The Rig Veda (III-55-11 & 15) cites several Asura qualities of the Divinities. Varuna, Mitra and several other gods were called Asuras. Later, when differences were accentuated between the two communities, Asura became equivalent to a spirit of evil and Sura came to signify a good spirit. The undivided Indo-Iranians must have passed a long time in their Central Asian home. The Indo-Iranian culture and religion have been reconstructed, at least in part, by comparing the Vedas with the Avesta.

Before the occupation of Iranian high lands by tribes from the Indo-Iranian original home, the plateau was the seat of a culture that was probably matriarchal, and the people worshipped snake-gods in the manner of India's primitive non-Aryans. It is likely that the pre-Aryan cultures of North-western India and Iran were alike in origin and spirit. This ancient cultural link between pre-Aryan Iran and pre-Aryan India, instead of getting strengthened by Aryan migration into the two countries, as could be normally expected, was to all appearances completely severed. Also, there is nothing to show that the Vedic Aryans of India maintained an active cultural relation with their brethren in Iran. In the earliest days, while the Aryans of India must have been connected with the Aryans of Iran as friends or as foes, actual historical contact cannot be asserted with any degree of probability.

The two peoples turned their backs upon each other, as it were, and developed their distinctive civilisations apparently without the least mutual influence, although in language, culture and religion their similarity in the earliest period had been little short of identity.

When, later in history, under the Achaemenids, Greeks, Bactrians and Sakas, the Iranians and the Indians were forced to meet as citizens of the same empire, they met as complete strangers, not as cousins or as scions from the same stock. The earliest literary productions of the Aryan settlers in India were the Rig Veda, Sama Veda (consisting of chants), Yajur Veda and the Atharva Veda (a composite religious and magical compilation) The Vedas comprise Mantras (hymns), Brahmanas (ritual and ceremonies), Aranyakas (forest speculations) and the philosophical Upanisads. In the context of this commonly accepted interpretation of the Vedas, it may be recalled that European Orientalists have too often considered them mainly from the theological, anthropological and sociological points of view. A study of the material in its religious aspect is difficult, since even the great commentary of Sayana is in terms of the ideas of his own age. On the presumption that the Vedas originated in primitive times, the Rig Veda hymns were regarded as the outpourings of child-like nature worship.

John Dowson in his Hindu Classical Dictionary observed: "The Aryan settlers were a pastoral and agricultural people, and they were keenly alive to those influences which affected their prosperity and comfort. They knew the effects of heat and cold, rain and drought, upon their crops and herds, and they marked the influence of warmth and cold, sunshine and rain, wind and storm, upon their own personal comfort. They invested these benign and evil influences with a personality; and behind the fire, the sun, the cloud, and the other powers of nature, they saw beings who directed them in their beneficent and evil operations. To these imaginary beings they addressed their praises, and to them they put up their prayers for temporal blessings. They observed also the movements of the sun and moon, the constant succession of day and night, the intervening periods of morn and eve, and to these also they gave personalities, which they invested with poetical clothing and attributes. Thus observant of nature in its various changes and operations, alive to its influences upon themselves, and perceptive of its beauties, they formed for themselves deities in whose glory and honour they exerted their poetic faculty."

But on a careful analysis of the Vedas it would be apparent that the Vedic view is more subtle and deeper in concept. The One Being whom the sages call by many names (Ekam-sat) is referred to in the neuter gender, signifying divine existence and not a divine individual. The monotheistic God stands in relation to man as a father and a patriarch, while in a Rig Veda hymn to Agni he is called "my father, my kinsman, my brother and my friend". Monotheism, it has been aptly stated "contemplates the Divine in heaven and polytheism contemplates the Divine in the universe. Polytheism believes in the assembly of gods, each possessing a character of his own. Max Muller coined the word henotheism for indicating the tendency of the Vedic seers to magnify the importance of the particular deity they are praising in a hymn at the expense of the other gods. This has been described as "opportunist monotheism". One deity is identified with another or different deities are identified with one divine entity, indifferently described as Ekam (one) and Tat Sat (the reality).

Vedic Concepts

Apart from these concepts, there are two basic ideas underlying the Vedas - Satya (truth) and Rta (eternal order); and every god or goddess exemplifies and represents these two ideas. As Abinash Chandra Bose says in his Call of the Vedas, Vedic theism is based on moral values which (also in the case of Buddhism) may be upheld in a nontheistic way. In India it is not the atheist who is denounced but the person who repudiates Dharma, moral law. The Rig Veda (X-85-1) states that the earth is sustained not by the will of God but by truth, and of this truth God is the supreme exponent, revealing Himself through Rta or eternal order. Examining the Vedic hymns as a whole, one discovers a doctrine, not of oneness, but of one divine substance pervading all. It is stated that the One Being is contemplated by the sages in many forms: Ekam santam bahudha kalpayanti (Rig Veda, X-114-5). It may also be observed that the Vedic ritual or Yajna is a uniform ceremonial; whatever deity is worshipped, the ritual is the same.

The universality of the Vedas is not often realised. The Rig Veda asserts that God is the God of Dasa as well as of Arya - "Lord God is he to whom both Arya and Dasa belong". (Rig Veda, Vlll-51-9). There is a special prayer for the forgiveness of sins against the foreigner (Rig Veda, V-35-7). According to the Atharva Veda, God is of the foreigner (Videsya) no less than of our own land (Samdesya). There are mantras which extend This principle to all living beings (sarvani bhutani) (Yajur Veda, 36-18) so that we come to a grand conception of universal peace and serenity - the harmony with Nature (sarvam santhi) (Yajur Veda, 36-17).

Many Schools of Thought

Panini is one of the world's earliest as well as the greatest of scientific grammarians. The consensus of opinion fixed his date not later than the 5th century B.C. At that period Yajna or sacrifice and the worship of various deities were current and popular, and theistic devotion to particular divinities, generally expressed by the term Bhakti, had become prevalent. Panini refers to Vasudev as the object of devotion, and Paramatma Devata Visesa, a form of the One Supreme Divinity. The doctrine which assumed great importance later - that custom has the force of law - is also exemplified by the twofold meaning, in Panini's Astadhyayi, attached to Dharma. Dharma is not only equivalent to Rta, primordial law, but also denotes custom (acara) as in the later Dharma Sutras.

Already in Panini's days different schools of thought had arisen, both theistic and non-theistic. A non-theistic doctrine described in Buddhist philosophy as the doctrine of non-causation and also as the doctrine of Yadrccha- (fortuitous accident), was current in Panini's time. That all existence was the result of chance was the doctrine of the Ahetuvadins. The Svetasvatara Upanisad which advocates the doctrine of the supreme spirit refers to other varieties of thought like those of the advocates of Svabhava or materialistic philosophy. Orthodox thought was later developed in the Samkhya philosophy and attained its climax in the Vedanta Sutras. Panini refers to Parasara Sutra, one of the earliest of the Vedanta treatises, and also to the atheistic school, known later as the Lokayata. There is mention also of Nihsreyasa which, in the Upanisads, denoted supreme bliss as also of Nirvana, possibly associated with Buddhism. From all these examples it is clear that, in the times of the Buddha and Panini, practically all the varieties of speculation which have flourished in India had already evolved.

Philosophical discourses and pursuits were at first specially developed by the Ksatriyas, but they soon became the prerogatives of the Brahmins. The Chandogya and Kausitaki Upanisads illustrate these successive stages. A solution of the ultimate problems of life is outlined in the early Upanisads, and it takes the form of Monism, absolute (according to Sankaracarya) or modified (according to Ramanuja). Filled with zeal for this doctrine of the Unity or Interdependence of all life, a social order was founded. Dr. Ananda Coomaraswamy in his Dance of Shiva says that the great Epics represented the desired social order as having actually existed in the golden past; they put into the mouths of their heroes not only the philosophy but the theory of its application in practice. This is evident, above all, in the long discourse of the dying Bhisma in the Santiparva of the Mahabharata.

"The heroes themselves they made ideal types of character for the guidance of all subsequent generations; for the education of India has been accomplished deliberately through hero-worship. In the Dharmashastra of Manu and the Arthashastra of Chanakya - perhaps the most remarkable sociological documents the world possesses -they set forth the picture of the ideal society, defined from the stand point of law. By these and other means they accomplished what has not yet been effected in any other country, in making religious philosophy the essential and intelligible basis of popular culture and national polity".

What, then, is this view of life? The inseparable unity of the material and spiritual world is made the foundation of Indian culture and that determines the whole character of Indian social ideals. Later Hindu thought is founded on the rhythmic nature of the world process, including evolution and involution, birth, death and rebirth, srsti and samhara. Every individual life - mineral, vegetable, animal, and human- has a beginning and an end; this creation and destruction, appearance and disappearance, are of the essence of the world process and equally originate in the past, present and future. According to this view, then, every individual ego (jivatman) or separate expression of the general will to life (icchatrsna) must be regarded as having reached a certain stage of its own cycle.

This is also true of the collective life of a nation, a planet or a cosmic system. It is further considered that the turning point of this curve is reached in man and hence the immeasurable value which Hindus (and Buddhists) attach to birth in human form. Before the turning point is reached - to use the language of Christian theology - the natural man prevails; after it, the regener man. To sum up, Indian philosophic thought developed in several stages. The Vedic period is generally placed between 2500 B.C. and 600 B.C. As already indicated, the four Vedas, the Bramanas, Aranyakas, and Upanishads are creations of the early sages.

The Upanishads

The Upanishads are diverse in character and outlook. They recognize intuition rather than reason as a path to ultimate truth. They also represent a strong reaction against the merely ritual and sacrificial duties on which stress had been laid earlier. The Upanishads are supposed to be 108 or more in number. Twelve of them are generally recognized as the principal units. The Isa Upanishad begins with the statement that whatever exists in this world is enveloped by the Supreme. It is by renunciation and absence of possessiveness that the soul is saved. In the Kena Upanishad, the Goddess Uma Haimavati in the form of Supreme Knowledge expounds the doctrine of the Brahman or Supreme Entity. The Katha Upanishad embodies the aspiration of Naciketas, who declined his father's offer of property and went into exile, making his way to the region of Yama, the God of Death. Naciketas, in his dialogue with Yama, declines all the worldly possessions and dignities offered by Yama and asserts that all enjoyments are transient and the boon he asks for is the secret of immortality. In This Upanishad occurs the famous saying "The knowledge of the Supreme is not gained by argument but by the teaching of one who possesses intuition."

In the Mundaka Upanishad occurs the verse which is the germ of the Bhagavad Gita. People who perform actions and are attached to the world are pursuing a futile path, and this Upanishad accordingly declares: "Let the wise man, having examined the world and perceived the motives and the results of actions, realize that as from a blazing fire sparks proceed, living souls originate from the indestructible Brahman and return to Him. All doubts disappear and the attachment to work subsides when the Supreme Being is cognized."

These basic doctrines are further expounded in the Taitiriya Upanishad, which contains This famous verse repeated in other Upanishad: May we both (teacher and disciple) be protected; may we both obtain sustenance; let both of us at the same time apply (our) energies (for the acquirement of knowledge); may our reading be illustrious; may there be no hatred (amongst us). Peace, peace, peace. In the more recent Svetasvatara Upanishad is found a summary of the main Upanishadic doctrines, and the idea of devotion to a personal God is also developed. The Chandogya Upanishad, one of the earliest, states that the main doctrines of the Upanishads, were first expounded by the Kshatriyas and not by the Brahmins. Later, as is evident from the Kausitaki Upanishad, the Brahmins took up the intensive study of philosophy. The contrast which is often drawn between Brahminism and Hinduism is therefore not based on a right appraisal of the facts.

The Epics

The period of the Epics succeeded the period of the Upanisads. In the Ramayana and the Mahabharata, philosophical doctrines were presented in the form of stories and parables. In these poems of the heroic age recounting the qualities and exploits of exalted individuals the Vedic gods are no longer supreme. Some have disappeared altogether. Indra retains a place of some dignity; but Brahma, Shiva and Vishnu have risen to preeminence. Even of these three, the first becomes subordinate. Vishnu and Shiva become the outstanding entities and are alternately elevated to supreme dignity and very often their ultimate oneness is proclaimed. Vishnu in the Vedas was the friend and companion of Indra and strode over the universe in three paces; in the Epics he often becomes the great deity of destruction as well as of renovation. Each of these two gods in his turn contends with and subdues the other; now one, now the other, receives the homage of his rival; and each in turn is lauded and honoured as the greatest of gods.

The Avatars

The Avatars, incarnations of Vishnu, assume a prominent place in the Epics, and more so in the Puranas. The first three, Matsya (fish), Kurma (tortoise) and Varaha (boar) have a cosmic character and are foreshadowed in the hymns of the vedas. The fourth incarnation, Nrsimha (man-lion), seems to belong to a later age, when the worship of Visnu had become established. The fifth, Vamana (dwarf), whose three strides deprived the Asuras of the domination of heaven and earth, is in character anterior to the fourth Avatara and the three strides are attributed to Vishnu in the Vedic text as Urukrama, the sixth, seventh and eighth, Parashurama. Ramchandra and Krishna, are mortal heroes whose exploits are celebrated in these poems so fervently as to raise the heroes to the rank of gods.

The ninth Avatara, the Buddha, is the deification of a great teacher. The tenth, Kalki, is yet to come; he resembles the manifestation referred to in the Biblical Revelation. The system of religious thought propounded in the Vedas and the Epics and especially in the Bhagavad Gita (a part of the Mahabharata) survived the Buddhist impact which led to a renunciation of much ritual and metaphysics on the part of a sizable proportion of the population. Buddhism was absorbed into the parent religion within a few centuries and Hinduism, as the Vedic religion had come to be called, adopted the theory of the Avataras or incarnations according to which the Buddha himself was accepted as Avatara. Jainism also became, in essence, a doctrinal modification and adaptation of the Vedic religion.

Dr. Toynbee has noted, in response to an ever more insistent craving in Indic souls to apprehend the unity of God, the myriad divinities gradually dissolved and colesced into one or other of the two mighty figures of Shiva and Vishnu. He adds that this stage on the road towards the apprehension of the unity of god was attained at least 1,500 years ago.

Buddhist Influence

We now come to the greatest contribution made by the Buddha to Indian thought and world culture. Dr. Radhakrishnan, in his edition of 'Dhammapada" (which embodies Buddhist teachings), has stated that, judged by intellectual integrity, moral earnestness and spiritual insight, the Buddha is undoubtedly one of the greatest figures in history. The same scholar pointed out that, altough ther were different streams of thought operating on men's minds in the 6th century B.C. philosophic thought was agreed at that time on certain fundamentals. Life does not begin at birth or end at death; it is a link in an infinite series of lives each of which is conditioned and determined by act done in previous existences. Relief from the round of births, resulting in life in eternity is the goal, indicated by such terms as Moksa (deliverance) and Nirvana (union with the Brahman). The means of attainment are prayer and worship; ritual and sacrifice; and Vidya (realization by knowledge).

Even though the Buddha accepted the doctrines of Karma

and rebirth and the non-reality of the empirical universe, he declined to speculate on Moksa and on the doctrine of the Atman and Paramatman. He laid stress on the supremacy of the ethical aspect, and his outlook was definitely practical and empirical. In fact, the Buddha did not tolerate any doctrines which, he thought, diverted the mind from the central problem of suffering, the cause of suffering and its removal, and the urgency of the moral task. He rejected the doctrine of the Vedanta that the ego is permanent and unchanging. At the same time, he did not countenance the view that, at death, it is destroyed. As Dr. Radhakrishnan says, the Buddha came to the conclusion that interest in the super-natural diverts attention and energy from the ethical values and the exploration of actual conditions: Karma builds the world and Dharma is an organic part of all existence.

The Bhagavad Gita

Every variety of Hindu philosophy has its source in the Upanisads, the Brahma Sutras of Badarayana of Vyasa and the Bhagavad Gita which forms a part of the Mahabharata. It was as a reaction to the tendencies exhibited by Buddhism and Jainism that the orthodox schools of Indian philosophy had their origin and the Bhagavad Gita is their epitome. This work contains the essence of Indian teaching about the duties of life as well as spiritual obligations. Everyone has his allotted duties of various kinds.

Sin arises not from the nature of the work itself but from the disposition with which the work is performed. When it is performed without attachment to the result, it cannot tarnish the soul and impede its quest. True Yoga consists in the acquisition of experience and the passage through life in harmony with the ultimate laws of equanimity, non-attachment to the fruits of action, and faith in the pervasiveness of the Supreme Spirit.

Absorption in that Spirit can be attained along several paths; and no path is to be preferred exclusively and none to be disdained. These doctrines have been interpreted as marking a Protestant movement which lays stress on the personality of God and His accessibility to devotion. While following the Hindu ideal of the Asramas, the Gita emphasizes the importance of knowledge, charity, penance and worship, and does not decry life as evil:

"Nor indeed can embodied beings completely relinquish action; verily, he who relinquisheth the fruit of action, he is said to be a true relinquisher."

The Dharma Shastras

Later, treatises on ethical and social philosophy known as the Dharma Sastras were compiled; they deal systematically with the proper conduct of life and describe social, ethical and religious obligations. The Sutras, of which the Brahma Sutra is the chief, are brief aphorisms or maxims. They contain interpretations of philosophic systems and refutations of opposing beliefs. It is remarkable that all philosophical systems in India are known as Darsanas, literally meaning calling insights or points of view. In the well known Sarvadar sanasangraha compiled by Madhavacarya, a great successor of Sankaracarya, the Carvaka or atheistic school, Buddhism, Jainism, the Vaisnava philosophy of Ramanuja and Madhva, the Shaiva system and several other doctrinal variants, are all described as Darshanas and as legitimate developments of Hindu thought: There are Sutras dealing with the Logical Realism of Nyaya, the Atomistic Pluralism of Vaisesika, the Evolutionism of Samkhya, the tech nique of Mind-control or Yoga, the ritualistic philosophy of Purva-Mimamsa and the metaphysics of Vedanta which attained its climax in the work of Sankara.

The Puranas

The Puranas cover the intermediate period between the Vedic and the Classical epochs. Cast in the form of parables and narratives, they became the scripture for the common people. Apart from their religious and often sectarian significance, they furnish a picture of social, political and cultural life and comprise an astonishingly varied repertory of folklore and information regarding diverse topics including philosophy, ethics, legal institutions, popular festivals, and several arts; they deal even with subjects like grammar, prosody, rhetoric, archery and care of horses and elephants; many of them also describe places of pilgrimage. At one time their historical value was discounted; but it is now being gradually appreciated.

Fusion with Non-Aryans

The Aryans marched en masse, guided by a leader who was often a poet, and came into contact with the Dasas and the Dasyus. The point to be noted is the speedy fusion of the Aryans with the non-Aryans. The process had three phases:

1. The elevation of non-Aryans and aboriginals by intermarriages with Aryans.
2. The incorporation of non-Aryans into Aryan society in various other ways.
3. Social reactions by which forms of life and modes of thought of the two groups under went a kind of osmosis, intensified by the Buddhist protestant reformation.

The Aitareya Brahmana gives an example of the manner in which progressive leaders of the Aryans facilitated the assimilation of other communities. An Rsi was performing a sacrifice on the banks of the Saraswati; and to this sacrifice was admitted one Kesava Ailusa, a Shudra, whose learning is stated to have put all the Brahmins to shame. The Vajasaneyi Samhita condemned intercommunal marriage, but it is narrated in that work (ch. 23, 30 and 31) that a Sudra was the lover of an Arya woman. By the time of the Mahabharata such great personages as Vyas and Vidura were described as the offspring of the connection of the Aryans with other groups. The story of Santanu and Satyawati, the vow of Bhisma as well as the story of Ambika and Ambalika and the birth of Vidura, also illustrate the above process.

Again, in the Mahabharata, it is narrated that Bhima married Hidimbi, a non-Aryan woman, and Arjuna married a Naga girl, Ulupi. A new class of Aryans called Utkrsta came into existence, and was admitted to the privileges of sacrifice. By the time of the Satapathabrahma Shudras became incorporated in the polity - a notable instance being the Nisadas. It is a curious fact (vide Panini's Grammar, ch. VI, 62, 58) that there were non-Aryan Brahmins as well.

Parasara, one of the great sages of India, married Satyavati, a fisher girl, who became the mother of Vyasa, the compiler of the Mahabharata and the Puranas. Such intermarriages or unions were frequent all through Indian history. Emperor Candragupta Maurya who belonged to a lower caste, married Kumara Devi of the Licchavi clan, who was either a Brahmin or a Kshatriya, and she was the grandmother of Ashoka.

It should be remembered that the groups which crystallized later into the Indian castes were initially not based on any gradation of superiority, the difference being functional rather than racial or communal. These groups, moreover, had their analogues in the Avesta, and the Iranian names do not suggest the idea of colour or superiority. Cooperation of all the classes was needed for administration, and a passage in the Mahabharata indicates that the King's Council included representatives of all classes of the people.

The current rigidity of the rules relating to intermarriage as also interdining among the Indian castes is a comparatively recent innovation. These lines found in several Puranas are significant: "The great sage Vasistha was born of a divine courtesan, but by austerity and penance he made himself recognized as a Brahmin. The transforming process was attained by self-imrovement." Another passage says, "Vyas was by birth a fisherman, Parasar was born in a dog-eating tribe, many non-Dvijas have in the past attained Brahmanhood by their merit." The Bhagavad Gita affirms: "Castes developed according to the differentiation of Guna and Karma", i.e., disposition or temperament and inherited instincts or aptitudes.

Both among the old Iranians and the Aryans of India the original caste system of three classes based on the practical distritution of functions was in existence. The Iranians, however, did not develop another class as the Hindus did - the Shudra. Clearly, the three Hindu caste divisions were not unalterably rigid. The definition of the word Dvija, twice-born, makes the position clear. Dvija is a person who has certain basic qualities: "If a man's activities be derived from his jati or birth, from his, occupation, from study and knowledge, and if all these are found combined, then he is to be called a Dvija, and not otherwise".

Cultural Synthesis

In their great trek to India the colonizing groups of Aryans encountered races who professed a firm belief in the doctrine of transmigration. It has indeed been suggested that this doctrine of metempsychosis itself, the cult of serpent worship, the worship of Ganesha, of Uma or Durga, of Skanda or Subrahmanya (the hunter-god) were all adopted by the Aryans from earlier settlers in India. Even the incarnation of Krishna, it has been said, was an adaptation from an aboriginal deity; his life is an instance of the mingling of the Aryans and the Yadavas. In any case, it seems clear that there was a good measure of synthesis of the thoughts and beliefs of the Aryan and pre-Aryan races.

There are widespread traditions of the southern migration of the Vedic sage, Agastya, the reputed author of several hymns of the Rig Veda. His asrama was located south of the Vindhyas; and he is said to have introduced the Vedic religion and literature in the South in his capacity as a uniifying factor between the Sanskritic and Dravidian tongues and ideals. When the Aryan colonisers in the wake of Agastya penetrated to the South, they found an advanced civilisation. The Ramayana describes Madurai as adorned with golden jewels. The grammarian Katyayana mentions the Pandyas and the Colas. Asoka's Buddhist missions were sent to the Pandya and Cola countries as far as Tamrapani River in the Tirunelveli District. An extensive commercial and cultural inter course grew up between the Aryans and the Dravidians, as also between the Dravidians and countries to the east and west of India.

The close contact between the Aryan and Dravidian elements continued all through history and manifested itself in every aspect of life. There is strong ground for the supposition that the importance of Shiva, Shakti and Skanda was due largely to Dravidian influence, since the cult of An (Shiva), Amma (Shakti) and Anil (Muruga or Skanda) was a cardinal belief from the beginning of Dravidian history.

These facts illustrate the composite character of Hindu civilisation. The Sama Veda spoke at length of the Vratyastoma (a particular sacrifice or ritual) by which non-Aryan Vratyas were admitted into Aryan society. The equalization of castes and communities was, of course, brought to a head by Gautama Buddha, though he was no opponent of the Brahminical civilisation. Both he and Mahavira, the expounder of Jainism, while admitting that the Brahmin ideal is the right one, led a crusade against certain aspects of Brahmin culture. Hindu civilisation itself adapted for its use many ideals and precepts of Buddhism and Jainism. For instance, among many communities, offerings of rice and ghee took the place of animal sacrifice - a compromise with the Vedic ritualism. The early Aryans had, of course, been meat-eaters, but probably under the influence of Buddhist and Jain ideas many groups of Brahmins as well as non-Brahmins became vegetarian.

Vaishnavism in the South

At a later period arose the fully organized Bhakti movement leading to Vaishnavism and Shaivism. The ancient Vaishnava mystics and saints in the South were known as Alvars, and the Vaishnavism teachers as Acaryas. They had a powerful exponent of these views in Ramanuja, who attacked the Advaita interpretation of the Upanishads and gave recognition to three ultimate realities, God, Soul and Matter, the last two being dependent on the first. As early as the 2nd century B. C. the renowned Besnagar Column had been erected by a Greek named Heliodorous, who had been converted to the Bhagavata or Vaishnava faith of which the Pancaratra doctrines then formed an integral part; its scriptures were Satvata Samhita, the Mahabharata, and the Bhagavata and Vishnu Puranas.

The origin of the Pancaratra doctrines which form the basis of Srivaishnava culture has been traced further back to the well known Purusasukta of the Rig Veda. The Satapatha Brahmana refers to the Pancaratra sacrifices performed by the primeval Narayana, the idea of Nara and Narayana (Primordial man and the deity Vishnu) being an integral part of ancient Indian thought. There are more than a dozen Vaishnava Upanishads. It was in the period from the 10th century up to the 17th that many Vaisnava works were produccd. The Vaishnavas regard the Pancaratra literature as almost equal to the Vedas.

The Vaishnava Samhitas and other works insist on knowledge of and devotion to, the supreme Godhead rather than on Vedic studies or sacrifices. It is worthy of note that in the Bhagavata Purana (11th Skanda) the Alvars were prefigured or adverted to; several great devotees of Vishnu, the Purana states, would appear on the banks of the Tamraparni, Krtamala (Vaigai), Payasvin (Palar), Kaveri (Cauvery), and Mahanadi (Periyar).

The Alvars lived between the 5th and the 12th centuries. The first group included Saroyogin or Poygaiyal var, Bhatayogin or Bhutattalvar, Mahadyogin or Peyalvr and Bhaktisara or Tirumalisai-Piran. Nammalvar or Satakopa, who came in the next group, was perhaps the greatest of the Alvars. Others in this group included Madhurakaviyalvar, Kulasekhara Perumal, Visnucitta (or Periyalvar) and Andal, his adopted daughter. In the last of the groups were Bhaktanghrirenu (Tondaradippodiyalvar), Yogivahana (Tiruppanalvar) and Parakala (Tirumangaiyalvar). The Divya Prabhandha constitutes the collection of the Alvars' compositions in the Tamil language.

The Advent of Shankara

The next important milestone is the advent of Shankara. In his short but marvelously active life, he travelled all through the country, refuting atheistic and materialistic systems of thought, wrote commentaries on the Upanisads, on the Brahma Sutra and on the *Gita*. He interpreted these scriptures and built up his thesis with wonderful clarity and depth of exposition. He remoulded Indian thought and destroyed many dogmas.

His great capacity for deep feeling and emotional expression was combined with relentless logic. Shankara's contribution to philosophy is his blending of the doctrines of Karma and Maya, which culminated in a logical exposition of the idea of nondualism.

The entire universe consisting of Namarupa, names and forms, is but an appearance; Brahman, infinite consciousness, is the sole reality. Its attainment and the annihilation of the great illusion of the universe called Maya, by a process of realization, were the objects of Sankara's quest. He revivified the doctrines of the Upanisads and, in Dr. Radhakrishnan's words, he was not a mere dreaming idealist but a practical visionary.

His Advaita doctrine is still a living force in India. Shankaracarya established several mathas in India to propagate the Vedantic or Advaita doctrine and the succesive heads of these mathas as well as later scholars like Madhusudana Sarasvati and the great polymath Appayya Diksita have produced important treatises, elucidating the Vedanta as propoundd by Shankaracarya. Shankara's outlook was based strictly on philosophical thought and logic; but even he has, in numerous compositions, dcscribed the supreme entity in a personal aspect as saviour, helper, friend and guide. He wrote poems dedicated to Narsimha, Sri Krishna, Laksmi, and Annapurna, and there is his celebrated lyrical homage to Parvati or Durga - the Saundaryalahari.

Shankara was followed by Ramanuja, Madhva and others who called themselves commentators but were indeed creators of new systems. Ramanuja's philosophy was termed qualified monism and Madhva's was a dualistic system. The three major forms of Vedanta developed respectively by Shankara,

Ramanuja, and Madhva are distinct philosophies, although each professes to have stemmed from the same three sources - the Upanisads, the Brahma Sutra and the *Gita*.

Ramanuja

Ramanuja, of course, was concerned much more with the personal aspect. His teachings may be regarded as a reaction against the tendency to view religion on the intellectual rather than the emotional plane. He assimilated many beliefs of the Dravidian civilisation and helped to encourage and promote temple worship and public festivals. Born early in the 11th century, Ramanuja was deeply influenced by the Tamil saints and Alvars - their ideas coloured his interpretation of the Upanishads and the Brahma Sutra. He put forward a theistic view of the Vedas as against the rigid Advaita point of view of Shankara. Basing his thoughts on Bodhayana and the theistic Upanishads, the Mahabharata (including the Bhagavad Gita), Vishnu Purana as well as the compositions of the Alvars and Acharyas, Ramanuja produced a number of works culminating in the Sribhasya.

He proclaimed the doctrine of salvation through Bhakti or faith. His earlier followers came to be known as Vadagala is. About two centuries later the Tengalais appeared; they, unlike the Vadagalais, did not concentrate on Sanskrit scriptures and traditions and regarded Tamil scriptures as equally canonical. There were several points of difference between Ramanuja and early Vaishnava teachers like Nadamuni and Yamunacarya. One was the importance attached to Swami Kripa, Grace of God. According to one school, this is spontaneous, not depending on any effort or merit of the devotee. The other school asserts that Grace also depends on the devotee's virtuous action.

The religious approach of Ramanuja was mainly based on self-surrender, which must result in universal charity and sympathy, and friendliness even to an enemy. He insisted that the performance of scriptural duties alone was not enough for salvation. Karma Yoga and Jnana Yoga, according to the Ramanuja School, only purify the mind in preparation for

Bhakti Yoga or devotion. Ramanuja's Saranagati Gadya is a notable contribution to the gospel of self-surrender, but it does not rule out caste functions and duties, and the doctrine of Karma.

Vedanta Desika, the greatest successor of Ramanuja, and a strong opponent of Sankara's Advaita doctrine, wrote a very controversial work, Satadusani. Pillai Lokacarya, the famous exponent of the Tengalai School, advocated passive surrender (Praptti) in preference to active faith (Bhakti), and the guidance of a spiritual preceptor, Manavala Maha Muni is the chief Saint of the Tengalais. This school built up a remarkable Tamil literature to which it ascribed an importance equal to that of the Vedas - it was called the Tamil Tirumurai or the Tamil Veda. In essence, however, there was no fundamental doctrinal divergence between the two sects. Differences in certain features such as caste marks on the forehead and temple ceremonials and usage became accentuated in later years.

Successors of Ramanuja

As the ideas of Ramanuja spread through India, men like Madhvacarya, Vallabhacarya, Caitanya, Ramananda, Kabir and Nanak came under their spell. Ramanuja and his followers opposed the doctrine of Maya and the interpretation of the world as purely phenomenal or illusory. They emphasized the distinction between the individual soul and the supreme Godhead and based their philosophy on man's conviction of sin, his responsibility for sin and the importance of grace emanating from the divine. In other words, they believed that salvation comes not specially through Jnana (knowledge) or karma (action), but through Bhakti (faith) and Prasada (grace). The Bhagavata doctrine of complete resignation to God was one of the articles of their faith. God was viewed alterlnately as father, mother, child, teacher and friend, and even as the beloved. Ramanuja declared that caste had nothing to do with the soul's quality; some of the Alvars were in fact non-Brahmins.

Ramanuja is said to have admitted even Harijans to the

temple at Melkote. One of his later followers, Ramananda, who lived in the 13th century, not only protested against caste distinctions but enjoined that no man should ask any devotee about his caste or sect: whoever worships God is God's own. Later followers of Ramanuja included a number of scholars who sustained his philosophic system through the centuries. While accepting the set rituals of initiation and worship, they admitted Jains, Buddhists, Shudras and Harijans into their fold. A celebrated successor of Ramanuja was Nimbarka, who lived about the same time as Madhvacarya. According to his philosophy, which is a type of Bhedabhedavada, that is, the theory of the Absolute as Unity-in-difference, Brahman or the Absolute has transformed itself into the world of matter and spirit.

As the Life-force, Prana manifests itself in the various cognitive sense functions, and yet keeps its own independence, integrity and difference, so the Brahman also manifests itself through the numberless spirits and matter, without losing itself in them. As the spider spins its web out of itself and yet remains independent of the web, so the Brahman splits itself up into numberless spirits and matter but retains its fullness and purity. The reaction against Shankara's Advaitism reached its climax in Madhvacarya's dualistic philosophy. It resembles Ramanuja's doctrine to some extent but stands for unqualified dualism. Madhva, also known as Purnapranjna and Anandatirtha, was born near Udipi in South Kanara in the 12th century. He draws a clear distinction between God and the individual soul, God and matter, individual soul and matter, one soul and another and one variety of matter and another.

Large groups in India follow this doctrine which bases itself on the feeling of absolutc dependence on God and love for Him. Madhvacarya attacked Shankara vehemently on the ground that his philosophy was a disguised variety of Buddhism. It is well known that Sankara was strongly influenced by Gaudapada, who had great regard for the Buddhist philosophy, and it is unquestionable that, while Sankara was opposed to Buddhist thought in general, he was perhaps unconsciously influenced by some of its tenets. Madhva, on the other hand, objected to Advaita: it seemed to him presumptuous for the individual soul to claim identity with Brahman. According to his doctrine, Vishnu is the only Supreme Being; and Bhakti is the primary essential for liberation. Among his great disciples was Purandaradasa, reputed as a social reformer and one of the creators of the Karnataka system of music. Vadiraja, a renowned writer, was another Madhva philosopher.

Vaishnavism in the North

One of the most influential Vaishnava cults was founded by Vallabhacarya, a Telugu Brahmin who lived in the 15th century. He migrated to the North and in his numerous works in the North he gave an interpretation of the Vedanta differing from that of Ramanuja, as also of Shankara. He called his doctrine Suddha Advaita, pure non-dualism. The world is real, and not an illusion. God is Nimitta-Karana, the causative being. Discarding the Maya theory Vallabhacarya asserts that God cannot be described by negatives but only by his holy and gracious attributes, and is personified in Krishna He is not only karta, creator, but also Bhokta, enjoyer.

Though he has no need to assume a bodily form, he often does so to please his devotees. Regarding Bhakti as the chief means of salvation and superior to Jnana, (knowledge) Vallabha opposed all kinds of asceticism. The body is the temple of God, he said. The famous Upanishadic precept Tatvamasi was by an ingenious interpretation, modified by Vallabha as Atatvamasi, "That thou art not". Vallabhacarya's doctrines were fully interpreted and expounded by his son Vitthala.

Later, in Northern India, there arose the Caitanya movement. Nimbarka had already elevated Radha, the consort of Krishna, to the highest position.

Jayadeva, the author of Gita-Govinda, and other poets like Vidyapati, Umapati and Candidas, adopted the Radha-Krishna cult. Caitanya, the great Vaishnava teacher of the 15th century transformed the Vaishnava faith and extended his influcnce in most parts of Northern India. He accepted converts from Islam, the foremost among them being Haridas, Rupa and Sanatana. Salvation, according to his doctrine, consists in the eternal experience of God's love. Caitanya exercised great influence over later Indian thought.

Shaktism

The cult of Shakti or the mother aspect of Godhead had its roots in the Vedas. The Rig Veda describes Shakti as the embodiment of power and the upholder of the universe. Shakti is represented as the sister of Krishna and the wife of Shiva. She is worshipped as Devi, who is one with Brahman.

The literature of Shaktism, called the Tantra, gives a high place to women and reacts strongly against caste distinctions. According to the doctrines of the Shakta cult (embodied in 77 Agamas), Siva or the supreme entity is impersonal and beyond activity. Shankara in his Saundaryalahari declares: "Shiva is able to function when united with Shakti; otherwise he is inert." He Shakta cult and philosophy has had great influence in Bengal and Assam, as well as in Malabar.

A variant of the Shaivite philosophy, which developed in Kashmir, is known as the Pratyabhijna system. Here, as Dr. Radhakrishnan says, Shiva is the subject as well as the object, the experiencer as well as the experienced. "As the consciousness on which all this resultant world is established, whence it issues, is free in its nature, it cannot be restricted anywhere. As it moves in the differentiated states of waking, sleeping, etc., identifying itself with them, it never falls from its true nature as the knower." In theme Godhead rather than on Vedic studies or sacrifices. It is worthy of note that in the Bhagavata Purana (11th Skanda) the Alvars were prefigured or adverted to; several great devotees of Vishnu, the Purana states, would appear on the banks of the Tamraparni, Krtamala (Vaigai), Payasvin (Palar), Kaveri (Cauvery), and Mahanadi (Periyar). The Alvars lived between the 5th and the 12th centuries. The first group included Saroyogin or Poygaiyal var, Bhatayogin or Bhutattalvar, Mahadyogin or Peya is the unchanging consciousness and Shakti its changing power, appearing as mind and matter.

Cultural fusions in the South

Early Indian history cannot be viewed in its true perspective unless the institutions of the South receive adequate treatment. The unity of India transcends the diversities of blood, fusions in colour, language, dress, manners and sects. It is seen in the fusion of Brahminical ideas and institutions with Dravidian cults. This unity, however, has been limited by the later developments of the caste system in a manner different from the original conception which was functional in character and elastic in scope.

A typical South Indian village almost invariably has a temple dedicated to Ayyanar or Hariharaputra or Hanuman or Anjaneya, or Ganesha. On many hilltops there are shrines dedicated to the Devi (Candi) or Kartikeya also named Subrahmanya. These exemplify the tolerant and assimilative outlook of the Aryans. In the context mention has already been made of the Vratyastoma (a particular sacrifice or ritual) by means of which masses of non-Aryans (Vratyas) were admitted into the Aryan society.

According to South Indian tradition, Tamil as first developed by the sage Agastya, to whom a grammar, a treatise on philosophy and many other works are ascribed. The oldest Tamil grammar now extant, the Tolkappiynm, is said to have been the work of one of his disciples. The Shaivite and Vaishnavite revival due to the Brahmins in Southern India, since the 8th century, brought about a counter-movement among the Jains. Early Buddhism in Northern India adopted the Prakrit or vernacular speech for its religious treatises. On the same analogy, Buddhism and Jainism in the South created works in the dialects of the people. The Dravidian Buddhists and Jains created a Tamil literature which was anti-Brahmanical in sentiment; and covered the period between the 9th and 13th centuries.

The Kural of Tiruvalluvar, dating not later than the 10th century A.D. is said to have been the work of a poet belonging to one of the depressed classes. It enforces the Samkhya philosophy in 1,330 poetical aphorisms based on three subjects: wealth, pleasure and virtue. To the sister of its author, the poetess Avvaiyar, are ascribed many compositions of the highest moral tone, and they have enjoyed perennial popularity in Southern India. The Jain period of Tamil literature includes works on ethics. In the same period a celebrated adaptation of the Ramayana was composed in Tamil by Kambar. This is a Tamil paraphrase rather than a literal translation of the ancient Sanskrit Epic.

Between this period and the 16th century, two encyclopaedic collections of Tamil hymns, deeply religious in spirit, were gradually formed. One collection was the work of Saivite devotees and their disciples who sought to uproot Jainism. Vaishnavite apostles of the same period were equally prolific in Tamil religious songs. Their Book of Four Thousand Psalms, Nalayira Prabandham, constitutes a hymnology dating from the 12th century.

Shaivite Sects

The development of Vaishnavism saw a parallel development of the Shaiva theism. A distinctive philosophy of Shaiva Siddhanta was evolved about the 11th century. The Shaiva Agamas were based on the Vedic concept of Rudra. A large number of inspired writers in the Tamil country were headed by Manikkavasagar. All their works have been collected and are venerated by the South Indian Shaivites. The first part of this collection, Tevaram, contains the hymns of Appar, Sambandar and Sundarar. The second part mainly comprises Manikkavasagar's Tiruvasakam. Sixty three Shaiva saints are recognized and their lives are recounted in the Periya Puranam Sekkilar.

Dr. Pope, the well known Tamil grammarian, has stated that Shaiva Siddhanta is one of the most influential and intrinsically valuable of the religious writings in India. The

Saiva Siddhanta recognizes three entities: God, the Soul or the aggregate of souls, and Bondage (Pati, Pasu and Pasa). The expression Bondage denotes the aggregate of the elements which fetter the soul and hold it back from union with God. In one of its aspects it is Malam, the taint clinging to the soul. In another aspect it is Maya, the material cause of the world. The peculiarity of the Shaiva Siddhanta doctrine which calls itself Suddhadvaita is its difference from the Vedanta Monism. God pervades and energizes all souls and, nevertheless, stands apart.

This concept of the absolute is clear from the Tamil word for God, Kadavul, meaning that which transcends (kada) all things and is yet the heart (ul) of all things. When the absolute becomes manifest, it is as Force (Shakti) of which the universe is the product. The Dvaita system, on the other hand, insists on a radical pluralism, and at the same time on the complete dependence of the souls and the world on God. One of the important Shaivite sects known as Virashaiva was founded by a Brahmin named Basava, who was for some time the minister of a ruler in Kalyan. The Basava Purana outlines Basava's life. This is also in Basava's own writings in Kannada describes the fundamentals of a doctrine based on rigid monotheism, Shiva being regarded as the supreme, limitless and transcendent entity.

Brahmana is the identity of "being", "bliss" and consciousness, and devoid of any form of differentiation. It is limitless and beyond all ways of knowledge. It is self-luminous and absolutely without any barrier of knowledge, passion or power. It is in Him that the whole world of the conscious and the unconscious remains, in a potential form untraceable by our senses, and it is from Him that the whole world becomes expressed or manifest of itself, without the operation of any other instrument. The Virashaivas, often called Lingayats, are distinguished by the Shivalinga and rudraksa on their person and they smear their bodies with ashes. They are strict vegetarians and abstain from drink. The Virashaiva doctrine has four schools, but the differences are of a minor kind. All believe in the efficacy of a Guru or preceptor. All assert the reality of the Universe and unity with Shiva, the only ultimate reality. The Virashaiva doctrine is prevalent in Mysore and in the southern regions of Maharashtra.

Great Movements of Reform

Side by side with these philosophical systems, a large body of devotional literature in the spoken languages of India has been developed. This was due to the advent of great reformers- Ramananda, Kabir, Nanak, Mirabai, Vallabhacarya, Caitanya, Tulasidasa, and Tukaram. Ramananda and his Muslim disciple Kabir emphasized the belief in a supreme deity and recognized no caste distinctions, although they accepted the doctrines of Karma and Samsara. Nanak founded the religion of the Sikhs. He was under the influence of Islam as well as of Hinduism and, like Kabir, he believed in Karma and Samsara, Maya and Moksa. He laid great stress on a personal God and a society of disciples not bound by caste or race restrictions. The militant character of Sikhism was a later development due to Aurangzeb's intolerance and persecution. The great saints of Maharashtra and Bengal created a wonderful literature of Bhakti based on the worship of Rama or of Krishna. Vallabhacarya, in particular, attacked Shankara's Advaita doctrine. He preached that by God's grace alone can man obtain release.

Caitanya, a contemporary of Vallabha, and his followers called Goswamis, were itinerant preachers whose sincerity of religious experience brought about a reformation in Bengal. The common features in Bhakti cults have been pointed out by D. S. Sharma in his Renaissance of Hinduism:

1. Belief in one supreme God of Love and Grace.
2. Belief in the individuality of every soul, which is nevertheless part of the Divine Soul.
3. Belief in salvation through Bhakti.
4. The exaltation of Bhakti above Jnana and Karma; and, also above, the performance of rites and ceremonies.
5. Extreme reverence paid to the Guru.
6. The doctrine of the Holy Name.

7. Initiation through a mantra and a sacramental meal.
8. The institution of sectarian orders of Sannyasins.
9. The relaxing of the rules of caste, sometimes even ignoring all caste distinctions.
10. Religious teaching through the vernaculars.

It was out of these Bhakti cults that the Sikh group transformed itself into a military brotherhood. Bhakti cults gave rise to such works as the Ramayana by Tulasidasa, the, Abhanga of Tukaram and the poems of devotees like Ramprasad of Bengal and Tayumanavar of South India and passionate outpouring of Mira Bai. All these helped to popularize the spirit of devotion and resulted in a great religious revival in many parts of India.

3

Renaissance in Hinduism

In the 18th century religion suffered a serious decline mainly because the impact of a completely different civilisation. English education destroyed the isolation of India and brought about an active ferment. Many Indians of the time became either sceptics who leaned towards Christianity, or reactionaries who sought to preserve at any cost the ancient forms and institutions.

Fortunately, at this time, enlightened Europeans like Sir William Jones, Sir Charles Wilkins, Colebrooke, Monier-Williams and Max Muller revealed by comment and by translation the treasures of ancient Indian wisdom. Their work was later supplemented by art lovers and art critics, who revealed the secrets of sacred and secular art-forms and concepts.

As an outcome of these influences and counter-influences, there arose a series of movements which have been rightly described as a renaissance of Hindu life and thought. Raja Ramamohun Roy was the most outstanding pioneer of these movements. He struck a note of universalism in tune with the spirit of the Upanishads. Born in Bengal in 1772, he studied Persian, Arabic and English. In 1803 he published a book in Persian, with a preface in Arabic, entitled Tuhfat-ul-Muwahhidin. It carried a protest against idolatory and sought to establish a universal religion based on the idea of the unity of Godhead.

He started a controversy with the Christian missionaries and published a book in which he tried to separate the moral teachings of Jesus from the miracles described in the Gospels. Rammohun Roy, along with David Hare, stressed the necessity of education in India on modern lines, in opposition to those who objected to English education and insisted on a return to the past.

He repeatedly declared that he had no intention of breaking away from the ancestral religion, and wished to see it restored to its original purity. In order to carry out his ideas he founded the Brahmo Samaj on the basis of theism. The Trust Deed of the Samaj lay down that "no graven image, statue or sculpture carving, painting, picture, portrait or the likeness of anything shall be admitted within the building."

The Brahmo Samaj

Debendranath Tagore, the next great leader of the Samaj, formulated the Brahmopadesa, comprising tenets from the Upanisads and Tantras. His successor, Keshub Chandra Sen, sought to incorporate Christian ideals into the Brahmo Samaj movement. He began the compilation of a scripture including passages from the Holy Books of many religions - Hindu, Buddhist, Hebrew, Christian, Muslim etc. Then he went to England in 1870, he was welcomed by many Christian organizations. As the result of secessions in the Brahmo Samaj, three institutions arose: The Adi Brahmo Samaj; the New Dispensation of Keshub Chandra Sen; and the Sadharan Brahmo Samaj founded by dissenters from the Keshub Church. The Sadharan Samaj, led by Shivanath Sastri and Ananda Mohun Bose, gave a rational, monistic interpretation of the Upanishads, admitting the essential unity of the universal self and the individual self. The following doctrines, as noted in Renaissance of Hinduism are common to all these varieties and offshoots of the Brahmo Samaj:

1. They have no faith in any scripture as an authority.
2. They have no faith in Avatars.
3. They denounce polytheism and idol-worship.

4. They are against caste restrictions.
5. They make faith in the doctrines of Karma and Rebirth optional.

Another offshoot of the Brahmo Samaj, the Prarthana Samaj was founded by Justice Ranade in Bombay. Its programme included disapproval of caste, recognition of widow marriage, and the encouragement of women's education. Dr. Atmaram Pandurang, Pandita Rama Bai, S. P. Kelkar and S. P. Pandit were the principal exponents of this Samaj.

The Arya Samaj

As a reaction against the influences typified by Raja Ramamohun Roy and Justice Ranade, the Arya Samaj was founded by Swami Dayanand Saraswati. It attacked the Brahmo Samaj for its pro-European and pro-Christian attitude. A great Sanskrit scholar and a believer in the doctrines of Karma and Rebirth, Swami Dayanand sought to revive the Vedic ideals and laid stress on Brahmacarya and Sannyasa. He believed implicitly in the ancient scriptures, disavowing Puranic Hinduism in favour of Vedic Hinduism. The Puranic texts, he said, had no Vedic sanction. Holding the Vedas alone as authoritative, he stated that God and the human soul are two distinct entities, different in nature and attributes, though they are inseparable from each other as the pervader and the pervaded.

The doctrine of Karma and Samsara is of course accepted by the Arya Samaj. One of its main activities is Suddhi, a purification ceremony, by which non-Hindus are converted to Hinduism. The depressed classes and Harijans are entitled to be invested with the sacred thread and are given equal status with other Hindus. The Arya Samaj also reclaimed many Hindus who had been converted to Islam and Christianity. Sanghatan, organization of the Hindus for self-defence, is one of the main principles of the Arya Samaj, and it has played its part as the church militant in the Hindu fold.

The Theosophical Society

The Theosophical Society, founded in 1875 by Col. Olcott and Madame Blavatsky, cooperated with the Arya Samaj and tried for a time to organize Indian life on national lines and check the activities of Christian missionaries. Col. Olcott and Madame Blavatsky went later to Ceylon, declared themselves Buddhists, and took part in a movement for the revival of Buddhism. Dr. Annie Besant joined the Society after a period of militant agnosticism, side by side with notable social service, and political work amongst the Fabians in England. She became the head of the Theosophical Society in 1891. Claiming that she had been a Hindu in her former birth, Annie Besant worked throughout her life for the regeneration and activisation of Hindu thought and Hindu life.

She published a translation of the *Bhagavad Gita* along with Dr. Bhagvan Das and popularized Hindu ideals in her numerous publications and marvellously eloquent speeches. A defender of many orthodox ideals, she turned later to social reform, which included the partial modification of the caste system. One of the main principles of Theosophy is the belief in a brotherhood of great teachers of the past who are supposed to be living still, watching over and guiding the evolution of humanity. The Theosophical Society under Dr. Besant's guidance spread the fundamental principles of the Hindu religion - Karma, Reincarnation, Yoga and spiritual evolution.

Sri Ramakrishna and Vivekananda

Sri Ramakrishna Paramhamsa, a great devotee and mystic, had a broad outlook of universalism. After accepting the discipline of Yoga and Tantric Sadhana, he underwent the discipline of the Vaisnava, the Christian and the Islamic ways of life. To rouse the religious feelings of the wordly-minded and reaffirm the ancient truths of Hinduism by an appeal to experience, he trained a devoted band of followers, the most outstanding of whom was Narendranath, Swami Vivekananda. Sri Ramakrishna's teachings were neither new nor heterodox. As Swami Vivekananda said on one occasion,

Ramakrishna brought old truths to light. He was an embodiment of the past religious thought of India. Like other great religious teachers of the world, he projected his ideas through parables or images.

Questioned, for instance, on the problem of evil, Sri Ramakrishna said:" Evil exists in God as poison in a serpent. What is poison to us is not poison to the serpent. Evil is evil only from the point of view of man." In other words, from the absolute standpoint, there is no evil, but from the relative standpoint evil is a terrible reality. Ramakrishna preached that realization is the essence of religion - and that all religions are paths leading to the same goal. He deprecated metaphysical subtleties and insisted on deep devotion - it was, he said, through his intense devotion to the image of the Divine Mother in Dakshineswar that realization had come to him. Swami Vivekananda said:" If men like Sankara, Caitanya and Ramakrishna found image worship helpful, there is no sense in declining it."

Ramakrishna's religion and the movement he founded by gathering around him a band of devoted workers were essentially practical. This aspect was expounded and universalized by Swami Vivekananda. Under the inspiration of Ramakrishna, he changed from scepticism to religious realization and travelled all over the world, preaching the essence of the truths of Hinduism. He dedicated himself to the service of India and particularly to the service of those who were starving, depressed, or beyond the social pale. The work for the uplift of the Indian masses was for him as important as meditation or Yoga.

At the Parliament of Religions in Chicago, Swami Vivekananda struck a note of universal toleration based on the Hindu belief that all religions lead to the same God. He also declared in Chicago that the religion of the Hindus is centered on self-realisation; idols, temples, churches and books are aids and nothing more. Swami Vivekananda strengthened the Ramakrishna organization by founding monasteries and centres of Hindu teaching in India and abroad. He reinterpreted Hinduism and stated that the abstract Advaita must become living. All through his life and especially during his travels abroad, he insisted that the essential features of Hinduism are its universality, its impersonality, its rationality, catholicity and optimism.

Above all, its authority is not affected by the historicity of any particular man. Swami Vivekananda told his countrymen that they had become weak and miserable because they did not bring their Vedanta out of the books into life itself. His great contribution to Hinduism lay in applying the Hindu creed to the elevation of the masses and abolishing India's isolation from the world, culturally, spiritually, and in many aspects of social life. He founded a great and worldwide organization, the Ramakrishna Mission, which has worked for the spiritual welfare and multiform amelioration of the living conditions of the people of India and other countries.

Sri Aurobindo

Sri Aurobindo Ghosh, one of the latest exponents and interpreters of Hinduism, has described ancient Indian philosophy as follows: "an ingrained and dominant spirituality, an inexhaustible vital creativeness and gusto of life, and, mediating between them, a powerful, penetrating and scrupulous intelligence, combined with the rational ethical and aesthetic mind at a high intensity of action, created the harmony of the ancient Indian culture." Sri Aurobindo gave new interpretations of the Vedas and the Vedanta, and in his *Essay on the Gita* he expounded what he called 'the integral view of life." His great work, *The Life Divine,* is a summing up of his philosophy of 'the Descent of the Divine into Matter." The importance of Sri Aurobindo's mission lies not only in his restatements of old ideals but also in his atternpt to explain the true methods of Yoga as apart from mere asceticism and illusionism.

Mahatma Gandhi

In the popularization of ancient Hindu ideals,

Rabindranath Tagore and Mahatma Gandhi have played significant parts. Tagore has made a suggestive interpretation of the Vedic religion and the substance of the Upanisads. The teachings of Mahatma Gandhi have led to vast social changes and to the uplift of the backward and depressed classes. He has stated that his whole religion is based on surrender to the will of God, the spirit of renunciation as embodied in the Isa Upanisad, the *Gita* and the ideals of practical service. He has given a new interpretation to the doctrine of non-violence which is as old as Hinduism, and tried to adapt it by means of Satyagraha to political and moral issues.

Mahatma Gandhi worked for the uplift of the depressed and backward classes and for the creation of national entity. Speaking in Travancore on the Temple Entry Proclamation enacted there in 1936, he said: "These temples are the visible symbols of God's power and authority. They are, therefore, truly called the houses of God,the houses of prayer. We go there in a prayerful mood and perform, first thing in the morning after ablution, the act of dedication and surrender. Scoffers and sceptics may say that all these are figments of the imagination, that we are imagining God in the images we see. I will say to these scoffers that it is so. I am not ashamed of confessing that imagination is a powerful factor in life. Now you can easily understand that, in the presence of God, the Ruler of the Universe, who pervades everything, even those whom we have called the lowest of the low, all are equal." A recent example of transcendental spiritual experience manifested in life is Shri Ramana Maharishi, who passed away in 1950. A man of powerful personality, he taught as much by his silence as by his sermons. He had a directness of approach and a universality of outlook, which were products of true enlightenment.

The Spirit of Tolerance

It may be noted that the comprehensive tolerance of Hinduism is exemplified remarkably in such instances as the following. In the temple of Dharmasthala in South Kerala the chief personage is a Jain - he is regarded as a hereditary oracle whose arbitration is sought by members of all Hindu and even Muslim communities. The temple itself has the Sivalinga as well as the Salagrama, or symbol of Visnu, the officiating priest being a Vaisnavite. In the shrine at Udipi the worship of Siva and Visnu alike is offered and the heads of the Udipi Math, although staunch Vaisnavites, are under the obligation to attend to two Siva shrines, in addition to officiating as the chief priests of the Krishna temple. It is believed that a person belonging to the Harijan community received special divine favour and attained union with God in the temple precincts.

The tradition of Chidambaram is similar- the Paraya saint, Nandan, who was refused admission by the Brahmin priests, became the object of divine favour and attained communion with God. In the temple of Jagannath at Puri, caste distinctions have been discarded. In Travancore there is a forest temple dedicated to Ayyappa or Hariharaputra - here, too, no caste distinctions are observed. Hindus, and even Muslims and Christians, perform vows in this shrine with belief in the efficacy of the god's protective help. It may be noted in this context that the usual invocation of Ayyappa, namely, Saranam Ayyappa, is reminiscent of the Buddhist prayer.

Hinduism is essentially an Indian phenomenon. It is the dominant faith of India, practised by over 80% of the population. Since religion is a way of life in India, Hinduism forms an integral part of the entire Indian tradition. It is not easy to define Hinduism, for it is much more than a religion in the Western sense.

According to some scholars, Hinduism is not exactly a religion. Also known to practitioners as Sanatana Dharma, which means everlasting or eternal religion / truth / rule, Hinduism can best be defined as a way of life based on the teachings of ancient sages and scriptures like the Vedas and Upanishads. The word 'dharma' connotes "that which supports the universe" and effectively means any path of spiritual discipline which leads to God.

Hindu Dharma, as one scholar analogizes, can be compared to a fruit tree, with its roots:

1. Representing the Vedas and Vedantas, the thick trunk.
2. Symbolizing the spiritual experiences of numerous sages, gurus and saints, its branches.
3. Representing various theological traditions, and the fruit itself, in different shapes and sizes.
4. Symbolizing various sects and subsects. However, the concept of Hinduism defies a definite definition because of its uniqueness.

Some of the more simplistic answers to this question include: Anyone born in India is automatically a Hindu (the ethnicity fallacy), if your parents are Hindu, then you are Hindu (the familial argument), if you are born into a certain caste, then you are Hindu (the genetic inheritance model), if you believe in reincarnation, then you are Hindu (forgetting that many non-Hindu religions share at least some of the beliefs of Hinduism), if you practice any religion originating from India, then you are a Hindu (the national origin fallacy).

The real answer to this question has already been conclusively answered by the ancient sages of Hinduism, and is actually much simpler to ascertain than we would guess. The two primary factors that distinguish the individual uniqueness of the great world religious traditions are a) the scriptural authority upon which the tradition is based, and b) the fundamental religious tenet(s) that it espouses. If we ask the question what is a Jew? For example, the answer is: someone who accepts the Torah as their scriptural guide and believes in the monotheistic concept of God espoused in these scriptures. What is a Christian? a person who accepts the Gospels as their scriptural guide and believes that Jesus is the incarnate God who died for their sins. What is a Muslim? Someone who accepts the Qur'an as their scriptural guide, and believes that there is no God but Allah, and that Mohammed is his prophet.

Scriptural Authority

In general, what determines whether a person is a follower of any particular religion is whether or not they accept, and attempt to live by, the scriptural authority of that religion? This is no less true of Hinduism than it is of any other religion on earth. Thus, the question of what is a Hindu is similarly very easily answered. By definition, a Hindu is an individual who accepts as authoritative the religious guidance of the Vedic scriptures, and who strives to live in accordance with Dharma, God's divine laws as revealed in the Vedic scriptures.

Only If You Accept the Vedas

In keeping with this standard definition, all of the Hindu thinkers of the six traditional schools of Hindu philosophy (Shad-darshanas) insisted on the acceptance of the scriptural authority of the Vedas (shabda-pramana) as the primary criterion for distinguishing a Hindu from a non-Hindu, as well as distinguishing overtly Hindu philosophical positions from non-Hindu ones. It has been the historically accepted standard that, if you accept the Vedas (and by extension *Bhagavad Gita,* Puranas, etc.) as your scriptural authority, and lived your life in accordance with the Dharmic principles of the Vedas, you are then a Hindu. Thus, an Indian who rejects the Veda is obviously not a Hindu. While an American, Russian, Indonesian or Indian who does accept the Veda obviously is a Hindu.

The Uniqueness of Hinduism

Hinduism does not have any one founder, and any one core doctrine to which controversies can be referred to for resolution. There is also no point in time when it could be said to have begun. It does not require its adherents to accept any one idea, and thus is cultural, not creedal. The unique concept of the Absolute "Brahman" that cannot be equated with "God" is also exclusive to Hinduism. Hinduism is also marked by an attitude which seems to accommodate religious and cultural perspectives other than one's own, and so is characterized by a rich variety of ideas and practices resulting in what appears as a multiplicity of religions under one term 'Hinduism'.

Hinduism is perhaps the only religious tradition that is so diverse in its theoretical premises and practical expressions that it is like a compilation of religions with a history contemporaneous with the peoples with which it is associated. According to philosopher Jeaneane Fowler, Hinduism can never be neatly slotted into any particular belief system — monism, theism, monotheism, polytheism, pantheism, panentheism — for all these systems is reflected in its many facets.

Theories about the Origin of Hinduism

According to historians, the origin of Hinduism dates back to 5,000 or more years. The word "Hindu" is derived from the name of River Indus, which flows through northern India. In ancient times the river was called the 'Sindhu', but the Persians who migrated to India called the river 'Hindu', the land 'Hindustan' and its inhabitants 'Hindus'. Thus the religion followed by the Hindus came to be known as 'Hinduism'. It was earlier believed that the basic tenets of Hinduism were brought to India by the Aryans who invaded the Indus Valley Civilization and settled along the banks of the Indus River about 2000 BC.

However, this theory has now been proved to be a flawed one and is considered nothing more than a myth. According to scholars, the evolution of Hinduism may be divided into three periods: the ancient (6500 BCE-1000 AD), the medieval (1000-1800 AD), and the modern (1800 AD to present). Hinduism is commonly thought to be the oldest religion in the history of human civilization.

The Main Tenets of Hinduism

Hinduism lacks any unified system of beliefs and ideas. It is a phenomenon and represents a broad spectrum of beliefs and practices which on one hand are akin to paganism, pantheism and the like, and on the other very profound, abstract, metaphysical ideas. Since religion and culture are nearly interchangeable terms in Hinduism, emotive expressions like 'bhakti' (devotion) or 'dharma' (what is right) and 'yoga' (discipline) are used to depict essential aspects of the religion. Hinduism believes in idol worship, reincarnation, karma, dharma and moksha. Some moral ideals in Hinduism include non-violence, truthfulness, friendship, compassion, fortitude, self-control, purity and generosity.

Human life is divided into four stages, and there are defined rites and rituals for each stage from birth till death. Traditional Hinduism has two life-long dharmas that one can follow: 'Grihastha Dharma' (Domestic Religion) and 'Sannyasin Dharma' (Ascetic Religion). The 'Grihastha Dharma' has four goals: 'kâma' (sensual pleasure), 'artha' (wealth and prosperity), 'dharma' (the laws of life), and 'moksha' (liberation from the cycle of births). The 'Sannyasin Dharma' recognizes 'moksha' as its ultimate goal.

The Sacred Texts of the Hindus

According to Swami Vivekananda, "the accumulated treasury of spiritual laws discovered by different persons in different times" constitutes the sacred Hindu texts. Collectively referred to as the Shastras, there are two types of sacred writings in the Hindu scriptures: Shruti (heard) and Smriti (memorized). Sruti literature refers to the habit of ancient Hindu saints who led a solitary life in the woods, where they developed a consciousness that enabled them to 'hear' or cognize the truths of the universe. Sruti literatures are of two parts: the Vedas and the Upanishads.

There are four Vedas:

- *The Rig Veda:* "Royal Knowledge"
- *The Sama Veda:* "Knowledge of Chants"
- *The Yajur Veda:* "Knowledge of Sacrificial Rituals"
- *The Atharva Veda:* "Knowledge of Incarnations"

There are 108 extant Upanishads, of which 10 are most important: *Isa, Kena, Katha, Prashna, Mundaka, Mandukya, Taitiriya, Aitareya, Chandogya, Brihadaranyaka.* Smriti Literature refers to 'memorized' or 'remembered' poetry and epics. They are more popular with Hindus, because they are easy to understand, explains universal truths through symbolism and mythology, and contain some of the most beautiful and exciting stories in the history of religion world literature.

The three most important of Smriti literature are:

- *The Bhagavad Gita:* The most well known of the Hindu scriptures, called the "Song of the Adorable One", written about the 2nd century BC and forms the sixth part of Mahabharata. It contains some of the most brilliant theological lessons about the nature of God and of life ever written.
- *The Mahabharata:* The world's longest epic poem written about 9th century BC, and deals with the power struggle between the Pandava and the Kaurava families, with an intertwining of numerous episodes that make up life.
- *The Ramayana:* The most popular of Hindu epics, composed by Valmiki around 4th or 2nd centuries BC with later additions up to about 300 CE. It depicts the story of the royal couple of Ayodha - Ram and Sita and a host of other characters and their exploits.

Hindu Beliefs

It is difficult to assign a dogmatic orthodoxy to Hinduism. Many variations have developed from Hinduism over the years, and many non-Hindu cults and religious movements gained their inspiration from Hinduism. Even in India today, the most orthodox divisions of Hinduism have changed significantly over the last three thousand years. One of the oldest aspects of Hinduism is as much social as religious, and that is the caste system. It is important to understand the caste system before delving into Hindu religious beliefs.

According to Hindu teaching, there are four basic castes, or social classes. Each caste has its own rules and obligation for living. The elite caste is the Brahman, or priest caste. Second are the Kshatriyas, or warriors and rulers. Third are the Vaisyas, or merchants and farmers. Finally, the fourth caste is the Shudras, or labourers.

Outside the caste system are the untouchables. The untouchables are the outcasts of Hindu society. Though outlawed in India in the 1940s, the untouchables are still a very real part of Indian society. One does not get decide his or her caste that matter is decided when one is born into a particular caste.

As previously stated, there is not a strict orthodoxy in Hinduism. There are however, several principles that share a commonality among the various sects. Virtually all Hindus believe in:

- *The three-in-one god known as Brahman, which is composed of:* Brahma (the creator), Vishnu (the Preserver), and Shiva (the Destroyer).
- The Caste System.
- Karma. The law that good begets good, and bad begets bad. Every action, thought, or decision one makes has consequences well or bad that will return to each person in the present life, or in one yet to come.
- Reincarnation. Also known as transmigration of souls, or samsara. This is a journey on the circle of life, where each person experiences as series of physical births, deaths, and rebirths. With good karma, a person can be reborn into a higher caste, or even to godhood. Bad karma can relegate one to a lower caste, or even to life as an animal in their next life.
- Nirvana. This is the goal of the Hindu. Nirvana is the release of the soul from the seemingly endless cycle of rebirths.

Hinduism is both polytheistic, and pantheistic. There are three gods that compose Brahman Brahma, Vishnu, and Shiva. Hindus also worship the wives of Shiva, such as Kali, or one of Vishnus ten incarnations (avatars). This is only the beginning. There are literally millions of Hindu gods and goddesses by some counts, as many as 330 million. At the same time, Hinduism teaches that all living things are Brahman in their core. In other words, all living things are Brahman, or god. Enlightenment is attained by becoming tuned in to the Brahman within. Only then can one reach Nirvana. The release from the wheel of life that allows access to Nirvana is known as moksha.

Hindus recognize three possible paths to moksha, or salvation. The first is the way of works or karma yoga. This is a very popular way of salvation and lays emphasis on the idea that liberation may be obtained by fulfilling ones familial and social duties thereby overcoming the weight of bad karma one has accrued.

The second way of salvation is the way of knowledge, or jnana yoga. The basic premise of the way of knowledge is that the cause of our bondage to the cycle of rebirths in this world is ignorance. According to the predominant view among those committed to this way, our ignorance consists of the mistaken belief that we are individual selves, and not one with the ultimate divine reality Brahman. It is this same ignorance that gives rise to our bad actions, which result in bad karma.

Salvation is achieved through attaining a state of consciousness in which we realize our identity with Brahman. This is achieved through deep meditation, often as a part of the discipline of yoga. The third way of salvation is the way of devotion, or bhakti yoga.

This is the way most favoured by the common people of India. It satisfies the longing for a more emotional and personal approach to religion. It involves the self-surrender to one of the many personal gods and goddesses of Hinduism. Such devotion is expressed through acts of worship, temple rituals, and pilgrimages. Some Hindus conceive of ultimate salvation as absorption into the one divine reality, with all loss of individual existence.

Others conceive of it as heavenly existence in adoration of the personal God. The Hindu scriptures are massive, and were written between 1400 B.C. and A.D. 500. The oldest of the Hindu scriptures is the Veda, which literally means wisdom or knowledge.

The Vedas contain hymns, prayers, and ritual texts

composed from about 1400 to about 400 B.C. The Upanishads are a collection of writings composed between 800-600 B.C. Over one hundred of them still exist. These writings marked a definite change from the sacrificial humans and magic formulas in the Vedas, to the mystical ideas about man and the universe specifically the Brahman, and the atman (the self or soul). The Upanishads had a great influence on Gautama Buddha, the founder of Buddhism.

The Ramayana is one of the two major epic tales of India, the other being the Mahabharata. A sage-poet named Valmiki wrote the Ramayana. The work consists of 24,000 couplets based upon the life of Rama, a righteous king who was supposedly an incarnation of the God Vishnu. The Mahabharata is the second epic.

It is an the story of the deeds of Aryan clans, and consists of some 100,000 verses and was composed over an 800-year period beginning about 400 B.C. contained within this work is a great classic, the *Bhagavad Gita,* or the "Song of the Blessed Lord."

The *Bhagavad Gita* is not only the most sacred book of the Hindus, but it is also the best known and the most read of all Indian works in the entire world, despite the fact it was added late to the Mahabharata, sometime in the first century A.D.

The story revolves around man's duty, which, if carried out, will bring nothing but sorrow. The significance this story has on Hindu belief is its endorsement of bhakti, or devotion to a particular god, as a means of salvation, since Arjuna, the story's main character, decides to put his devotion to Vishnu above his own personal desires. The *Gita* ends with Arjuna devoted to Vishnu and ready to kill his relatives in battle.

Nine Beliefs of Hinduism

Our beliefs determine our thoughts and attitudes about life, which in turn direct our actions. By our actions, we create our destiny. Beliefs about sacred matters—God, soul and cosmos—are essential to one's approach to life. Hindus believe many diverse things, but there are a few bedrock concepts on which most Hindus concur. The following nine beliefs, though not exhaustive, offer a simple summary of Hindu spirituality.

1. Hindus believe in a one, all-pervasive Supreme being who is both immanent and transcendent, both Creator and Unmanifest Reality.
2. Hindus believe in the divinity of the four Vedas, the world's most ancient scripture, and venerate the Agamas as equally revealed. These primordial hymns are God's word and the bedrock of Sanatana Dharma, the eternal religion.
3. Hindus believe that the universe undergoes endless cycles of creation, preservation and dissolution.
4. Hindus believe in karma, the law of cause and effect by which each individual creates his own destiny by his thoughts, words and deeds.
5. Hindus believe that the soul reincarnates, evolving through many births until all karmas has been resolved, and moksha, liberation from the cycle of rebirth, is attained. Not a single soul will be deprived of this destiny.
6. Hindus believe that divine beings exist in unseen worlds and that temple worship, rituals, sacraments and personal devotionals create a communion with these devas and Gods.
7. Hindus believe that an enlightened master, or satguru, is essential to know the Transcendent Absolute, as are personal discipline, good conduct, purification, pilgrimage, self-inquiry, meditation and surrender in God.
8. Hindus believe that all life is sacred, to be loved and revered, and therefore practice ahimsa, no injury, in thought, word and deed.
9. Hindus believe that no religion teaches the only way to salvation above all others, but that all genuine paths are facets of God's Light, deserving tolerance and understanding.

Hinduism, the world is oldest religion, has no beginning—it precedes recorded history. It has no human founder. It is a mystical religion, leading the devotee to personally experience the Truth within, finally reaching the pinnacle of consciousness where man and God are one. Hinduism has four main denominations—Shaivism, Shaktism, Vaishnavism and Smartism.

Fundamental Principles of Hinduism

The beliefs of Hindu thought are wide and varied, and have been expounded upon by saints and writers throughout the centuries. The two essays by Swami Vivekananda, Duty to masses and why we differ, provide tremendous insights into Hindu beliefs. Vivekananda was very instrumental in removing the aura of mysticism that had surrounded Hinduism for centuries and bringing the authority of the Vedas to the forefront for the masses. He exhorted Hindus to develop faith instead of superstition and to seek the paths of knowledge and reason. His non-dualistic explanation of Hinduism was an endorsement of the *Advaita* philosophy - man is not just made in the image of God but is God - all is *Brahman*. Vivekananda also preached that the way to salvation is that one must see God.

The essence of Hinduism can be found in the *Bhagavad Gita*. The seminal interpretation of the *Gita* was provided by Shankaracharya and the core principles taught by him include the process of obtaining liberation or *moksha* by:

- Purifying the heart
- Developing true detachment
- Distinguishing between *maya* and *gyana*
- Realizing the truth
- Obtaining *nivritti* and, finally, *sanyaasa*

Personal God(s) and Caste System in Hinduism

The concept of the personal God is fundamental to Hinduism and is often misunderstood as polytheism. One explanation is provided in the *Bhagavad Gita* by Lord Krishna:

For the protection of the good, for the destruction of the wicked and for the establishment of righteous Dharma, I come into being from age to age.

Over the ages, these various incarnations of the Godhead gave rise to various sects in Hinduism e.g. shaivism (followers of Lord Shiva) and vaishnavism (followers of Lord Krishna).

The concept of the caste system is also explained in the *Bhagavad Gita:*

The four-fold order was created by Me according to the divisions of quality and work. The emphasis is on guna (aptitude) and karma (function) and not on jaati (birth). The *Varna* or the order to which we belong is independent of sex, birth or breeding. A caste is determined by temperament and vocation - not by birth or heredity.

Hence, the origin of the caste system is clarified as one of functional classification - it was never meant to be abused as a system of repression of the so-called "lower" castes by the "higher" castes.

Sacred Texts in Hinduism

Festivals, holidays and ritual form an integral part of Hinduism. Every religion needs its mythology in addition to its fundamental truths and philosophies. Most Hindu festivals are based on the lunar calendar and celebrate the traditions laid out in mythology via the series of books called the *Puranas.* The cornerstone principles of Hinduism are contained in the sacred texts called the *Vedas* (meaning 'knowledge') and the *Upanishads* (meaning 'secret texts'). There are four principal *Vedas* (Rg, Sama, Yajur and Atharva) and several principal *Upanishads.*

Karma and Re-incarnation in Hinduism

The Hindu concept of *karma* is derived from one of the four purposes of life i.e. *karma* (pursuit of pleasure), *artha* (pursuit of propserity), *dharma* (faith or way of life) and *moksha* (liberation). The life of the Hindu is divided into four stages or *ashramas* which are perhaps aligned with the attainment of these four purposes:

- *Brahmacharya:* The life of the student and the pursuit of education
- *Grahastha:* The life of the householder and the pursuit of family life
- *Vanaprastha:* The transition from householder to ascetic and the process of detachment from possessions, desires and relations begins in this stage
- *Sanyaasa:* The final stage of renunciation and the pursuit of penance and meditation. This stage is rarely practised in modern times.

The sum-total of positive and negative experiences in the pursuit of the four purposes of life during the four stages of life is said to be responsible for accumulation of *karma*. Hence, it can be viewed as a means of keeping a score-sheet of a person's actions during this lifetime and beyond. The concept of reincarnation follows naturally from the concept of *karma*. The Hindu belief is that while the physical body may decay and eventually die, the soul of the person cannot be "killed". The *karma* from past lives is carried by the soul from one birth to another and the purpose of life is to accumulate enough positive *karma* by following the path of *dharma* so that one may attain liberation from rebirth, or *moksha*.

The common beliefs underlying all schools of thought in Hinduism are beliefs concerning:

- The evolution of the physical world
- The law of karma and rebirth
- The four-fold goal of human life

The four-fold goal of human life is the:

- Purusharthas-Dharma (Righteousness)
- Artha (Worldly Prosperity)
- Kama (Enjoyment), and
- Moksha (Liberation)

Beliefs of Hinduism

Hindus believe in many gods and goddesses. Some of them are human (e.g. Krishna, Rama, some animals (e.g. fish, monkey, rat, snake), (some animal-humans as in the case of Ganesh who has the head of elephant with trunk and the body of a human), and some others are natural phenomena (e.g. dawn, fire, sun). Their number is generally believed to be 330 million. According to Hinduism beliefs, god incarnates, i.e., takes the form of human being and other animals and appears in this earth in that form. Gods and goddesses were born like human beings and had wives and children. No god possesses absolute power; some of the gods are weaker than the sages and some others even weaker than the monkey (e.g. Rama).

Another aspect about Hindu gods is that the status of their godhood is not fixed. One finds that some gods were worshipped for a time and then abandoned and new gods and goddesses were adopted instead. The gods and goddesses worshipped now-a-days in Hindu homes and temples are not Vedic. The Vedic gods like Agni (fire), Surya (sun) Usha (dawn) are completely rejected and the gods and goddesses mentioned in the Puranas are worshipped by modern Hindus. Similarly, Rama who is currently receiving increasing acceptance among Hindus in India because of the wide propagation of the official and other media was never worshipped as a deity until the eleventh century.

Hinduism's complexity stems from the many forms of three primary deities: Shiva, Creator and Destroyer of all Existence, Vishnu, Protector or Preserver of the Universe and Shakti, the Divine Feminine. Each sect views its deity as the "Supreme Personified Godhead," surrounded by a mythology that includes the texts, rituals and social and cultural observances. Depending on their needs, worshippers may appeal to many different deities, but all acts of devotion have the common goal of summoning the universal. The above facts clearly explains the sacred elements of Hinduism and beliefs of Hinduism.

Hinduism and the Belief in Rebirth

According to Hinduism a soul reincarnates again and again on earth till it becomes perfect and reunites with it

Source. During this process the soul enters into many bodies, assumes many forms and passes through many births and deaths. This concept is summarily described in the following verse of the *Bhagavad Gita*:

"Just as a man discards worn out clothes and puts on new clothes, the soul discards worn out bodies and wears new ones."

According to Hinduism a being has to live many lives and under go many experiences before it attains perfection and becomes one with the Divine. The Hindu theory of creation suggests that creation begins when the individual souls becomes separated from the undifferentiated One. It continues as the evolution of life and consciousness in matter progresses. During this process some of souls journey back to God through the transformation of matter or prakriti in which they were hidden. The remaining souls continue their existence and rejoin Him in the end, not through transformation but through a process of great destruction. Thus the great cycle of creation, stretching over millions of years, comes to its logical end.

Once the creative process is switched on, the individual soul hides behind the false personality called Jiva, the subtle body and an outer personality called the mind and the body or the ego. The Jiva is made up of the subtle body, the subtle mind and a little bit of discretionary intelligence called buddhi. The ego is made up of the gross physical body, the surface consciousness consisting of innumerable desires and impulses. Since the Jiva and the ego have no idea of Truth or reality, they suffer from ignorance and illusion. They succumb to illusion and suffer from the delusion of the outer mind. They behave selfishly as if they are different from the rest of creation and end up with suffering, indulging in acts of self perpetuation.

At the end of each life, the physical body and the gross mind return to the elements of the earth. But the Jiva and the soul survive death. Depending upon the nature of their past deeds, and the number of subtle bodies it has developed, the

Jiva either ascends to the heaven or descends into the hell. Hiding the indwelling spirit in its core, the Jiva stays in these worlds till it exhausts the fruits of its good or bad actions. Having learned some new lessons, it then returns to the earth again to take another birth.

Thus the Jiva undergoes innumerable births and deaths. It becomes bound to the mortal life and the laws of nature. Death provides temporary relief, but exposes the individual Jiva to the risk of falling into greater depths of suffering.

Even the Buddha who founded Buddhism did not discard this theory, though he was silent on the existence of God and did not confirm the existence of soul. The Buddha preached that not soul but the ever changing individual character, which moves from one birth to another birth, till all changing and becoming comes to an end, through the transformation of character on the lines of the Eightfold path. Hinduism speaks of the existence of heavens above and hells below. The former are sun filled, inhabited by gods and innumerable divine souls. The latter are dark worlds (asurya lokas) and populated by all the dark and demonic forces. The individual souls go into these worlds according to their deeds. But they do not stay there permanently till the end of destruction. They go there basically as a consequence of their actions, either to enjoy or to suffer. In either case they learn the lesson and come back to earth to start a new earthly life all over again.

Thus according to Hinduism, life in heaven may be longer, but still it is a mortal life only. There, a Jiva may enjoy extreme pleasures, but it would not last for ever. Once its karma is exhausted, the Jiva is thrown back from the heights of heavenly glory into the turmoil of unstable earthly life. The Hindu concept of reincarnation is alien to western people. It is mostly misunderstood and misinterpreted, partly because of ignorance and partly because of some inherent mental blockage natural to the single minded pursuit of religious faith along rutted paths. It generated a lot of controversy because it directly challenges the western notion of one life, one heaven and the final day of judgement.

Today this fundamental concept of Hinduism is finding many new adherents and believers all over the world. The reasons are many. Firstly, a great mass of evidence is gathering in favour of reincarnation through the personal experiences of many who chanced to remember their past lives and was able to record their experiences in stunning details for the posterity. Secondly the modern theories of hypnotic regression are gaining acceptance in many parts of the world. There are now many institutions, which help interested individuals to remember their past lives as a part of their spiritual awakening. Thirdly many enlightened psychic masters like Edgar Cayce confirmed beyond doubt that reincarnation is not just a theory or imagination, but a definite reality.

The Hindu concept of reincarnation is based upon the logical notion that life on earth did not emerge suddenly, but evolved gradually, involving great epoch of time and a vast multitude of beings. During this process the static and inert consciousness of matter yielded place to the dynamic movement of life and consciousness. The animal tendencies gave way to human reason and humane thoughts. Extending the same logic we may further say that in future, from this part animal, part human and part divine being, there would emerge a spiritual man of divine consciousness, the Superman of Sri Aurobindo, with supra mental consciousness.

If you look at the personality of an ordinary human being, you will realize that there is a lot in him, that is grosser and denser which cannot be purified and transformed in the shorter time of one life span. What is a hundred years or less than a hundred of life on a scale of millions of years of continuous evolution of life on earth? Does not it sound illogical to say that we would remain static from the evolutionary point of view; while change is the nature of life and every thing else all around us is changing and evolving constantly?

Hinduism does not accept the premise that under normal circumstances an individual soul can free itself completely from the entanglement with Samsara and unite with its Creator in just one life time. The Jiva has to progressively evolve through the cycle of innumerable births and deaths before the soul can liberate itself. From inert matter to inert consciousness and then to dynamic consciousness, from ignorance to semi awareness and then to self awareness, from attachment to detachment and then to complete freedom, from illusion to awareness and then to reality, from darkness to dawn and then into light, from mortality to immortality: this is the forward movement of life in the whole creation. And all this cannot happen just in a few hundred years.

It is very obvious that God did not create the worlds and the beings in His likeness, but in exact opposite to it. If He would have created everything in His true likeness then there would have been no differentiation and no possibility of any movement. Creation would have remained static, without an aim and purpose, offering no scope for movement and change.

It is true that God is hidden in every aspect of His creation. But that which is visible and sensible is not His true self. It is His negative and false self, which tries to compete with Him and fight for its own individuality, and finally, having lost the battle, would move towards Him in total obedience. Thus the whole drama of creation seems to start with the creation of His individual selves that hide themselves in His negative selves so that a movement away from Him and then again back to Him can be initiated and sustained. The Hindu scriptures describe this process variously with such expressions as: "the true self hides behind the false self, God enters into Prakriti, self becomes enveloped with ignorance".

The awakening comes after wards. When the soul stirs and makes its vibrations felt by the ignorant consciousness, the seeds of spiritualization of the being are sown. The movement that began away from God now becomes reversed. It then starts moving away from illusion and ignorance towards God and Truth.

The inexorable law of karma operates through out this grand drama. Karma is the correction mechanism, the chisel with which the negative self, the inert stone, is chiselled away till the hidden deity comes out of it and enters the temple of God. In the ordinary circumstances, awakening of a sleeping self cannot take place through miracles but through trial and error. Good actions lead to good future, and bad actions to the opposite. An awareness of this very law is the first great awakening and the first sure leap towards the Light.

All this cannot take place in one simple life, but over a period of time involving many lives. It cannot happen on the strength of a life time's learning but in the light of a great mass of accumulated wisdom. It cannot happen if the purpose of whole life is to move towards light and truth. This is where the idea of reincarnation of soul perfectly fits in. If we accept the whole creation as a grand process stretching over a vast period of time, we cannot over look the importance and the role of man in it. Man cannot make a brief appearance on earth, live just one life and then disappear forever into the cozy corners of some safe heaven, or the vast dungeons of some burning hell, leaving creation, God and Nature to themselves.

At the individual level, the movement of creation and evolution need not universally progressive. Since the whole movement is regulated on the principle of trial and error, of learning and improvement through such learning, some times, a retrogressive movement may also take place. Due to some unfortunate error of judgment, instead moving towards the light, a being may move away from it. Thus depending upon the merits of the previous deeds, a being may evolve into higher life forms or regress temporarily into a lower life form. However, due to some peculiar circumstances, if an individual takes birth as a lower life form, he can still reverse the process. He can change his present actions and establish a basis for his forward movement again.

The Jiva thus drifts, sailing in the boat of his own karma, in a sea of worldly illusion (samsara sagaram), towards the shores of liberation, through trial and error, self effort and assisted by invisible laws and mysterious forces, with the soul remaining as its silent, witnessing companion. That the theory of reincarnation is not a mere theory, but an actual fact is being now established beyond reasonable doubt. Many instances have now come to light where individuals were able to recollect their past lives through a process of regression or by other means. The theory still baffles many, while many others refuse to acknowledge it because of intense prejudice.

4

World Religion

Buddhism and its Belief System

Buddhism

Although Buddhism never developed a missionary movement, Buddha's teachings nevertheless spread far and wide on the Indian subcontinent and from there throughout Asia. In each new culture it reached, the Buddhist methods and styles were modified to fit the local mentality, without compromising the essential points of wisdom and compassion. Buddhism, however, never developed an overall hierarchy of religious authority with a supreme head. Each country to which it spread developed its own forms, its own religious structure and its own spiritual head. The most well-known and internationally respected of these authorities at present is His Holiness the Dalai Lama of Tibet.

There are two major divisions of Buddhism. The Hinayana, or Modest Vehicle, emphasizes personal liberation, while the Mahayana, or Vast Vehicle, stresses working to become a fully enlightened Buddha in order to be best able to help others. Each has many sub-divisions. At present, however, three major forms survive: one Hinayana, known as Theravada, in South East Asia, and two Mahayana, namely the Chinese and Tibetan traditions. The Theravada tradition spread from India to Sri Lanka and Burma in the third century

B.C.E., and from there to Yunnan in southwest China, Thailand, Laos, Cambodia, South Vietnam and Indonesia. Pockets of Indian merchants practicing Buddhism were soon found on the coast of the Arabian Peninsula and even as far as Alexandria, Egypt. Other forms of Hinayana spread from that time to modern-day Pakistan, Kashmir, Afghanistan, eastern and coastal Iran, Uzbekistan, Turkmenistan and Tajikistan.

These were the ancient states of Gandhara, Bactria, Parthia and Sogdia. From this base in Central Asia, they spread further in the second century C.E. to East Turkistan (Xinjiang) and Inner China, and in the late seventh century to Kyrghyzstan and Kazakhstan. These forms of Hinayana were later combined with Mahayana aspects that also came from India so that Mahayana eventually became the dominant form of Buddhism in most of Central Asia. The Chinese form of Mahayana later spread to Korea, Japan and North Vietnam. Another early wave of Mahayana, mixed with Shaivite forms of Hinduism, spread from India to Nepal, Indonesia, Malaysia and parts of South East Asia starting in about the fifth century. The Tibetan Mahayana tradition, which, starting in the seventh century, inherited the full historical development of Indian Buddhism, spread throughout the Himalayan regions and to Mongolia, East Turkistan, Kyrghyzstan, Kazakhstan, northern Inner China, Manchuria, Siberia and the Kalmyk Mongol region near the Caspian Sea in European Russia.

Spread of Buddhism

The expansion of Buddhism throughout most of Asia was peaceful and occurred in several ways. Shakyamuni Buddha set the precedent. Being primarily a teacher, he traveled to nearby kingdoms to share his insights with those who were receptive and interested. Likewise, he instructed his monks to go forth in the world and expound his teachings. He did not ask others to denounce and give up their own religion and convert to a new one, for he was not seeking to establish his own religion. He was merely trying to help others overcome the unhappiness and suffering that they were creating for themselves because of their lack of understanding. Later generations of followers were inspired by Buddha's example and shared with others his methods that they found useful in their lives. This is how what is now called "Buddhism" spread far and wide.

Sometimes the process evolved organically. For example, when Buddhist merchants visited and settled in different lands, some members of the local populations naturally developed interest in these foreigners' beliefs, as with the introduction of Islam to Indonesia and Malaysia. Such a process occurred with Buddhism in the oasis states along the Silk Route in Central Asia during the two centuries before and after the Common Era. As local rulers and their people learned more about this Indian religion, they invited monks from the merchants' native regions as advisors or teachers and, in this manner, eventually adopted the Buddhist faith. Another organic method was through the slow cultural assimilation of a conquering people, such as the Greeks into the Buddhist society of Gandhara in present-day central Pakistan during the centuries following the second century B.C.E.

Often, however, the dissemination was due primarily to the influence of a powerful monarch who had adopted and supported Buddhism himself. In the mid-third century B.C.E, for example, Buddhism spread throughout northern India as the result of the personal endorsement of King Ashoka. This great empire-builder did not force his subjects to adopt the Buddhist faith. But by posting edicts engraved on iron pillars throughout his realm exhorting his people to lead an ethical life and by following these principles himself, he inspired others to adopt Buddha's teachings. King Ashoka also actively proselytized outside his kingdom by sending missions to distant lands. On some occasions, he acted upon the invitation of foreign rulers, such as King Tishya of Sri Lanka. On others, he sent monks as envoys at his own initiative. These visiting monastics, however, did not forcefully pressure others to convert, but simply made Buddha's teachings available, allowing people to choose for themselves.

This is evidenced by the fact that in such places as South India and southern Burma, Buddhism soon took root, while in others, such as the Greek states in Central and West Asia, there is no record of any immediate impact. Other religious kings, such as the sixteenth century Mongol potentate Altan Khan, invited Buddhist teachers to their realm and proclaimed Buddhism the official creed of the land in order to help unify their people and consolidate their rule. In the process they may have prohibited certain practices of non-Buddhist, indigenous religions and even persecuted those who followed them, but these heavy-handed moves were primarily politically motivated. Such ambitious rulers never forced their subjects to adopt Buddhist forms of belief or worship. This is not part of the religious creed.

If Shakyamuni Buddha told people not to follow his teachings out of blind faith, but to examine them carefully themselves before accepting them, how much less so should people accept Buddha's teachings out of coercion from zealous missionaries or royal decree? Thus, for instance, when Toyin Neiji in the early sixteenth century tried to bribe Eastern Mongol nomads into following Buddhism by offering them livestock for each verse they memorized, people complained to the highest authorities. In the end, this overbearing teacher was punished and exiled.

Main Events in the Life of Gautama Buddha:

- Birth (Lumbini) - 624 B.C.E.
- Marriage (Kapilavastu) - 608 B.C.E
- Renunciation (Kapilavastu) - 595 B.C.E
- Enlightenment (Bodh Gaya) - 589 B.C.E
- 1st Year after Enlightenment (Sarnath) - 588 B.C.E.
- Death / Parinirvana at Kushinagar - 544 B.C.E

Soon after Buddha's death or parinirvana, five hundred monks met at the first council at Rajagrha, under the leadership of Kashyapa. Upali recited the monastic code (Vinaya) as he remembered it. Ananda, Buddha's cousin, friend, and favorite disciple — and a man of prodigious memory—recited Buddha's lessons (the Sutras). The monks debated details and voted on final versions. These were then committed to memory by other monks, to be translated into the many languages of the Indian plains. It should be noted that Buddhism remained an oral tradition for over 200 years. In the next few centuries, the original unity of Buddhism began to fragment.

The most significant split occurred after the second council, held at Vaishali 100 years after the first. After debates between a more liberal group and traditionalists, the liberal group left and labeled themselves the Mahasangha — "the great sangha." They would eventually evolve into the Mahayana tradition of northern Asia. The traditionalists, now referred to as Sthaviravada or "way of the elders" (or, in Pali, Theravada), developed a complex set of philosophical ideas beyond those elucidated by Buddha. These were collected into the Abhidharma or "higher teachings." But they, too, encouraged disagreements, so that one splinter groups after another left the fold. Ultimately, 18 schools developed, each with their own interpretations of various issues, and spread all over India and Southeast Asia. Today, only the school stemming from the Sri Lankan Theravada survives.

Ashoka

One of the most significant events in the history of Buddhism is the chance encounter of the monk Nigrodha and the emperor Ashoka Maurya. Ashoka, succeeding his father after a bloody power struggle in 268 BC, found himself deeply disturbed by the carnage he caused while suppressing a revolt in the land of the Kalingas. Meeting Nigrodha convinced Emperor Ashoka to devote himself to peace. On his orders, thousands of rock pillars were erected, bearing the words of the Buddha, in the brahmi script — the first written evidence of Buddhism. The third council of monks was held at Pataliputra, the capital of Ashoka's empire.

There is a story that tells about a poor young boy who, having nothing to give the Buddha as a gift, collected a handful of dust and innocently presented it. The Buddha smiled and accepted it with the same graciousness he accepted the gifts of wealthy admirers. That boy, it is said, was reborn as the Emperor Ashoka. He sent missionaries all over India and beyond. Some went as far as Egypt, Palestine, and Greece. St. Origen even mentions them as having reached Britain. The Greeks of one of the Alexandrian kingdoms of northern India adopted Buddhism, after their King Menandros (Pali: Milinda) was convinced by a monk named Nagasena — the conversation immortalized in the Milinda Pañha.

A Kushan king of north India named Kanishka was also converted, and a council was held in Kashmir in about 100 AD. Greek Buddhists there recorded the Sutras on copper sheets which, unfortunately, were never recovered. It is interesting to note that there is a saint in Orthodox Christianity named Josaphat, an Indian king whose story is essentially that of the Buddha. Josaphat is thought to be a distortion of the word bodhisattva.

Sri Lanka and Theravada

Emperor Ashoka sent one of his sons, Mahinda, and one of his daughters, Sanghamitta, a monk and a nun, to Sri Lanka (Ceylon) around the year 240 BC. The king of Sri Lanka, King Devanampiyatissa, welcomed them and was converted. One of the gifts they brought with them was a branch of the bodhi tree, which was successfully transplanted. The descendants of this branch can still be found on the island.

The fourth council was held in Sri Lanka, in the Aloka Cave, in the first century BC. During this time as well, and for the first time, the entire set of Sutras were recorded in the Pali language on palm leaves. This became Theravada's Pali Canon, from which so much of our knowledge of Buddhism stems. It is also called the Tripitaka (Pali: Tipitaka), or three baskets: The three sections of the canon are the Vinaya Pitaka (the monastic law), the Sutta Pitaka (words of the Buddha), and the Abhidamma Pitaka (the philosophical commentaries).

In a very real sense, Sri Lanka's monks may be credited with saving the Theravada tradition: Although it had spread once from India all over Southeast Asia, it had nearly died out due to competition from Hinduism and Islam, as well as war and colonialism. Theravada monks spread their tradition from Sri Lanka to Burma, Thailand, Malaysia, Cambodia, and Laos, and from these lands to Europe and the west generally.

Mahayana

Mahayana began in the first century BC, as a development of the Mahasangha rebellion. Their more liberal attitudes toward monastic tradition allowed the lay community to have a greater voice in the nature of Buddhism. For better or worse, the simpler needs of the common folk were easier for the Mahayanists to meet. For example, the people were used to gods and heroes. So, the Trikaya (three bodies) doctrine came into being: Not only was Buddha a man who became enlightened, he was also represented by various god-like Buddhas in various appealing heavens, as well as by the Dharma itself, or Shunyata (emptiness), or Buddha-Mind, depending on which interpretation we look at — sort of a Buddhist Father, Son, and Holy Ghost.

More important, however, was the increased importance of the Bodhisattva. A Bodhisattva is someone who has attained enlightenment, but who chooses to remain in this world of Samsara in order to bring others to enlightenment. He is a lot like a saint, a spiritual hero, for the people to admire and appeal to. Along with new ideas came new scriptures. Also called Sutras, they are often attributed to Buddha himself, sometimes as special transmissions that Buddha supposedly felt were too difficult for his original listeners and therefore were hidden until the times were ripe. The most significant of these new Sutras are these:

- Prajñaparamita or Perfection of Wisdom, an enormous collection of often esoteric texts, including the famous Heart Sutra and Diamond Sutra. The earliest known piece of printing in the world is, in fact, a copy of the Diamond Sutra, printed in China in 868 AD.
- Suddharma-pundarika or White Lotus of the True

Dharma, also often esoteric, includes the Avalokiteshwara Sutra, a prayer to that Bodhisattva.

- Vimalakirti-nirdesha or Vimalakirti's Exposition is the teachings of and stories about the enlightened householder Vimalakirti.
- Shurangama-samadhi or Hero's Sutra provides a guide to meditation, shunyata, and the bodhisattva. It is most popular among Zen Buddhists
- Sukhavati-vyuha or Pure Land Sutra is the most important Sutra for the Pure Land Schools of Buddhism. The Buddha tells Ananda about Amitabha and his Pure Land or heaven, and how one can be reborn there.

There are many, many others. Finally, Mahayana is founded on two new philosophical interpretations of Buddhism: Madhyamaka and Yogacara.

Madhyamaka

Madhyamaka means "the middle way." You may recall that Buddha himself called his way the middle way in his very first sermon. He meant, at that time, the middle way between the extremes of hedonistic pleasure and extreme asceticism. But he may also have referred to the middle way between the competing philosophies of eternalism and annihilationism — the belief that the soul exists forever and that the soul is annihilated at death or between materialism and nihilism.... An Indian monk by the name of Nagarjuna took this idea and expanded on it to create the philosophy that would be known as Madhyamaka, in a book called the Mulamadhyamaka-karika, written about 150 AD.

Basically a treatise on logical argument, it concludes that nothing is absolute, everything is relative, nothing exists on its own, and everything is interdependent. All systems, beginning with the idea that each thing is what it is and not something else (Aristotle's law of the excluded middle), wind up contradicting themselves.

Rigorous logic, in other words, leads one away from all systems, and to the concept of shunyata. Shunyata means emptiness. This doesn't mean that nothing exists. It means that nothing exists in and of itself, but only as a part of a universal web of being. This would become a central concept in all branches of Mahayana. Of course, it is actually a restatement of the central Buddhist concepts of anatman, anitya, and dukkha.

Yogacara

The second philosophical innovation, Yogacara, is credited to two brothers, Asanga and Vasubandhu, who lived in India in the 300's AD. They elaborated earlier movements in the direction of the philosophy of idealism or chitta-matra. Chitta-matra means literally mind only. Asanga and Vasubandhu believed that everything that exists is mind or consciousness. What we think of as physical things are just projections of our minds, delusions or hallucinations, if you like. To get rid of these delusions, we must meditate, which for the Yogacara School means the creation of pure consciousness, devoid of all content. In that way, we leave our deluded individual minds and join with the universal mind, or Buddha-mind.

Tantra

The last innovation was less philosophical and far more practical: Tantra. Tantra refers to certain writings which are concerned, not with philosophical niceties, but with the basic how-to of enlightenment, and not just with enlightenment in several rebirths, but enlightenment here-and-now. In order to accomplish this feat, dramatic methods are needed ones which, to the uninitiated, may seem rather bizarre. Tantra was the domain of the siddhu, the adept — someone who knows the secrets, a magician in the ways of enlightenment.

Tantra involves the use of various techniques, including the wellknown mandalas, mantras, and mudras. Mandalas are paintings or other representations of higher awareness, usually in the form of a circular pattern of images, which may provide the focus of one-pointed meditation. Mantras are words or phrases that serve the same purpose, such as the famous "Om mani padme hum." Mudras are hand positions that symbolize certain qualities of enlightenment.

Less well known are the yidams. A yidam is the image of a god or goddess or other spiritual being, either physically represented or, more commonly, imagined clearly in the mind's eye. Again, these represent archetypal qualities of enlightenment, and one-pointed meditation on these complex images lead the adept to his or her goal. These ideas would have enormous impact on Mahayana. They are not without critics, however: Madhyamaka is sometimes criticized as word-play, and Yogacara is criticized as reintroducing atman, eternal soul or essence, to Buddhism. Tantra has been most often criticized, especially for its emphasis on secret methods and strong devotion to a guru. Nevertheless, these innovations led to a renewed flurry of activity in the first half of the first millenium, and provided the foundation for the kinds of Buddhism we find in China, Tibet, Japan, Korea, Vietnam, and elsewhere in East Asia.

China

Legend has it that the Chinese Emperor Ming Ti had a dream which led him to send his agents down the Silk Road — the ancient trade route between China and the west — to discover its meaning. The agents returned with a picture of the Buddha and a copy of the Sutra in 42 Sections. This Sutra would, in 67 AD, be the first of many to be translated into Chinese.

The first Buddhist community in China is thought to be one in Loyang, established by "foreigners" around 150 AD, in the Han dynasty. Only 100 years later, there emerges a native Chinese Sangha. And during the Period of Disunity (or Era of the Warring States, 220 to 589 AD), the number of Buddhist monks and nuns increase to as many as two million. Apparently, the uncertain times and the misery of the lower classes were fertile ground for the monastic traditions of Buddhism.

Buddhism did not come to a land innocent of religion and philosophy, of course. China, in fact, had three main competing streams of thought: Confucianism, Taoism, and folk religion. Confucianisim is essentially a moral-political philosophy, involving a complex guide to human relationships. Taoism is a life-philosophy involving a return to simpler and more "natural" ways of being. And the folk religion — or, should we say, religions — consisted of rich mythologies, superstitions, astrology, reading of entrails, magic, folk medicine, and so on. (Please understand that I am simplifying here: Certainly Confucianism and Taoism are as sophisticated as Buddhism.)

Although these various streams sometimes competed with each other and with Buddhism, they also fed each other, enriched each other, and intertwined with each other. Over time, the Mahayana of India became the Mahayana of China and, later, of Korea, Japan, and Vietnam.

Pure Land

The first example historically is Pure Land Buddhism (Ching-T'u, J: Jodo). The peasants and working people of China were used to gods and goddesses, praying for rain and health, worrying about heaven and hell, and so on. It wasn't a great leap to find in Buddhism's cosmology and theology the bases for a religious tradition that catered to these needs and habits, while still providing a sophisticated philosophical foundation.

The idea of this period of time as a fallen or inferior time — traditional in China — led to the idea that we are no longer able to reach enlightenment on our own power, but must rely on the intercession of higher beings. The transcendent Buddha Amitabha, and his western paradise ("pure land"), introduced in the Sukhavati-vyuha Sutra, was a perfect fit.

Ch'an

Another school that was to be particularly strongly influenced by Chinese thought was the Meditation School — Dhyana, Ch'an, Son, or Zen. Tradition has the Indian monk Bodhidharma coming from the west to China around 520

AD. It was Bodhidharma, it is said, and who carried the Silent Transmission to become the First Patriarch of the Ch'an School in China.

From the very beginning, Buddha had had reservations about his ability to communicate his message to the people. Words simply could not carry such a sublime message. So, on one occasion, while the monks around him waited for a sermon, he said absolutely nothing. He simply held up a flower. The monks, of course, were confused, except for Kashyapa, who understood and smiled. The Buddha smiled back, and thus the Silent Transmission began. Zen Buddhism focuses on developing the immediate awareness of Buddha-mind through meditation on emptiness. It is notorious for its dismissal of the written and spoken word and occasionally for his rough-house antics. It should be understood, however, that there is great reverence for the Buddha, the Dharma, and the Sangha, even when they are ostensibly ignoring, poking fun, or even turning them upside-down.

Zen has contributed its own literature to the Buddhist melting-pot, including The Platform Sutra, written by Hui Neng, the Sixth Patriarch, around 700 AD., The Blue Cliff Record, written about 1000 AD., and The Gateless Gate, written about 1200 AD. And we shouldn't forget the famous Ten Ox-Herding Pictures that many see as containing the very essence of Zen's message.

The Blossoming of Schools

During the Sui dynasty (581-618) and T'ang dynasty (618-907), Chinese Buddhism experienced what is referred to as the "blossoming of schools." The philosophical inspirations of the Madhyamaka and Yogacara, as well as the Pure Land and Ch'an Sutras, interacting with the already sophisticated philosophies of Confucianism and Taoism, led to a regular renaissance in religious and philosophical thought. We find the Realistic School, based on the "all things exist" Hinayana School; the Three-Treatises School, based on Madhyamaka; the Idealist School, based on Yogacara; the Tantric School;

the Flower Adornment School (Hua-Yen, J: Kegon), which attempted to consolidate the various forms; and the White Lotus School (T'ien-T'ai, J: Tendai), which focused on the Lotus Sutra.

All the Chinese Schools had their representatives in neighboring countries. Korea was to develop its own powerful form of Ch'an called Son. Vietnam developed a form of Ch'an that incorporated aspects of Pure Land and Hinayana. But it was Japan that would have a field day with Chinese Buddhism, and pass the Mahayana traditions on to the US and the west generally.

Japan

Again, we begin with the legendary: A delegation arrived from Korea with gifts for the Emperor of Japan in 538 AD., including a bronze Buddha and various Sutras. Unfortunately a plague led the Emperor to believe that the traditional gods of Japan were annoyed, so he had the gifts thrown into a canal. But the imperial court on the 600's, in their constant effort to be as sophisticated as the courts of their distinguished neighbors, the Chinese, continued to be drawn to Buddhism.

Although starting as a religion of the upper classes, in the 900's, Pure Land entered the picture as the favorite of the peasant and working classes. And in the 1200's, Ch'an, relabeled Zen, came into Japan, where it was enthusiastically adopted by, among others, the warrior class or Samurai. Zen was introduced into Japan by two particularly talented monks who had gone to China for their educations: Eisai (1141-1215) brought Lin-chi (J: Rinzai) Ch'an, with its koans and occasionally outrageous antics; Dogen (1200-1253) brought the more sedate Ts'ao-tung (J: Soto) Ch'an. In addition, Dogen is particularly admired for his massive treatise, the Shobogenzo.

Ch'an has always had an artistic side to it. In China and elsewhere, a certain simple, elegant style of writing and drawing developed among the monks. In Japan, this became an even more influential aspect of Zen. We have, for example, the poetry, calligraphy, and paintings of various monks – Bankei (1622-1698), Basho (1644-1694), Hakuin (1685-1768), and Ryokan (1758-1831) – which have become internationally beloved. One last Japanese innovation is usually attributed to a somewhat unorthodox monk named Nichiren (1222-1282). Having been trained in the Tendai or White Lotus tradition, he came to believe that the Lotus Sutra carried all that was necessary for Buddhist life.

More than that, he believed that even the name of the Sutra was enough. So he encouraged his students to chant this mantra: Namu-myoho-renge-kyo, which means "homage to the Lotus Sutra." This practice alone would ensure enlightenment in this life. In fact, he insisted, all other forms of Buddhism were of little worth. Needless to say, this was not appreciated by the Buddhist powers of the day. He spent the rest of his life in relative isolation. The Nichiren School nevertheless proved to be one of the most successful forms of Buddhism on the planet.

Tibet

Finally, let's turn out attention to the most mysterious site of Buddhism's history, Tibet. Its first encounter with Buddhism occurred in the 700's AD, when a Tantric master, Guru Rinpoché, came from India to battle the demons of Tibet for control. The demons submitted, but they remained forever a part of Tibetan Buddhism – as its protectors. During the 800's and 900's, Tibet went through a "dark age," during which Buddhism suffered something of a setback. But, in the 1000's, it returned in force. And in 1578, the Mongol overlords named the head of the Gelug School the Dalai Lama, meaning "guru as great as the ocean." The title was made retroactive to two earlier heads of the school.

The fifth Dalai Lama is noted for bringing all of Tibet under his religious and political control. The lineage continues down to the present 14th Dalai Lama, Tenzin Gyatso, born 1935. In 1989, he was awarded the Nobel Peace Prize for his efforts on behalf of his people and nation, which had been taken ovemr by the Communist Chinese in 1951.

The West

It was in the latter half of the 1800's that Buddhism first came to be known in the west. The great European colonial empires brought the ancient cultures of India and China back to the attention of the intellectuals of Europe. Scholars began to learn Asian languages and translate Asian texts. Adventurers explored previously shutoff places and recorded the cultures. Religious enthusiasts enjoyed the exotic and mystical tone of the Asian traditions.

In England, for example, societies sprang up for devotees of "orientalia," such as T. W. Rhys Davids' Pali Text Society and T. Christmas Humphreys' Buddhist Society. Books were published, such as Sir Edwin Arnold's epic poem The Light of Asia (1879). And the first western monks began to make themselves know, such as Allan Bennett, perhaps the very first, who took the name Ananda Metteya. In Germany and France as well, Buddhism was the rage.

In the United States, there was a similar flurry of interest. First of all, thousands of Chinese immigrants were coming to the west coast in the late 1800's, many to provide cheap labor for the railroads and other expanding industries. Also, on the east coast, intellectuals were reading about Buddhism in books by Europeans. One example was Henry Thoreau, who, among other things, translated a French translation of a Buddhist Sutra into English.

A renewal of interest came during World War II, during which many Asian Buddhists — such as the Zen author D.T. Suzuki — came to England and the U.S., and many European Buddhists — such as the Zen author Alan Watts — came to the U.S. As these examples suggest, Zen Buddhism was particularly popular, especially in the U.S., where it became enmeshed in the Beatnik artistic and literary movement as "beat Zen."

One by one, European and Americans who studied in Asia returned with their knowledge and founded monasteries and societies, Asian masters came to Europe and America to found monasteries, and the Asian immigrant populations from China, Japan, Vietnam and elsewhere, quietly continued their Buddhist practices. Today, it is believed that there are more than 300 million Buddhists in the world, including at least a quarter million in Europe, and a half million each in North and South America. I say "at least" because other estimates go as high as three million in the U.S. alone. Whatever the numbers may be, Buddhism is the fourth largest religion in the world, after Christianity, Islam, and Hinduism. And, although it has suffered considerable setbacks over the centuries, it seems to be attracting more and more people, as a religion or a philosophy of life.

Buddhist Beliefs

The Three Signs of Being

Buddhists believe that these three signs are at the root of all human existence:

- *Annica:* (impermanence) everything is unstable, changing and, eventually ceases to exist.
- *Anatta:* (no soul) there is no permanent, unchanging soul in any one. In effect, existence is an illusion.
- *Dukkha:* (suffering) suffering is part of the human condition.
- The Four Noble Truths.
- The teaching of Siddartha Gautama (who became known as the Buddha) is summarised in the Four Noble Truths.
- *Dukkha:* (suffering) all life is suffering. All are born to suffer.
- *Samudaya:* (cause of dukkha) suffering is caused by Tanha, which means 'craving' or 'desire'. Because Buddhists believe there is no permanent self/soul and nothing has any real existence, then no desire can be really satisfied. Misery and suffering are the result.
- *Nirodha:* (cessation of dukkha) suffering can be eliminated if people learn to live without craving or desire.

- *The Middle Way:* Gautama had lived, as a prince, in luxury. Then he had lived as an ascetic in extreme deprivation. Neither satisfied him. He, therefore, concluded that the answer was to be found in the Middle Way, between the two extremes. He mapped out such a life style in the Eightfold Path.
- *Right Understanding:* Viewing things as they really are (Annica, anatta, dukkha).
- *Right Thought:* Compassion and love towards all.
- *Right Speech:* No lies or insults.
- *Right Action:* No harm to others.
- *Right Livelihood:* Earning living in morally right way.
- *Right Effort:* To follow Eightfold Path without distractions.
- *Right Mindfulness:* Full attention to own actions and to needs of others.
- *Right Concentration:* Mind focussed on one thing through meditation.

The Triple Refuge

Buddhists, when they need help or encouragement, say that there are three Jewels (Trisharana). They say that for refuge they go to the Buddha, they go to the Dhamma and they go to the Sangha. This is the Tiratana, the Triple Refuge.

Buddha

Gautama was the man who claimed to have been enlightened, and taught the way for others to follow.

Dhamma

This means the Universal Law, and is the teaching of Buddha as contained in the Four Noble Truths and the Eightfold Path.

Sangha

The community of those who try to live according to the teachings of Buddha.

Past, Present and Future

- Kamma (aka Karma) is the idea that past actions (from previous existences) are responsible for the person's present state. Similarly, present actions will affect future ones.
- Samsara is the continual and repeated cycle of life, suffering, death and rebirth.
- Nibbana (aka Nirvana) is the ultimate goal of Buddhists. It represents that final state when the Buddhist has extinguished all desire and is freed from the illusion of existence. Ideas of nibbana vary from a peaceful state of existence to its not being a state of existence at all - i.e. non-existence.

The Basics Buddhism Beliefs

The basic practices and beliefs of Buddhism are credited to Siddhartha Guatama, born in Nepal in 563 B.C. Troubled by the suffering amongst the common people, Guatama departed from his Hindu studies and gods. He chose to live off of alms while devoting him to extreme somberness. This brought him to a weakened state of mind and body and not to the peace he had hoped for. He began intense meditation, claiming it brought him into a god-like state of "Nirvana." Though difficult to reach, Nirvana is said to be achieved by totally denying self, entering a state of illumination, joy, and harmony. However, it is said that to do so brings release from desires for self that causes all bodily pain and sorrow. By claiming to have done so, Guatama proclaimed himself to be an "enlightened one" or a Buddha. A Buddha is someone regarded as embodying divine wisdom and virtue, but not a god.

Buddhist beliefs and Christianity differ in many ways:

- Buddhists do not believe in a Divine being, therefore they have no concept of salvation and atonement for wrong doings. Compare those beliefs to Christianity, wherein God provided His Son Jesus as redemption for our sins.

- While Buddhism claims there is no beginning and end, we are shown through Christianity and Judaism the Creation and God's plan for our eternity.
- The philosophies of Buddha were written 400 years after his death. The Bible was written with numerous prophecies hundreds of years before Jesus was born.
- There are no directives or absolutes to the path of Nirvana. Yet Jesus taught that while our physical bodies will die, our soul will ascend to be with the Lord in Heaven. We must simply accept His gift of salvation to be redeemed for this assurance. Buddhists contend that people do not have individual souls and hold to the belief that achievements in life will continue on and on into your next bodily form, striving to get it right (reincarnation). In Buddhism, there is no forgiveness or mercy from a loving God.

Buddhist beliefs: Where is the hope? In Buddhism, there is no hope for eternal safety. In Christianity, however, Jesus gave us directives and absolutes. Eternal joy is achievable through accepting Him.

He tells us in John 10:9a (KJV), "I am the door: by me if any man enter in, he shall be saved..." and Romans 10:9-13, "That if you confess with your mouth,' Jesus is Lord' and believe in your heart that

God raised him from the dead, you will be saved and it is with your heart that your believe and are justified, and it is with your mouth that you confess and are saved. As the Scripture says, 'Anyone who trusts in him will never be put to shame.' For there is no difference between Jew and Gentile — the same Lord is Lord of all and richly blesses all who call on him, for 'Everyone who calls on the name of the Lord will be saved.'"

Buddhism, as a religion, lays great emphasis on the adherence to the basic beliefs. The basic Buddhist belief comprise of the basic teachings and concepts of Buddhism. Lord Buddha urged His followers to concentrate on the Four Noble Truths, which helps in attaining freedom from suffering.

In the following lines, we have provided more information on the basic Buddhism beliefs.

Basic Points of Buddhism

Chief monks belonging to both the Theravada sect and the Mahayana sect met in Sri Lanka in the year 1966 and approved the following "Basic Points Unifying the Theravada and Mahayana":

- Buddha is our only Master.
- We take refuge in the Buddha, the Dhamma and the Sangha.
- This world is not created and ruled by a God.
- The purpose of life is to develop empathy for all living beings without prejudice and to work for their good, happiness, and peace. Last but not the least; we need acquire acumen that will lead to the realization of Ultimate Truth.
- We accept the Four Noble Truths of Buddhism.
- All accustomed things (samskaara) are transient (anitya) and dukkha and all conditioned and unconditioned things (dharma) are without self (anaatma).
- The Thirty-seven qualities helpful in Enlightenment are different aspects of the path taught by the Buddha.
- There are three ways of attaining Enlightenment, namely as a Disciple, as a Pratyeka-Buddha and as a Samyaksam-Buddha. The life of a Bodhisattva, who is striving to become a Samyak-sam-Buddha, is the highest, noblest and the most heroic.
- The different Buddhist beliefs, practices, rites and ceremonies, customs and habits followed in different countries should not be confused with the essential teachings of Buddha.

Theistic or Atheistic

Buddhism does not believe in the existence of a God who created the universe. As per Lord Buddha, one should emphasize on the practical ways of life, which will help a person in attaining enlightenment. However, at the same time,

Buddha did not rule out the existence of a God or gods altogether. With the growth and spread of Buddhism, local deities and religious practices were included in it. Today, Tibetan Buddhist cosmology talks about a large number of 'Divine Beings', believed to be representative of the psychic life. One of the six realms of the Tibetan cosmology is the realm of Gods, who must take birth on earth as humans to attain enlightenment.

Buddhist Deities

Theravada sect of Buddhism does not believe in the existence of deities. However, as per the Mahayana sect, celestial Buddhas and bodhisattvas occupy the universe as Gods and Goddesses. The most popular Buddhist deities include the Laughing Buddha, the Medicine Buddha, Kuan Yin, the Green and White Taras, etc.

Human Nature

As per Buddhism, there is nothing such as a soul or atman. Rather, a human being is believed to be constituted of five elements, namely physical form, feelings, ideations, mental developments and awareness. These components combine to form a human being at the time of birth. However, since Buddhism believes in reincarnation and karma, one finds a little contradiction here.

The Purpose of Living

The main aim of life, as per Buddhism, is the extinction of suffering. By recognizing the four noble truths of life and following the noble eightfold path, one can end the suffering in life.

The Noble Eightfold Path

In Buddhism, it is believed that one can escape from the vicious cycle of birth and death by following the noble eightfold path, consisting of the following eight steps:

- Right Actions

- Right Concentration
- Right Effort/Exercise
- Right Livelihood
- Right Mindfulness/Awareness
- Right Speech
- Right Thoughts
- Right Understanding

The Four Noble Truths

The Four Noble Truths, forming the essence of Buddhism, are:

- The Noble Truth of Suffering (Dukkha)
- The Noble Truth of the Origin of Suffering (Samudaya)
- The Noble Truth of the Cessation of Suffering (Nirodha)
- The Noble Truth that leads to the Extinction of Suffering (Magga)

Belief of Reincarnation

Two of the basic beliefs of Buddhism are the principles of rebirth and karma. There now follows a brief introduction to these topics taken from Geshe Kelsang's book, *Eight Steps to Happiness*:

"The mind is neither physical, nor a byproduct of purely physical processes, but a formless continuum that is a separate entity from the body. When the body disintegrates at death, the mind does not cease. Although our superficial conscious mind ceases, it does so by dissolving into a deeper level of consciousness, call 'the very subtle mind'.

The continuum of our very subtle mind has no beginning and no end, and it is this mind which, when completely purified, transforms into the omniscient mind of a Buddha. Every action we perform leaves an imprint, or potential, on our very subtle mind, and each karmic potential eventually gives rise to its own effect.

Our mind is like a field, and performing actions is like

sowing seeds in that field. Positive or virtuous actions sow the seeds of future happiness, and negative or non-virtuous actions sow the seeds of future suffering.

This definite relationship between actions and their effects - virtue causing happiness and non-virtue causing suffering - is known as the 'law of karma'. An understanding of the law of karma is the basis of Buddhist morality. After we die our very subtle mind leaves our body and enters the intermediate state, or 'bardo' in Tibetan. In this subtle dream-like state we experience many different visions that arise from the karmic potentials that were activated at the time of our death. These visions may be pleasant or terrifying depending on the karma that ripens. Once these karmic seeds have fully ripened they impel us to take rebirth without choice.

It is important to understand that as ordinary samsaric beings we do not choose our rebirth but are reborn solely in accordance with our karma. If good karma ripens we are reborn in a fortunate state, either as a human or a god, but if negative karma ripens we are reborn in a lower state, as an animal, a hungry ghost, or a hell being. It is as if we are blown to our future lives by the winds of our karma, sometimes ending up in higher rebirths, sometimes in lower rebirths.

This uninterrupted cycle of death and rebirth without choice is called 'cyclic existence' or 'samsara in Sanskrit. Samsara is like a Ferris wheel, sometimes taking us up into the three fortunate realms, sometimes down into the three lower realms. The driving force of the wheel of samsara is our contaminated actions motivated by delusions, and the hub of the wheel is self-grasping ignorance.

For as long as we remain on this wheel we shall experience an unceasing cycle of suffering and dissatisfaction, and we shall have no opportunity to experience pure, lasting happiness. By practicing the Buddhist path to liberation and enlightenment, however, we can destroy self-grasping, thereby liberating our self from the cycle of uncontrolled rebirth and attaining a state of perfect peace and freedom. We shall then be in a position to help others to do the same."

Basic Beliefs

What are the basic beliefs of Buddhism? Buddhism is a complex religious tradition. It is hard to cover all the beliefs that Buddhists have, as there are many schools and branches which differ in many aspects between each other. Here, I'm going to talk about the basic teachings that are commonly attributed to the Buddha Siddharta Gautama.

- *The Doctrine of Reincarnation:* I think most of you know what I'm talking about here. Human beings don't live just one life, but cycle around again and again, life after life, death after death, in a process of death and rebirth. Indian civilization view reincarnation not as a single life, or two or three lives strung together, but sees it on a time scale that involves millions and millions of lifetimes. They see it as a burden, as a problem to be solved. This is known in India as Samsara. The Buddha changed a bit the way they see reincarnation. He said that beings don't have soul. Indians believed that when someone died, his soul was reincarnated in another body. The Buddha rejected that and said that there wasn't a permanent soul that went through one life to another, but it was just a stream of causes. (To read more about this, go to the article The Doctrine of Reincarnation).
- *The Law of Karma:* In India, the word Karma simply means "action". The cycle of death and rebirth, the cycle of Samsara, is driven by an inexorable law. What you do now, will produce some result in a future life. You have to find some way to work with this law in order to permit some positive solution to the problem of Samsara. (To read more about this, go to the article The Law of Karma).
- *The Realms of Rebirth:* Where Karma can lead you? Six realms are considered into which you can be born. You can be born as a god, as a demigod or a lesser category of gods sometimes referred as demons, as a human being, as a ghost, as an animal, or as a spirit in hell. Yes, hell. It is a place where you can really be punished for the

bad actions you have done. (To read more about this, go to the article The Real Meaning of Reincarnation).

The Teachings of the Buddha

Now, let's talk about the teachings of the Buddha. The traditional summary of the teaching is given in four categories, the so called Four Noble Truths:

- *The Truth of Suffering (Dukkha):* The truth of suffering is expressed in the simple claim that All is Suffering. All the things in human experience cause suffering.
- *The Arising of Suffering (Samudaya):* It says that suffering arises essentially from ignorance. From that ignorance comes desire or craving. And then, out of that craving or desire comes reincarnation. Ignorance leads to desire, desire leads to birth.
- *The Cessation of Suffering (Nirodha):* This is Nirvana. Nirvana means literally to blow out. You might say that Nirvana is the cessation, is the extinction of "self" that wanders constantly from one life to the next. What's so great about this? You must remember that the process of reincarnation is a burden for Buddhists and Indian religious people in general. They see it as a really serious problem, and Nirvana is the final solution.
- *The Truth of the Way (Marga):* The Path of Nirvana is often divided in eight categories, The Noble Eightfold Path. It includes the concept of right understanding, right intention, right speech, right action, right livelihood, right effort, right mindfulness and right concentration.

The Path becomes a little bit clearer if we take these eight categories and reduce them or group them together into three:

- *Sila (moral conduct):* No killing, no stealing, no lying, no abuse of sex and not drinking intoxicants. Pretty simple.
- *Samadhi (mental concentration):* This is to meditate or concentrate the mind. It is a way to stop all of those distractions and all of those negative tendencies that tie you to the experience of death and rebirth.
- *And Panna (wisdom):* This is to try to know the nature of

the world and to know where it is going, so you can become detached from it and begin the process that leads to Nirvana.

Theravada: The Doctrine of the Elders

Theravada is a word that means "doctrine of the Elders". It is the oldest surviving school. It is said that it was founded around one hundred years after the Buddha's Parinirvana. They accept as their scripture the Pali Canon. The Pali Canon is the mother of all Buddhist scriptures; it is accepted by the other branches of Buddhism (of course, including other additional scriptures).

What is the Pali Canon about? Well, the Pali Canon contains what are considered the traditional teachings of the Buddha, what we here in the West commonly think of when we hear the word Buddhism. The Buddha said that his teaching was suffering, its origin and cessation. Well, it took him many and many life times to find and fully grasp the meaning of suffering. What he understood is summarized in the so called Four Noble Truths:

- *The Truth of Suffering:* the Buddha said that all in life causes suffering, no matter how pleasurable or good something seems. Everything ultimately leads to suffering.
- *The Truth of the Origin of Suffering:* the Buddha talked about a complex chain of causes that originates suffering. This is synthesized by pointing out the most important links in the chain: Ignorance, desire, birth. This means that all suffering is ultimately rooted in ignorance. This ignorance about reality of our selves leads to desire. This desire is what causes suffering and keep us in the cycle of deaths and rebirths.
- *The Truth of the Cessation of Suffering:* the Buddha said that the cessation of suffering is Nirvana. Nirvana is a concept difficult to grasp. It literally means to extinguish. Extinguish what? Extinguish the causes that lead us to suffering and to rebirth.
- *The Truth of the Path:* the Buddha also taught about what

to do to achieve Nirvana. He talked about moral conduct, mental concentration and wisdom. Moral conduct and mental concentration are like supporting elements to achieve wisdom, which is what will lead us to Nirvana.

These are the teachings of the Buddha according to the Theravada. This paradigm makes it difficult to lay people to seek Nirvana. In traditional Buddhism and in the Theravada tradition, the goal of lay people is to get good karma and consequently a good rebirth that may get them closer to Nirvana.

They also have to support the monastic community, as monks and nuns can't work in lay activities. Monks and nuns are the ones who seek Nirvana really seriously. They have an additional series of regulations. For example, they can't sleep in soft beds. They also can't carry food from one day to the next. Everyday they have to get for their food and eat it in that moment.

The Path

Until now, we've just mentioned what people have to do to achieve Nirvana. They have to abide some rules of moral conduct; they have to engage in mental concentration or meditation and to try to find wisdom. The ultimate goal of Theravada is to achieve wisdom, which will lead to Nirvana. What is this wisdom about? What should we know? The Buddha taught about the nature of reality and, more importantly, about the nature of the self. In this case, we should say the non-nature of the self, because the Buddha said that what we commonly identify as our "self" does not exist.

Self does not exist? What does this mean? It means that nothing lasts from one moment to the next. Nothing has an identity that endures from one moment to the next, including persons. Now you are not the same person that you were ten years ago. You are not the same person that you were one second ago. We don't have an identity that endures from one moment to the next. Then, you may ask, if there is no self, who is reading this article? The Buddha said that what we commonly call our "self" is a bundle of momentary phenomena. These skhandas, as the Buddha called them, are: matter, sensation, perception, mental formations and consciousness. If we identity with one or more of these phenomena suffering arises. Following this, suffering is extinguished by relinquishing attachments to any of these phenomena. This is wisdom.

Mahayana Buddhism: A New Paradigm

The Mahayana, or "Great Vehicle", changes the style, the tone and the content of Buddhist practice in profound ways. It opens up the practice of Buddha hood to lay people as well as to monks and nuns. It also involves a far more extended vision of the cosmos than anything that came before. Theravada Buddhism in South East Asia is in some ways very different from Buddhist practice at the time of the Buddha, but still represents, quite deliberately, a conservative option. The name Mahayana comes from the literature of the movement itself. It is a name that is used to distinguish itself from what it saw as the Buddhism that came before. The basic premise of the Mahayana is that the Buddha gave his final and real teachings to a select group of followers. These teachings were not recorded in the Pali Canon, but in numerous "Sutras".

The Boddhisattva Ideal

So, what is new with the Mahayana? The fundamental teaching of Mahayana Buddhism is what is called the Boddhisattva Ideal. A Boddhisattva is a Buddha-to-be, somebody who isn't a Buddha yet but plans to be one in a future life. A Boddhisattva in the Mahayana tradition doesn't attempt to go straight to Nirvana but he turns to this world and attempts to help others along the path to salvation. This means that Boddhisattvas can include lay men as well as monks and nuns, because all of us can be understood as being part of the path to Buddhahood. Boddhisattvas that come back like this to this world to help others cultivate two important virtues.

One is wisdom, that great virtue that was discussed in the early accounts of the Buddhist path that leads you to Nirvana. In addition to that, Boddhisattvas explicitly develop the virtue of compassion. The word is Karuna, a crucial Mahayana word. So, Boddhisattvas cultivate two virtues. Wisdom, a contemplative and quiet virtue that has to do with the understanding of the nature of the self and the world and compassion, a virtue that has to do with actively seeking the welfare of others. How is the Boddhisattva ideal expressed in ritual and in philosophy?

The most important concept to express the Boddhisattva ideal is the concept of the Bodhicitta, a word we translate as the "mind that seeks enlightenment" or simply the aspiration to seek enlightenment for the sake of all other beings. Boddhisattvas who enter the Boddhisattva path start with some kind of gut feeling. "I want to be enlightened in order to bring that enlightenment to others". This mind of enlightenment is generated and cultivated as the Boddhisattva path proceeds.

The Lay Boddhisattvas

Boddhisattvas described in Mahayana literature are often human beings just like us. In the earlier tradition we always were talking largely about monks and nuns. The ideal practitioners of the Buddhist path were monks and nuns who engaged in an act of renunciation and pursued a monastic life.

Now, this tradition was opening up explicitly for lay people. This is a way of saying that lay Buddhist values and the lay Buddhist life is a place where you can pursue the fundamental teaching of the Buddha. You can become a Boddhisattva and bring to ordinary lay life all the values of Buddhist life.

You can go out and have a couple of beers, you may live with your family, you may even go to a gambling hall, but you always do it in a way that is going to bring Buddhist values into that place. The Boddhisattva is engaged in the world. This is a crucial shift of the basic understanding of Buddhist life and it had a radical effect on Buddhism throughout Asia.

The Celestial Bodhisattvas and Buddhas

The Mahayana begins to imagine a universe that is not populated just by human boddhisattvas, people like you and me, but also by celestial boddhisattvas and Buddhas that have infinitely greater power than we have. These celestial boddhisattvas have the ability to intervene in this world and save people as if they were gods. Here we are going to talk about these "deities" and how they affect the lives and practices of Buddhists in the Mahayana world.

All living beings have the same basic wish to be happy and avoid suffering, but very few people understand the real causes of happiness and suffering. We generally believe that external conditions such as food, friends, cars, and money are the real causes of happiness, and as a result we devote nearly all our time and energy to acquiring these. Superficially it seems that these things can make us happy, but if we look more deeply we shall see that they also bring us a lot of suffering and problems.

Happiness and suffering are opposites, so if something is a real cause of happiness it cannot give rise to suffering. If food, money, and so forth really are causes of happiness, they can never be causes of suffering; yet we know from our own experience that they often do cause suffering. For example, one of our main interests is food, but the food we eat is also the principal cause of most of our ill health and sickness.

In the process of producing the things we feel will make us happy, we have polluted our environment to such an extent that the very air we breathe and the water we drink now threaten our health and wellbeing. We love the freedom and independence a car can give us, but the cost in accidents and environmental destruction is enormous. We feel that money is essential for us to enjoy life, but the pursuit of money also causes immense problems and anxiety. Even our family and friends, with whom we enjoy so many happy moments, can also bring us a lot of worry and heartache.

In recent years our understanding and control of the external world have increased considerably, and as a result we have witnessed remarkable material progress; but there has not been a corresponding increase in human happiness. There is no less suffering in the world today, and there are no fewer problems. Indeed, it could be said that there are now more problems and greater unhappiness than ever before. This shows that the solution to our problems, and to those of society as a whole, does not lie in knowledge or control of the external world.

Why is this? Happiness and suffering are states of mind, and so their main causes cannot be found outside the mind. The real source of happiness is inner peace. If our mind is peaceful, we shall be happy all the time, regardless of external conditions, but if it is disturbed or troubled in any way, we shall never be happy, no matter how good our external conditions may be. External conditions can only make us happy if our mind is peaceful. We can understand this through our own experience. For instance, even if we are in the most beautiful surroundings and have everything we need, the moment we get angry any happiness we may have disappears. This is because anger has destroyed our inner peace.

We can see from this that if we want true, lasting happiness we need to develop and maintain a special experience of inner peace. The only way to do this is by training our mind through spiritual practice – gradually reducing and eliminating our negative, disturbed states of mind and replacing them with positive, peaceful states. Eventually, through continuing to improve our inner peace we shall experience permanent inner peace, or 'nirvana'. Once we have attained nirvana we shall be happy throughout our life, and in life after life. We shall have solved all our problems and accomplished the true meaning of our human life.

5

World Religion

Islam and its Belief System

The literal meaning of Islam is peace; surrender of one's will i.e. losing oneself for the sake of God and surrendering one's own pleasure for the pleasure of God. The message of Islam was revealed to the Holy Prophet Muhammad (peace and blessings on him) 1, 400 years ago. It was revealed through angel Gabriel (on whom be peace) and was thus preserved in the Holy *Quran*.

The Holy *Quran* carries a Divine guarantee of safeguard from interpolation and it claims that it combines the best features of the earlier scriptures. The prime message of Islam is the Unity of God, that the Creator of the world is One and He alone is worthy of worship and that Muhammad (peace and blessings on him) is His Messenger and Servant.

The follower of this belief is thus a Muslim - a Muslim's other beliefs are: God's angels, previously revealed Books of God, all the prophets, from Adam to Jesus (peace be on them both), the Day of Judgement and indeed the Decree of God. A Muslim has five main duties to perform, namely; bearing witness to the Unity of God and Muhammad (peace and blessings on him) as His Messenger, observing the prescribed prayer, payment of Zakat, keeping the fasts of Ramadhan and performing the pilgrimage to Mecca.

Islam believes that each person is born pure. The Holy

Quran tells us that God has given human beings a choice between good and evil and to seek God's pleasure through faith, prayer and charity. Islam believes that God created mankind in His image and by imbuing the attributes of God on a human level mankind can attain His nearness. Islam's main message is to worship God and to treat all God's creation with kindness and compassion. Rights of parents in old age, orphans and the needy are clearly stated. Women's rights were safeguarded 1,400 years ago when the rest of the world was in total darkness about emancipation. Islamic teachings encompass every imaginable situation and its rules and principles are truly universal and have stood the test of time. In Islam virtue does not connote forsaking the bounties of nature that are lawful.

On the contrary one is encouraged to lead a healthy, active life with the qualities of kindness, chastity, honesty, mercy, courage patience and politeness. In short, Islam has a perfect and complete code for the guidance of individuals and communities alike. As the entire message of Islam is derived from the Holy *Quran* and indeed the Sunnah and Hadith (the traditions and practices of the Holy Prophet, peace and blessings on him) it is immutable in the face of change in time and place. It may appear rigid to the casual eye, in actual fact it is most certainly an adaptable way of life regardless of human changes. Islam teaches that the path to spiritual development is open to all. Any individual who searches the One Creator can seek nearness to God through sincere and earnest worship; it is central to establishing a relationship with the Almighty. This positive message for humanity fills hearts with hope and courage. At present there are 1.5 billion Muslims worldwide and they form the majority in more than 50 countries of the world. Today Islam is the fastest growing faith in the world - its beautiful message is reaching millions in the far corner of the earth.

The Spread of Islam

From the oasis cities of Makkah and Madinah in the

Arabian Desert, the message of Islam went forth with electrifying speed. Within half a century of the Prophet's death, Islam had spread to three continents. Islam is not, as some imagine in the West, a religion of the sword nor did it spread primarily by means of war. It was only within Arabia, where a crude form of idolatry was rampant, that Islam was propagated by warring against those tribes which did not accept the message of God—whereas Christians and Jews were not forced to convert. Outside of Arabia also the vast lands conquered by the Arab armies in a short period became Muslim not by force of the sword but by the appeal of the new religion. It was faith in One God and emphasis upon His Mercy that brought vast numbers of people into the fold of Islam.

The new religion did not coerce people to convert. Many continued to remain Jews and Christians and to this day important communities of the followers of these faiths are found in Muslim lands. Moreover, the spread of Islam was not limited to its miraculous early expansion outside of Arabia. During later centuries the Turks embraced Islam peacefully as did a large number of the people of the Indian subcontinent and the Malay-speaking world. In Africa also, Islam has spread during the past two centuries even under the mighty power of European colonial rulers. Today Islam continues to grow not only in Africa but also in Europe and America where Muslims now comprise a notable minority.

General Characteristics of Islam

Islam was destined to become a world religion and to create a civilization which stretched from one end of the globe to the other. Already during the early Muslim caliphates, first the Arabs, then the Persians and later the Turks set about to create classical Islamic civilization. Later, in the 13th century, both Africa and India became great centers of Islamic civilization and soon thereafter Muslim kingdoms were established in the Malay-Indonesian world while Chinese Muslims flourished throughout China.

Global Religion

Islam is a religion for all people from whatever race or background they might be. That is why Islamic civilization is based on a unity which stands completely against any racial or ethnic discrimination. Such major racial and ethnic groups as the Arabs, Persians, Turks, Africans, Indians, Chinese and Malays in addition to numerous smaller units embraced Islam and contributed to the building of Islamic civilization. Moreover, Islam was not opposed to learning from the earlier civilizations and incorporating their science, learning, and culture into its own world view, as long as they did not oppose the principles of Islam. Each ethnic and racial group which embraced Islam made its contribution to the one Islamic civilization to which everyone belonged.

The sense of brotherhood and sisterhood was so much emphasized that it overcame all local attachments to a particular tribe, race, or language—all of which became subservient to the universal brotherhood and sisterhood of Islam. The global civilization thus created by Islam permitted people of diverse ethnic backgrounds to work together in cultivating various arts and sciences. Although the civilization was profoundly Islamic, even non-Muslim "people of the book" participated in the intellectual activity whose fruits belonged to everyone. The scientific climate was reminiscent of the present situation in America where scientists and men and women of learning from all over the world are active in the advancement of knowledge which belongs to everyone.

The global civilization created by Islam also succeeded in activating the mind and thought of the people who entered its fold. As a result of Islam, the nomadic Arabs became torch-bearers of science and learning. The Persians who had created a great civilization before the rise of Islam nevertheless produced much more science and learning in the Islamic period than before. The same can be said of the Turks and other peoples who embraced Islam. The religion of Islam was itself responsible not only for the creation of a world civilization in which people of many different ethnic backgrounds participated, but it played a central role in developing intellectual and cultural life on a scale not seen before.

For some eight hundred years Arabic remained the major intellectual and scientific language of the world. During the centuries following the rise of Islam, Muslim dynasties ruling in various parts of the Islamic world bore witness to the flowering of Islamic culture and thought. In fact this tradition of intellectual activity was eclipsed only at the beginning of modern times as a result of the weakening of faith among Muslims combined with external domination. And today this activity has begun anew in many parts of the Islamic world now that the Muslims have regained their political independence.

The literal meaning of Islam is peace; surrender of one's will i.e. losing oneself for the sake of God and surrendering one's own pleasure for the pleasure of God. The message of Islam was revealed to the Holy Prophet Muhammad (peace and blessings on him) 1, 400 years ago. It was revealed through angel Gabriel (on whom be peace) and was thus preserved in the Holy *Quran*. The Holy *Quran* carries a Divine guarantee of safeguard from interpolation and it claims that it combines the best features of the earlier scriptures. The prime message of Islam is the Unity of God, that the Creator of the world is One and He alone is worthy of worship and that Muhammad (peace and blessings on him) is His Messenger and Servant.

The follower of this belief is thus a Muslim - a Muslim's other beliefs are: God's angels, previously revealed Books of God, all the prophets, from Adam to Jesus (peace be on them both), the Day of Judgement and indeed the Decree of God. A Muslim has five main duties to perform, namely; bearing witness to the Unity of God and Muhammad (peace and blessings on him) as His Messenger, observing the prescribed prayer, payment of Zakat, keeping the fasts of Ramadhan and performing the pilgrimage to Mecca. Islam believes that each person is born pure.

The Holy *Quran* tells us that God has given human beings a choice between good and evil and to seek God's pleasure through faith, prayer and charity. Islam believes that God created mankind in His image and by imbuing the attributes of God on a human level mankind can attain His nearness.

Islam's main message is to worship God and to treat all God's creation with kindness and compassion. Rights of parents in old age, orphans and the needy are clearly stated. Women's rights were safeguarded 1,400 years ago when the rest of the world was in total darkness about emancipation. Islamic teachings encompass every imaginable situation and its rules and principles are truly universal and have stood the test of time. In Islam virtue does not connote forsaking the bounties of nature that are lawful. On the contrary one is encouraged to lead a healthy, active life with the qualities of kindness, chastity, honesty, mercy, courage patience and politeness. In short, Islam has a perfect and complete code for the guidance of individuals and communities alike.

As the entire message of Islam is derived from the Holy *Quran* and indeed the Sunnah and Hadith (the traditions and practices of the Holy Prophet, peace and blessings on him) it is immutable in the face of change in time and place. It may appear rigid to the casual eye, in actual fact it is most certainly an adaptable way of life regardless of human changes. Islam teaches that the path to spiritual development is open to all.

Any individual who searches the One Creator can seek nearness to God through sincere and earnest worship; it is central to establishing a relationship with the Almighty. This positive message for humanity fills hearts with hope and courage. At present there are 1.5 billion Muslims worldwide and they form the majority in more than 50 countries of the world. Today Islam is the fastest growing faith in the world - its beautiful message is reaching millions in the far corner of the earth.

Islamic Beliefs and Eschatology

Islam has a world-following in excess of one billion devotees; about 20% are in the Middle East, with the largest concentration of Muslims in Indonesia. There are over 4 million

Moslems living in America—which means that there are about twice as many Moslems in the US as Episcopalians. There has been an active Muslim contingent in North America for over 300 years, since the time the religion arrived with West African slaves. The Arabic term Islam literally means "surrender," or "submission." Islam's believers (known as "Muslims" from the active participle of "islam"), accept surrender to the will of Allah (the Arabic word for God). Allah is viewed as a unique God—creator, sustainer, and restorer of the world. The will of God to which man is to submit is made known through the Qur'an (the Koran), revealed to his messenger Muhammad.

Muhammad, it is claimed was the last of the great prophets which included Adam, Noah, Moses, Jesus and some others. The basic belief of Islam is expressed in the shahadah, the Muslim confession of faith, "There is no god but God; Muhammad is the prophet of God." Founded in the 7th century AD, Islamic fundamental beliefs include belief in angels, the revealed books and Scriptures, a series of prophets, and a Last Day (of Judgment). Muslim duties include five daily prayers, a welfare tax called zakat, fasting (during the month of Ramadan), and a pilgrimage (hajj) to Mecca; these four elements plus the profession of faith are called the Five Pillars. The Encyclopedia Britannica is a good resource for understanding the roots of Islam. Mecca at the time the prophet was born was inhabited by the tribe of Quraysh (Koreish) to which the clan of Hasim belonged.

The city was a mercantile center with shrines to many gods, chief of whom was Ilah. The Ka'bah sanctuary in the city square guaranteed the safety of those who came to trade. The pre-Islamic deities of Arabia which were most venerated were astral deities, especially the triad of the moon god, the sun goddess, and the god associated with the planet Venus. The moon god was the chief and was protector of the cities. These deities were given various names; however the moon god was evidently originally the Babylonian moon god Sin. To end division among his people in Mecca, Muhammad elevated the moon god Al Ilah to the chief and only god. (It is not widely known in Islam that Allah was a sexual being, having fathered three daughters—this is documented in the E.B.).

Among the visitors and residents of Mecca in the time of the prophet were Jews as well as Christians. Muhammad's thinking was further heavily influenced by these followers of Abraham, as well as by special revelations which were (it is said) communicated to him by the angel Gabriel. The God of Abraham was not Ilah, however, but Yahweh. Abraham was called by Yahweh from Ur of the Chaldees (Babylon) and told to renounce the pagan gods of his family which were the gods of Babylon. In fact Babylon was the seat of all false religion after the Flood of Noah and from Babylon idolatry spread throughout the rest of the ancient world. Muhammad assigned to the moon god of Mecca some of the attributes of the god of Abraham; however the pagan and occultic roots of pre-Islamic religion were not discarded. Alexander Hislop's classic book The Two Babylons remains a good reference on the Babylonian Mystery Religion which has now permeated the entire world.

Abu al-Qasim Muhammad ibn 'Abd Allah ibn 'Abd al-Muttalib ibn Hasim was persecuted for his teachings in Mecca and fled to Medina in 622 AD, his teachings were soon accepted and the community-state of Islam emerged. From the date of Muhammad's flight, called the hijrah, Muslims begin their calendar—AH (Anno Hegirae) 287 is the same as AD (Anno Domini) 900. During the early period Islam acquired its characteristic ethos as a religion uniting itself in both the spiritual and temporal aspects of life and seeking to regulate not only the individual's relationship to God but human relationships in a social setting as well. Thus, there is not only an Islamic religious institution (private) but also an Islamic code/law governing society (public).

The dual religious and social character of Islam, expressing itself as a religious community commissioned by God to bring its own value system to the world through jihad (holy war or holy struggle). Muhammad died in 632 AD and through jihad, Islam spread within a century from Spain to India.

During the Muslim conquests Jews and Christians were assigned a special status as communities possessing Scriptures and are known to Muslims as "people of the Book" (ahl al-kitab) or dhimmis (protected people). Christians, Jews, and later Hindus and Zoroastrians were allowed religious autonomy, but had to pay a per capita tax called the jizyah. Many people converted to Islam to avoid the jizyah tax. In the 12 century the Muslim mystics, known as Sufis, were primarily responsible for spreading Islam to India, China, Central Asia, Turkey, and sub-Saharan Africa.

Islamic traders were responsible (by the 14th century) for extending Islam to Indonesia, Malaya, and China. Under Islam, land once possessed by Islam, if subsequently lost to an invader, remains land that is holy to Islam. It is especially imperative that such lost lands be restored to the rightful rule of Islam. Historically, of course, such lost lands now lost to Islam include not only Israel but large portions of Southern Europe, Spain and North Africa. Since Allah's will is for the entire world to come under subjection to the rule of Islam, Muslims are known for their zeal in spreading their religion, whether by peaceful means or by the sword.

Islamic doctrine/law/thinking are based upon fundamental principals/sources: the Qur'an, the sunnah (traditions), the ijma (community consensus), and ijtihad (individual thought). The Qur'an (which is Arabic for reading or recitation) is regarded by Muslims as The Word of God, delivered to Muhammad by the angel Gabriel. The Qur'an is divided into 114 surahs (chapters), the early surahs revealed in Mecca are ethical and spiritual teachings and the Day of Judgment, whereas the later surahs are concerned with social legislation and the politico-moral principals of community. The sunnah (a clear and welltrodden path, of traditions) denote tribal/common law and the examples of the Prophet, his words and deeds. Six collections of the Hadith (a collection of the sayings of Muhammad) compiled in the 3rd century AH (9th century AD) are regarded as especially authoritative by the Sunni Muslims; whereas Shi'ah Muslims have a different set of sayings in their Hadith.

The ijma standardizes Islamic law and since the 3rd century AH, have been primarily closed to further interpretation. Accepted interpretations of the *Qur'an* and the actual content of the sunnah all rest finally upon the ijma. The transformation of the ijma into a conservative mechanism and the acceptance of a definitive body of Hadith virtually eliminated ijtihad (individual thought). The Islamic doctrine of God, expressed in the *Qur'an* is rigorously monotheistic. God is one and unique; he has no partner or equal. Trinitarianism, the Christian belief that God is three persons in one substance, is vigorously repudiated by Muslims. Muslims believe although Allah's presence is everywhere, he does not indwell anything or anyone. He is the sole Creator, and sustainer of the universe, wherein every creature bears witness to his lordship and unity.

He is also just, merciful, majestic, sovereign, and has endowed every creation with a definite and defined nature which allows the myriad of creation to function as a whole. This "nature" of creation, sets limits; and the limitedness of everything is one of the most fixed points in both the cosmology and the theology of the *Qur'an*. According to the *Qur'an*, God created two apparently parallel species, man and jinn. Man was created from clay and jinn were created from fire. The jinn are endowed with reason and responsibility but are more prone to evil than man. The *Qur'an* is primarily directed at man, and is self described as the guide for the human race. Despite man's lofty position, the *Qur'an* describes human nature as frail and faltering. Man is viewed as rebellious and full of pride, arrogating to himself the attributes of self-sufficiency. Pride, thus, is viewed as the cardinal sin of man, because by not recognizing in himself his essential creaturely limitations he becomes guilty of ascribing to himself partnership with God and thereby violating the unity of God. True faith (identified as iman), consists of belief in the immaculate Divine Unity and Islam is in one's submission to the Divine will.

According to the Qur'an, the being who became Satan had previously occupied a high station but fell from grace by refusing to honour Adam when ordered by Allah to do so. Since then, Satan's work has been to beguile man into error and sin. Satan is a contemporary of man, and his act of disobedience is construed to be the sin of pride. Satan's machinations will cease on the Last Day. The *Qur'an* reveals that messengers from God have, throughout history, been calling man back to God; yet few men have accepted the truth; most have rejected it and have become disbelievers (the kafir, the ungrateful). In Islam there is no point of no return, God is always willing to offer pardon based upon genuine repentance.

All prophets of Islam are human and never part of divinity; they are simply recipients of revelation form God. God never speaks directly to man, he sends angels or inspiration. In Islamic doctrine, on the Last Day when the world will come to an end, the dead will be resurrected and judgment will be pronounced on every person in accordance with his deeds. Those condemned will burn in hellfire, and those saved will enjoy the abiding pleasures of paradise. Besides suffering in physical fire, the damned will also experience a fire "in their hearts"; similarly, the blessed, besides physical enjoyment, will experience the greatest happiness of divine pleasure.

In Islamic life hoarding of wealth without recognizing the rights of the poor is threatened with the direst punishments in the hereafter and is declared to be one of the main causes of the decay of societies in this world. The practice of usury is forbidden. Islam is the concept of the community of the faithful. The mission of the community of the faithful is to "enjoin good and forbid evil" so that "there is no mischief and corruption" on earth, the doctrine of jihad, in view of the constitutional of the community as the power base is the logical outcome. The objective of jihad is not the conversion of individuals to Islam, but rather gaining of political control over the collective affairs of societies to run them in accordance with the principles of Islam. Individual conversion occurs as a byproduct of the power structure of the community passing to the hands of the Muslim community. Under Islam, it is forbidden to wage wars for the sake of acquiring worldly glory, power, or rule.

The Muslim sect of Kharijite once held that "decision belongs to God alone," and insisted on waging continuous and relentless jihad, but the followers of this sect were virtually destroyed during the internecine wars of the 8th century. The Kharijis sect (and the more moderate Ibadis sect) believed that the basis of rule was righteous character and piety, any Muslim, irrespective of race creed or colour could become ruler-provided he or she satisfy the conditions of piety. This is in contrast to the claims of the Shi'ah that the ruler must belong to the family of the Prophet, and in contrast to the Sunnis that the head of state must belong to the Prophet's tribe. Sunni political theory is essentially a product of circumstance-an after-the-fact rationalization of historical developments. Thus, between the Shi'ah legitimism that restricts rule to Ali's family, and the Kharji democratism, Sunnism holds to the position that the rule belongs to the Quraysh (the Prophet's tribe), the condition that actually existed.

The Sunni sect embraces the principle of toleration, making it possible for diverse sects to recognize and coexist with one another. Sunni theologians place emphasis on divine omnipotence at the expense of the freedom and efficacy of the human wills, a deterministic outlook on life characteristic of the Sunni (and invigorated by the Sufi) teaches that nothing exists except God. The Sunnites support the concept that "Muslims must obey even a tyrannical ruler." The Shi'ah, probably under Gnostic and Old Iranian influences, expanded their belief that the ruler must be from the family of the Prophet, and that the perfect leader (imam) is transformed into a metaphysical manifestation of God. The imam, alone, is infallible and can reveal the hidden and true meaning of the *Qur'an*.

The Shi'ah recognise a dozen imams throughout history and believe that knowledge derived from sources other than the imam is useless. Shi'ism in contrast to Sunnism adopted the doctrine of freedom of the human will and the capacity of human reason to know good and evil. In the sphere of law Shi'ism differs from Sunni law mainly in allowing temporary marriage, legally contracted for a fixed period of time based upon a fixed dower. From a spiritual point of view, perhaps the greatest difference between Shi'ism and Sunnism is the Shi'ah concept of the "passion motive." The violent death of Ali's son, Husayn, in 680 AD, at the hands of Umayyad troops is celebrated by the Shi'ah with moving orations, passion plays, and processions in which the participants (in an emotional frenzy of self-flagellation) beat their breasts with heavy chains and sharp objects.

The cities of Mecca and Medina are holy shrines of Islam. The fifth pillar of Islam, the pilgrimage (hajj) to Mecca, begins on the 7th and ends on the 10th month of the Dhu al-Hijjah. When the pilgrim is ten kilometers from the Holy City (Mecca) he enters the state of ihram, he wears two seamless garments and neither shaves nor cuts his hair or nails until the ceremony ends. The principal activities consist of a visit to the Ka'bah sanctuary or the Sacred Mosque; the kissing of the Hajar al-Aswad (the Black Stone); seven circumambulations of the Ka'bah; and the ascent of and running seven times between Mt. Safa and Mt. Marwah (not really mountains but topographic elevations in the desert). At the second stage of the ritual, the pilgrim proceeds from Mecca to Mina, a few miles away; and from there he goes to Arafat, where it is essential to hear a sermon and spend one afternoon.

The last rites consist of spending the night at Muzdalifah (between Arafat and Mina) and offering sacrifice on the last day of ihram, which is the id (festival) of sacrifice. The sacred places of Islam include: the Ka'bah sanctuary at Mecca built by Abraham; the Prophet's mosque in Medina; and Jerusalem from where Muhammad (mi'raj) ascended to heaven (which was the direction to which the early Moslems prayed before the "qiblah" was changed to the Ka'bah in Mecca). For the Shi'ah, Karbala in Iraq (the place of martyrdom of Ali's son,

Husayn) and Meshed in Iran (where Imam Ali ar-Rida is buried) are considered places of special veneration. In Baghdad the tomb of saint Abd al-Qadir al-Jilani is visited every year by pilgrims from throughout the Muslin world, as are numerous Sufi shrines.

The general religious life of the Muslims is centered on the mosque. Friday is the weekly Muslim holy day. The most important and comprehensive concept of Islam, at the practical level, is that of the Shari'ah (the path leading to the watering place). In religious terms it means the highway of life leading to God. The virtue of chastity is regarded as of prime importance by Islam. The Qur'an advanced its universal recommendation of marriage as a means to ensure a state of chastity (ihsan) which is held to be induced by a single free wife. Adultery and false accusations of adultery are severely punished. With regard to Islamic art, the most important principal is aniconism, the prohibition of figurization and representation of living creatures. Underlying this prohibition is the assumption that God is the sole author of life and that a person who makes a picture of a living being seeks to rival God. Architecture and poetry are the richest of the Islamic art forms.

Perhaps the least understood element of Islam is the doctrine of jihad (holy war). The classical Islamic position holds that the world is divided into three spheres: the zone of Islam (dar al-Islam); the zone of peace (dar as-sulh—those nations with whom Muslim nations have peace pacts); and the zone of war (dar al-harb—the rest of the world). In modern times the jihad has appeared primarily as a defense against colonialism, rather than as a program of offense. In classical Islamic law, Shari'ah, offenses against the person, from homicide to assault, are punishable by retaliation—the offended being subject to precisely the same treatment as the victim. For six specific crimes the punishment is fixed (hadd): death for apostasy (renunciation of religious faith) and for highway robbery; amputation of the hand for theft; death by stoning for extramarital sexual relations where the offender is a married person and 100 lashes for unmarried offenders; 80 lashes for an unproven accusation of unchastity/adultery, or for consumption of any alcoholic beverage.

Islamic belief has obviously drawn heavily on information available to the prophet Muhammed from local Jews and Christians living in Arabia during his. The principle claim that the revelation given to the Prophet came from an angel is not unusual among world religions or cults, and is consistent with the warning of the Apostle Paul given in 2 Corinthians. "I feel a divine jealousy for you, for I betrothed you to Christ to present you as a pure bride to her one husband. But I am afraid that as the serpent deceived Eve by his cunning, your thoughts will be led astray from a sincere and pure devotion to Christ...And what I do I will continue to do, in order to undermine the claim of those who would like to claim that in their boasted mission they work on the same terms as we do. For such men are false apostles, deceitful workmen, disguising themselves as apostles of Christ? And no wonder, for even Satan disguises himself as an angel of light. So it is not strange if his servants also disguise themselves as servants of righteousness. Their end will correspond to their deeds.

Islam attributes mercy and compassion to Allah, but has no provision for the certain salvation of the individual, no sacrifice for sin and of course no risen Lord to indwell and guide the believer through this life and the next. Allah is notoriously unpredictable and whimsical in his actions and the Koran sufficiently vague so as to give little assurance or guidance for daily life beyond strong, harsh legalistic restrictions and punishments taken out of context from the Law of Moses. On many points Islam differs radically from Christianity. To cite but one important instance, the church of Jesus Christ is not to bear the sword, nor to ally itself with the state, but to concentrate on "calling out (of the world) a people for His name."

Orthodox Christianity proclaims the coming of the kingdom of God among men, but not Christian Dominionism. Compassion, understanding and tolerance is to be extended to everyone, not from an attitude of superiority, but of service, following the example of her Lord who said, "The Son of man came not to be served, but to serve and to give his life as a ransom for many"; and, "The Son of man came to seek and to save that which was lost." God will see to it that His rule on earth eventually is universal, but in the meantime He is full of mercy and very longsuffering towards all the sons of Adam. Islam's claim as far as Israel is concerned is to assume (without any Biblical basis of course) that Ishmael, not Isaac, is the legitimate heir to whom the Abrahamic promises were passed.

Islamic Eschatology

Although not commonly appreciated by most Christians and Jews, the various sects of Islam, in their oral tradition, and from the Koran, maintain a complex and intricate eschatology dealing with the end of the age and the coming of a great world leader, or Mahdi. The center of these events at the end of the age is Jerusalem, not Mecca, and Jesus is one of the principle participants in the coming great judgment, according to Muslim belief. Since the destruction of the Second Jewish Temple in 70 AD, Jews have been unable to offer any blood sacrifice for sins, however the Moslems observe to this day an annual sacrifice of many thousands of lambs which are slain during the pilgrimage to Mecca:

"Midway through the pilgrimage rites, pilgrims move into tents outside the city of Mecca for the ceremony of standing in the Valley of Arafat at the foot of the Mount of Mercy. This celebrated standing ceremony, which lasts throughout an entire afternoon, creates in the minds of the devout a profound sense of the presence of God in their lives and of divine forgiveness of their sins. They remember, too, that Muhammad visited this spot and preached here on his final pilgrimage. So meaningful is this ceremony that many authorities regard it as the climactic or central event of the entire pilgrimage. In the evening, pilgrims gather forty-nine small stones which they take to Mina the next morning, in order to hurl them at one of three stone pillars representing the devil and his powers of temptation. By this rite (Jamrat) they recall the way Ishmael, on his way to be sacrificed by his father (Muslin tradition substitutes Ishmael for Isaac as the son whom Abraham nearly sacrificed), turned back the suggestions of Iblis that he flee."

"The slaughtering of a small animal on the field of sacrifice is a way of remembering that Allah accepted Abraham's sacrifice of a ram in place of his son." (Quoted from *Islam: A Survey of the Muslim Faith* by C. George Fry and James R. King, Babwer Press, Grand Rapids, 1980).

Muslim belief draws more on Old Testament Jewish belief than on Christian influence, though both Jewish synagogues and Christian assemblies existed in Arabia when the Prophet received the angelic revelations which lead him to write the Koran.

"Christians are interested to learn of the high regard Muslims have for Jesus (Isa, in Arabic). Jesus, it is taught, was born of a virgin, without human father, and lived a sinless life. He is given titles of honor bestowed on no other prophet and He is pictured as a wandering preacher who performed miracles and spoke beautiful words. To Him was given a book for His people, the Gospel, but the book was lost (or hopelessly distorted) and Jesus Himself was rejected. His people attempted to crucify Him, but Jesus was saved when someone took His place on the cross or tree and He ascended into heaven, having promised to send a comforter (Muhammad)."

"In Muslin piety many legends surround Jesus. Some Muslims believe that at some time in the distant future He will return to earth and marry. A grave site has been reserved for Him. Others declare that Jesus will judge the world at the end of time—or that He will help Muhammad with his work of judgment. Still another tradition, from the Ahmadiyya Muslims of South Asia, has it that Christ fled Palestine for India, where He gathered many followers, died at a ripe old age, and was buried at Srinagar, where His tomb was recently uncovered."

A recent study of Muslim beliefs concerning the end time says: "The Imamite doctrine of the Mahdi at one point merges with the return of Jesus, another prominent figure of Islamic eschatology. The doctrine of the return of Jesus, as described in the Sunnite sources and cited by the Shiite traditionists is explained in a more or less uniform manner."

"He will descend in the Holy Land at a place called Afiq with a spear in his hand; he will kill with it al-Dajjal (the Antichrist of Islamic eschatology) and go to Jerusalem at the time of the morning prayer.

The Imam will seek to yield his place to him, but Jesus will refuse and will worship behind him according to the Sharia of Muhammad. Thereafter he will kill the swine, break the cross, and kill all the Christians who do not believe in him. Once al-Dajjal is killed, all the Peoples of the Book (i.e., Jews and Christians) will believe in him and will form one single umma of those who submit to the will of God. Jesus will establish the rule of justice and will remain for forty years, after which he will die. His funeral will take place in Medina, where he will be buried beside Muhammad, in a place between Abu Bakr and Umar."

"The Muslim eschatological tradition is unanimous in assigning to both Jesus and the Mahdi a significant role in the doctrine of the qiyama (resurrection). As a matter of fact, many exegetes of the *Quran* in explaining the verse, "He (Jesus) is surely knowledge of the Hour" (43:61), state that the descent of Jesus during the rulership of the Mahdi will make the approach of the Hour known. In the development of the eschatological role of the Mahdi in Shiite traditions, much emphasis was laid on the function of the Mahdi as the descendant of Muhammad and the Imam, who will be followed in the prayer by Jesus. The latter point is repeatedly emphasized in the Shiite eschatological tradition. This distinguished the roles of the Mahdi and Jesus, which at times became confusingly alike.

On the other hand, some Sunnites, in their polemics against the Shiites, related a tradition attributed to the

Prophet: 'There is no Mahdi save Jesus, son of Mary.' This tradition was evidently used to undermine the chiliastic hopes of the Shiites and to minimize the eschatological importance of the Mahdi, which was emphatically maintained by the Shiites. The group who used the above tradition in their polemics argued that while there was no mention of Mahdi in the Ouran, the return of Jesus was well established in the signs of the Hour, and he, not the Mahdi, would kill the Dajjal.

"In the Shiite traditions the function of killing the Dajjal is reserved for al-Mahdi. In a long tradition Ali is reported to have answered a question regarding al-Dajjal, whose features are vividly described thus: He is one-eyed, his eye being in his forehead and shining like the morning star. On his forehead is written: "This is the kafir (non-believer)," which will be legible to both literate and illiterate persons. His emergence will be preceded by a time of great hardship. Then Ali describes the manner in which he will appear on a donkey, and his call will be heard from one end of the earth to the other. He will tell the people that he is their creator and their lord.

"Those who follow him on that day will be the enemies of God, who will be wearing something green on their heads. God will cause them to be killed in Syria at a spot named Afiq, on Friday, three hours after the sunrise, at the hands of the one behind whom Jesus will worship. Beware that his death will be followed by a great event. This great event is the revolution of the twelfth Imam, commencing from the direction of Safa in the precinct of the Keba. Thereafter no repentance will be accepted. Al-Dajjal's role at the End of Time is almost identical with that of Satan, as explained in traditional sources, because he will tempt people by bringing food and water, which will be scarce at that time. The Prophet is reported to have said that since the time of Noah there has been no umma on earth who did not fear al-Dajjal and his temptations; every prophet has warned his community against this tempter. The episode of al-Dajjal's emergence, at the time of the zuhur, has been interpreted as a test for sifting the true believers of God from the false ones".

In their book *The Islamic Understanding of Death and Resurrection*, Jane Idleman Smith and Yvonne Yaybeck Haddad, State University Press of Albany, New York (1981) quote from an earlier work, The Religion of Islam, by Ahmad Galwash: "It has been well known (and generally accepted) by all Muslims in every epoch, that at the end of time a man from the family (of the Prophet) will without fail make his appearance, one who will strengthen the religion and make justice triumph. The Muslims will follow him, and he will gain domination over the Muslim realm. He will be called the Mahdi. Following him, the Antichrist will appear, together with all the subsequent signs of the Hour (the Day of Judgment), as established in (the sound tradition) the Sahih. After (the Mahdi), Isa (Jesus) will descend and kill the Antichrist; or, Jesus will descend together with the Mahdi, and help him kill (the Antichrist), and have him as the leader in his prayers."

One can not expect that all Moslems everywhere are so well read in matters of their own faith that they all have worked out a personal view of eschatology. But what is interesting is that Islam does has a belief system about the end of the ages, the coming of a great Iman Mahdi, a great judgment, a heaven and hell, and a God who is basically merciful and compassionate. As we approach the end of the age and consider the building of a Third Jewish Temple in Jerusalem as well as mounting messianic expectations in Israel, it is interesting to consider the possibility that a charismatic, religiously persuasive, and inspiring Jewish false messiah might conceivably also fulfill Muslim expectations for their own long-awaited Mahdi and thus expedite the final false and misleading Middle Eastern peace treaty spoken of by the ancient Hebrew prophets.

The end of the age we live in is marked by deception on a worldwide scale-because truth has been so widely and universally rejected by mankind. This is the clear statement of Paul when he speaks about the appearing of the man of sin.

"Let no one deceive you in any way; for that day will not come, unless the apostasy comes first, and the man of lawlessness is revealed, the son of perdition, who opposes and exalts himself against every so-called god or object of worship, so that he takes his seat in the temple of God (in Jerusalem), proclaiming himself to be God. Do you not remember that when I was still with you I told you this? And you know what is restraining him now so that he may be revealed in his time.

For the mystery of lawlessness is already at work; only he who now restrains it will do so until he is out of the way. And then the lawless one will be revealed (unveiled), and the Lord Jesus will slay him with the breath of his mouth and destroy him by his appearing and his coming. The coming of the lawless one by the activity of Satan will be with all power and with pretended signs and wonders, and with all wicked deception for those who are to perish, because they refused to love the truth and so be saved. Therefore God sends upon them a strong delusion, to make them believe what is false (lit: "the lie"), so that all may be condemned who did not believe the truth but had pleasure in unrighteousness. (2:3-12)

The word "Islam" in Arabic Language means "submission" and "peace" A Muslim is a person who submits to the will of Allah and finds therein peace. Islam is derived from the Arabic word "salaam" meaning peace. Who are the Muslims? The common answer is "the Arabs." This is a mistaken impression that is true only insofar as Islam arose among the Arabs, its Prophet and many of its adherents were and are Arabs, and its scripture, the Holy *Quran*, must be recited in original Arabic form. The Arabs comprise only 25 % of the present population of Islam. They form majority of the population in roughly thirty-six countries and nearly half of the population in five others. The estimated strength of Islam is estimated to be one billion people, almost one fifth of world population. Islam is the world's third largest religion, behind Christianity and Buddhism, and its present rate of growth and vitality rivals both traditions.

Muslims represent many races and socioeconomic settings. There have been however significant divisions of opinion within the umma (commonwealth of Islam or Islamic Community). Despite these differences, Islam brings unity by incorporating divergent interpretations of basic beliefs.

SUNNI: The recorded practice and teachings of Prophet Mohammad were early regarded as his Sunnah, meaning 'path' or 'way.' These traditions became powerful symbols for the Islamic religion, models of right belief and practice. The collection of Prophet Mohammad's sayings is called "Hadith" comprising Sunnah or "authoritative examples." These required further interpretations and application to a variety of situations of everyday life. Majority of Muslims following Sunnah of Prophet Mohammad are termed "Sunnis." Islam developed four schools of jurisprudence whose functions were to decide upon the proper application of Holy *Quran* and Sunnah to virtually all aspects of life of the community. Each of the four schools takes its name from early jurist to whom later followers trace many of the school's distinctive opinions. The four schools are:

1. Hanifi's (after Abu Hanifa, d.767)
2. Maliki's (after Malik ibn Anas, d.795)
3. Shafi'is (after Muhammad al-Shafi'i d.819)
4. Hanbali's (after Ahmad ibn Hanbal d.855)

The learned scholars of law are called "Ulema."They are highly respected for their learning in the religious sciences. Islam has no clergy or priesthood as such. The basic principles of Islamic Law are established by the following:

i. The Holy *Quran*
ii. The Prophet's Sunnah
iii. The learned consensus of Ulema
iv. Reasoning by analogy from accepted interpretations of i) & ii) to new problems not directly addressed therein.

All of the four above form a concept of revelation of God's will to the community of Islam. This concept is called, Shari'a, it is more than scripture; it implies a composite source of teaching and practice involving the Holy *Quran*, the Sunnah of the Prophet Muhammad and authoritative human interpretation and application.

SHI'IA: A significant minority of Muslims, 10-15 %, differ on certain religious and political matters almost since the beginning of Islam. They are known as Shi'ia's. The historical and religious differences do not obscure the broad lines of agreement between Shi'ias and Sunnis. Shi'ias differs little from Sunnis in belief and practice. Their differences lie mainly in the modes of leadership and piety. Although Islam united the Arabs of North and South under the same banner but the cultural and traditional differences remained strong and surfaced at the time of choosing the successors of Prophet Muhammad after His death. The majority believed in choosing from the closest companions of Prophet Muhammad while others sought guidance in political and religous matters from Hazart Ali, Prophet Muhammad's cousin and son-in-law. Hazart Ali was chosen as the fourth Caliph (leader of Islamic community) but was assassinated in 661. The civil strife resulted left and indelible mark upon Islamic Umma (community).

Shi'ias believe Prophet Muhammad passed on a significant part of his teachings directly to Hazart Ali, and hence to subsequent Imams (sprititual leaders). Although the twelfth and last Imam disappeared late in the ninth century expected to return before the Judgement Day. The Shia Ulema carry on the distinctive teachings and interpretations they trace back through the Imams to Prophet Muhammad. The teachings of the sixth Imam, Jafar al-Sadiq (d.765) became the basis of Jafari schools among Sunnis.

The emotional intensity that characterizes Shi'ia beliefs culminates on the tenth day of Muharram (the first month of Islamic calendar). On this date in Karbala, Iraq, in 680, Hazart Husayn, son of Hazart Ali and grandson of Prophet Muhammad, was brutally murdered by troops of Ummayyad Caliph, Yazid. For nine days, Yazid's troops besieged the camps and deprived Hazart Husayn and his followers (72 of them) of any water. Remembering the tragedy of Hazart Husayn on every year on 10th of Muharram is done by Sunnis as well as Shi'ias.

Five Pillars of Islam

The pillars of Islam are considered obligatory for all Muslims although Sunni and Shia schools of law have slight variations. The pillars of Islam play important roles in intellectual and social dimensions of Islamic life. The five pillars of faith and practice are:

1. The Shahada (Witness)
2. The Salat (Prayer)
3. The Zakat (Alms)
4. The Sawm or Siyam (Fasting)
5. The Hajj (Pilgrimage)

SHAHADA (Witness): The Shahada is: In Arabic "La ilah ha il Allah, Muhammadan Rasul-Allah" Translation: "(There is) No diety but Allah (and) Muhammad is His Messenger" or,

"There is no God but Allah" and "Muhammad is His Apostle."

Islam is one of the three monotheistic religions to arise in the Middle East; along with the other two - Judaism and Christianity- it stresses the oneness and uniqueness of God. The world 'Allah' means 'The God.'

The second phrase of the Shahada declares that Muhammad is God's messenger to humankind. Accepting the Judaeo-Christian Biblical tradition in large part, Muslims believe that God had sent prophets and messengers to other nations in the past with the same revealed message Muhammad was to recite to the Arabs. Muhammad's mission brought the final positing of divine Truth, and thus Muhammad is regarded as the "Seal of the Prophets."

SALAT (Payer): Performing daily prayers is an act of communication between humans and God. Five daily prayers are considered a duty for all Muslims, and on these occasions preparations in ritual purity are required. The prayers are Fajr (early morning before the sun rise), Zuhr (afternoon), Asr (later afternoon), Maghrib (after sunset) and Isha (evening). The prayers must be said while facing in the direction of Mecca. The congregational prayer of Friday afternoon is compulsory and must be said in a Mosque, Muslim's place of worship. There is a sermom and then the prayers in uniform rows.

ZAKAT (Alms): The Zakat is a form of giving to those who are less fortunate. It is obligatory upon all Muslims to give 2.5 % of wealth and assets each year (in excess of what is required) to the poor. This is done before the beginning of the month of Muharram, the first of New Year. Giving the Zakat is considered an act of worship because it is a form of offering thanks to God for the means of material wellbeing one has acquired.

SAWM or SIYAM (Fasting): Another form of offering thanks to God is fasting. It is duty to all Muslims to fast during the ninth month of Islamic calendar, Ramadan. During this month, Muslims refrain from food, drink during daylight. Excepts are those ill health, pregnant women and travelers. One is to make up lost days of fasting at a later time. The time of fasting is from just before sunrise to just after sunset. The breaking of fast is joyous occasion. Sawm during Ramadan or any time is recognized as physically demanding but spiritually rewarding.

HAJJ (Pilgrimage): The pilgrimage season begins in the tenth month, the month following Ramadan, and lasts through the middle of twelveth month, Dhu al-Hijja.

This fifth pillar requires all Muslims who are physically and financially capable to make Hajj to Mecca once during their lives. The actual rites and prayers take place at the sacred Ka'ba in Mecca and at nearby locations. Muslims associate the origin of the Hajj and the founding of the Ka'ba with the prophet Abraham. Nearly two million Muslims perform Hajj each year.

JIHAD (Striving): Although it is not a pillar of Islam but is a duty in one form or another. The most common media misconception is of calling Jihad a 'Holy War.' The general meaning of the term is "striving for moral and religious perfection." The broader meaning of this term encompasses one's life and community. The constant struggle of striving to remain on the path of Islam by observing the above five pillars of Islam is Jihad. One who strives is Mujahid.

Being a Mujahid, a striver for moral and religious perfection, involves numerous forms of public and private devotion that charaterizes the 'practice' of Islam. This includes respecting the dietry laws against eating pork and drinking alcohol, respecting parents and elders, helping to provide for close relatives and kins, giving to the poor and disadvantaged. On the other side, theft, murder, fornication, adultery, lying, cheating, wrongly accusing or testifying are strictly forbidden by Shari'a (Islamic Law). In technical sense, Islam means 'the pratice of the religious and social duties' outlined above.

IMAN (Faith): The faith, like Five Pillars, can be divided in six parts. It means belief in the following:

1. God and His Attributes
2. Prophets
3. Angels
4. Sacred Books
5. The Judgement Day
6. Predestination

Basic Beliefs

The teachings of *Quran* and Hadith (sayings of Prophet Mohammad) revolve around two Arabic words namely, Emaan (Faith) and Amaal (Acts). Emaan is like the roots of a tree and Amaal are the stems, leaves or other parts of it. Just as without the roots, the tree cannot survive, similarly, without faith, the acts are useless.

The teachings of *Quran* emphasize mostly on the beliefs and an overview the acts, whereas the Hadith explains both beliefs and acts in details. Muslims believe that although there may be reservations in the Hadith, but *Quran* is free from all the mistakes and is infallible.

Quran is comprised of 114 Surahs (chapters) and 6236 Ayats (verses). *Quran* was preserved through writing and memorization. Undoubtedly, today *Quran* is the only book which is fully memorized by more than 10 million people all over the world.

The teachings of *Quran* confirm the revelations of other books and scriptures on various prophets. But, at the same time, all these books are considered to be corrupted with time and do not contain the original script of God.

Six Articles of Faith

The six articles of faith are the main doctrines of Islam. All Muslims share beliefs in the following:

1. *God:* Islam preaches that there is only one Supreme, Eternal, Infinite and Unparallel entity, Allah (God). He alone is the creator of the entire universe. *Quran* declares "That is God, your Lord. There is no god but Him, the Creator of everything. So worship Him. He is responsible for everything." (6:102)
2. *Angels:* Muslims believe in angels. They are comprised of light, and each have different purposes. Angel Gabriel brought the divine message to Mohammad. Two angels (Kiraaman and Katibeen) are assigned to record the actions of the human beings; one records good deeds, the other bad deeds. The angel of death (Azrael) takes the soul out of the body. Angels Munkir and Nakir question each person in grave.
3. *Scriptures:* It refers to believing in all the four books; the Torah (Moses), the Psalms (David), the Gospel (Jesus) and the Qur'an (Mohammad). Muslims also believe that all other books are alteration with time by its followers. Muslims believe that *Quran* is the only book which can never be distorted as God has himself taken the responsibility of its protection, "We have, without doubt,

sent down the Message; and We will assuredly guard it (from corruption)." (15:9)

4. *Prophets:* It is obligatory on every Muslim to believe in all the messengers from Adam to Mohammad without any discrimination. *Quran* treats all the prophets equally, "Say (O Muslims), we believe in Allah and that which is revealed unto us and that which was revealed unto Abraham, and Ishmael, and Isaac, and Jacob, and the tribes, and that which Moses and Jesus received, and that which the Prophets received from their Lord. We make no distinction between any of them, and unto Him we have surrendered." (2:136)
5. *Resurrection:* Muslims have faith that after the end of the world, every human will be resurrected from the grave. They will be held accountable for whatever they have done in their lives. The day is known as the Day of Judgment. On this day, justice will be done to every individual soul. The innocent ones will stay in Heaven, whereas, the corrupted ones will go to hell. *Quran* testifies it by saying, "This day We seal up mouths, and hands speak out and feet bear witness as to what they used to earn." (36:65)
6. *Divine Creed:* It is one of the main aspects of Islam. Believing in divine creed refers to predestination. Muslims believe that unlike living beings, God is not limited to anything; even with time. Everything that has happened, is happening, or will happen is evident to Him. Living beings are being given a free choice to do whatever they want to do, but God knows what choice they will make. It must also be clear that God's knowing does not restrict anyone from making a free choice. *Quran* proclaims, "Knowest thou not that Allah knows all that is in heaven and on earth? Indeed it is all in a Record, and that is easy for Allah."

The Five Pillars of Faith

The five pillars of faith are duties each Muslim performs to demonstrate his or her faith.

1. *Testimony of Faith (Kalima):* One must state, "There is no god, but Allah, and Muhammad is the Prophet of Allah." It consists of three parts:
   a. To reject all the false gods.
   b. To accept Allah as the only sole creator of everything.
   c. To Mohammad as the last messenger of Allah.

   Quran declares, "Say: He is Allah, the One and Only! Allah, the Eternal, Absolute; He begetteth not nor is He begotten. And there is none like unto Him. "

2. *Prayer (Salat):* It is compulsory for every Muslim to pray five times a day at respective timings facing towards the direction of Mecca. During the prayer, Muslims narrate verses from the Holy *Quran,* specially the following prayer which is recited at least 17 times a day,

   "All praise is due to Allah, Lord of the worlds, The Most Gracious, the Most Merciful, and Sovereign of the Day of Judgment. It is You alone we worship and You alone we ask for help. Guide us to the straight path; The path of those upon whom You have bestowed favor, not of those who have evoked Your anger or of those who are astray." (1:1-7)

   Quran tells about those who will get eternal success by stating that, "Certainly will the believers have succeeded, they who are during their prayer humbly submissive" (23:1-2)

3. *Almsgiving (Zakat):* The word Zakat means "to grow" or "to purify". It literally means to gain Allahs blessings and purify the wealth by helping the needy. It is mandatory on every Muslim to give 2.5% of their yearly savings (or excess money) for charity.

   Quran emphasizes the importance of zakat on various occasions, "Alms are for the poor and the needy, and those employed to administer the (funds); for those whose hearts have been (recently) reconciled (to Truth); for those in bondage and in debt; in the cause of Allah and for the wayfarer: (thus is it) ordained by Allah, and Allah is full of knowledge and wisdom." (9:60)

4. *Fasting (Sawm)*: Following zakat, every Muslim is required to fast during the month of Ramadan from sunrise to sunset. During this period, Muslims are forbidden to eat, drink, smoke or have an intercourse. It not only physical discipline in ones life, but it is also a way to feel the afflictions of the poor.

   Quranic verses explain fasting in detail, "O ye who believe! Fasting is prescribed to you as it was prescribed to those before you, that ye may (learn) self-restraint" (2:183)

   "Ramadhan is the (month) in which was sent down the Qur'an, as a guide to mankind, also clear (Signs) for guidance and judgment (Between right and wrong). So every one of you who is present (at his home) during that month should spend it in fasting, but if any one is ill, or on a journey, the prescribed period (Should be made up) by days later. Allah intends every facility for you; He does not want to put to difficulties. (He wants you) to complete the prescribed period, and to glorify Him in that He has guided you; and perchance ye shall be grateful." (2:185)

5. *Pilgrimage (Hajj):* Hajj literally means to "set out for place". For Muslim, it is a pilgrimage to Kaaba (House of Allah) in Makkah. It is the responsibility of every physically and financially able Muslim to perform this offering at least once in a lifetime. Hajj is performed on the 10th day of Dhu al-Hijjah (the 12th and the final month of the Islamic calendar). Hajj is the symbol of unity among the Muslims. Millions of believers from all over the world participate in the ritual irrespective of their caste, color, creed or tradition. It tears down the difference of social status and brings all the Muslims on one platform. During this occasion, men only wear two unstitched clothes; one covers the lower part, and the other is wrapped around the shoulders. Women wear simple white dress and headscarf.

   Allah says in the Holy *Quran,* "For Hajj are the months

well known. If any one undertakes that duty therein, Let there be no obscenity, nor wickedness, nor wrangling in the Hajj. And whatever good ye do, (be sure) Allah knoweth it. And take a provision (With you) for the journey, but the best of provisions is right conduct. So fear me, o ye that are wise." (2:197)

The Beliefs and Laws of Islam

Origins Islam is the religion of allegiance to God and his prophet Mohammed, who lived around 570-632 and came from a family of traders at Mecca. The religion's book of revelation, mediated by the prophet, is the Koran. The word Islam derives from the same Semitic root as the Hebrew word Shalom, which means peace. Islam means "entering into a condition of peace and security with God, through allegiance or surrender to him". Mohammed is said to have received his revelations over a period of 23 years from the Angel Jibreel, or Gabriel, who was relaying the word of God. It was not a completely new faith but is the third great monotheistic religion. In Muslim eyes, Mohammed completes a succession of prophets, including Abraham, Moses and Jesus, each of whom refined and restated the message of God.

The Koran therefore corroborates updates and expands the Old and New Testaments. It contains 114 chapters, written in vivid, rhyming prose, and was settled in its current form within 30 years of Mohammed's death. Main tenets Central to Islam is the absolute sense that there can only be one God - Allah - and that he is the source of all creation and disposer of all lives and events. Hence, there is no God but God and Mohammed is his messenger. All people should become a single Umma - community - witnessing to that fact. On the Day of Judgment, all will rise from the dead and be sent to heaven or hell. The Koran contains many moral exhortations, forming the basis of Islamic (sharia) law. It lays down generosity and fairness and the requirements for daily prayer, alms giving, and abstinence during daylight hours in the month of Ramadan and pilgrimage to Mecca.

The five pillars of the Islamic faith - the fundamental constituents of Muslim life - are: (i). Shahada, the profession of faith in the uniqueness of Allah and the centrality of Mohammed as his prophet, (ii). Salat, formal worship or prayer, (iii). Zakat, the giving of alms for the poor, assessed on all adult Muslims as 2.5% of capital assets once a year, (iv). Hajj, pilgrimage to Mecca, which every Muslim should undertake at least once in their lifetime; the annual hajj takes place during the last 10 days of the 12th lunar month every year and (v). Sawm, fasting during Ramadan, the holy ninth month of the lunar year. Early history In 622, Mohammed travelled from Mecca to Medina in the hijrah (emigration) - this forms the starting point in the Muslim dating system.

After the prophet's death his community split into followers of the caliph Abu Bakr and those who supported Mohammed's closest relative, his son-in-law, Ali ibn Abi Talib. This division between Shia (followers of Ali) and Sunni (followers of the custom of the caliphate) persists to this day. Although both share most of the customs of the religion, Shiites place more emphasis on the guiding role of the imam. About 90% of the world's Muslims are Sunni and about 10% Shia.

Sharia

The Sharia is the divine law of Islam by which Muslims should live their lives.It embraces every aspect of life, including family relations, inheritance, taxation, purification and prayer and observes no distinction between secular and religious law. How far modern Islamic states follow this principle depends on the degree of secularisation they permit. It is essentially laid down by the Koran but has been updated and extended by fatwa (legal opinion), consensus and custom.

Concept of God in Islam

It is a known fact that every language has one or more terms that are used in reference to God and sometimes to lesser deities. This is not the case with Allah. Allah is the personal name of the One true God. Nothing else can be called Allah. The term has no plural or gender. This shows its uniqueness when compared with the word "god," which can be made plural, as in "gods," or made feminine, as in "goddess." It is interesting to notice that Allah is the personal name of God in Aramaic, the language of Jesus and a sister language of Arabic.

The One true God is a reflection of the unique concept that Islam associates with God. To a Muslim, Allah is the Almighty Creator and Sustainer of the universe, Who is similar to nothing, and nothing is comparable to Him. The Prophet Muhammad was asked by his contemporaries about Allah; the answer came directly from God Himself in the form of a short chapter of the *Qur'an,* which is considered to be the essence of the unity or the motto of monotheism. This is chapter 112, which reads:

In the name of Allah, the Merciful, the Compassionate.

Say (O Muhammad), He is God, the One God, the Everlasting Refuge, who has not begotten, nor has been begotten, and equal to Him is not anyone.

Some non-Muslims allege that God in Islam is a stern and cruel God who demands to be obeyed fully and does not love and kind. Nothing could be farther from the truth than this allegation. It is enough to know that, with the exception of one, each of the 114 chapters of the *Qur'an* begins with the verse, "In the name of God, the Merciful, and the Compassionate." In one of the sayings of Prophet Muhammad (PBUH), we are told that "God is more loving and kind than a mother to her dear child."

On the other hand, God is also Just. Hence, evildoers and sinners must have their share of punishment, and the virtuous must have God's bounties and favors. Actually, God's attribute of Mercy has full manifestation in His attribute of Justice. People suffering throughout their lives for His sake should not receive similar treatment from their Lord as people who oppress and exploit others their whole lives. Expecting similar treatment for them would amount to negating the very belief in the accountability of man in the Hereafter and thereby negate all the incentives for a moral and virtuous life in this world. The following Qur'anic verses are very clear and straightforward in this respect. Verily, for the Righteous are gardens of Delight, in the Presence of their Lord. Shall we then treat the people of Faith like the people of Sin? What is the matter with you? How judge you? (68:34-36)

Islam rejects characterizing God in any human form or depicting Him as favoring certain individuals or nations on the basis of wealth, power or race. He created the human-beings as equals. They may distinguish themselves and get His favor through virtue and piety only. The concepts that God rested on the seventh day of creation, that God wrestled with one of His soldiers, that God is an envious plotter against mankind, and that God is incarnate in any human being are considered blasphemy from the Islamic point of view.

The unique usage of Allah as a personal name of God is a reflection of Islam's emphasis on the purity of the belief in God that is the essence of the message of all God's messengers. Because of this, Islam considers associating any deity or personality with God as a deadly sin that God will never forgive, despite the fact that He may forgive all other sins. The Creator must be of a different nature from the things created because if He is of the same nature as they are, He will be temporal and will therefore need a maker. It follows that nothing is like Him. If the maker is not temporal, then he must be eternal. But if he is eternal, he cannot be caused, and if nothing caused Him to come into existence, nothing outside Him causes Him to continue to exist, which means that he must be self-sufficient. And if He does not depend on anything for the continuance of His own existence, then this existence can have no end. The Creator is therefore eternal and everlasting: "He is the First and the Last."

He is Self-sufficient or Self-subsistent, or, to use a Qur'anic term, Al-Qayyum. The Creator does not create only in the sense of bringing things into being, He also preserves them and takes them out of existence and is the ultimate cause of whatever happens to them. God is the Creator of everything. He is the guardian over everything. Unto Him belong the keys of the heavens and the earth. (39:62-63) No creature is there crawling on the earth, but its provision rests on God. He knows its lodging place and its repository. (11:16)

God's Attributes

If the Creator is eternal and everlasting, then His attributes must also be eternal and everlasting. He should not lose any of His attributes nor acquire new ones. If this is so, then his attributes are absolute. Can there be more than one Creator with such absolute attributes? Can there be, for example, two absolutely powerful Creators? A moment's thought shows that this is not feasible.

The *Qur'an* summarizes this argument in the following verses: God has not taken to Himself any son, nor is there any god with Him: for then each god would have taken of that which he created and some of them would have risen up over others. (23:91)

And why, were there gods in earth and heaven other than God, they (heaven and earth) would surely go to ruin. (21:22)

The Oneness of God

The *Qur'an* reminds us of the falsity of all alleged gods. To the worshippers of man-made objects it asks:

Do you worship what you have carved yourself? (37:95)

Or have you taken unto yourself others beside Him to be your protectors, even such as have no power either for good or for harm to themselves? (13:16)

To the worshippers of heavenly bodies it cites the story of Abraham: When night outspread over him, he saw a star and said, "This is my Lord." But when it set, he said, "I love not the setters." When he saw the moon rising, he said, "This is my Lord." But when it set, he said, "If my Lord does not guide me, I shall surely be of the people gone astray." When he saw the sun rising, he said, "This is my Lord; this is greater." But when it set, he said, "O my people, surely I quit that which you associate, I have turned my face to Him who originated the heavens and the earth; a man of pure faith, I am not one of the idolaters." (6:76-79)

The Believer's Attitude

In order to be a Muslim, that is, to surrender one to God, it is necessary to believe in the oneness of God, in the sense of His being the only Creator, Preserver, Nourisher, etc. But this belief, later called *Tawhid Ar-Rububiyyah,* is not enough. Many of the idolators knew and believed that only the Supreme God could do all this. But this was not enough to make them Muslims. To *tawhid ar-rububiyyah,* one must add *tawhid al-'uluhiyyah,* that is, one acknowledges the fact that it is God alone who deserves to be worshipped, and thus abstains from worshipping any other thing or being.

Having achieved this knowledge of the one true God, man should constantly have faith in Him, and should allow nothing to induce him to deny truth. When faith enters a person's heart, it causes certain mental states that result in certain actions. Taken together, these mental states and actions are the proof for the true faith. The Prophet said, "Faith is that which resides firmly in the heart and which is proved by deeds."

Foremost among those mental stated is the feeling of gratitude towards God, which could be said to be the essence of *ibada* (worship). The feeling of gratitude is so important that a non-believer is called *'kafir'*, which means 'one who denies a truth' and also 'one who is ungrateful'.

A believer loves, and is grateful to God for the bounties He bestowed upon him, but being aware of the fact that his good deeds, whether mental or physical, are far from being commensurate with Divine favors, he is always anxious lest God should punish him, here or in the Hereafter. He, therefore, fears Him, surrenders himself to Him and serves Him with great humility. One cannot be in such a mental state without being almost all the time mindful of God. Remembering God is thus the life force of faith, without which it fades and withers away.

The Qur'an tries to promote this feeling of gratitude by repeating the attributes of God very frequently. We find most of these attributes mentioned together in the following verses of the Qur'an: He is God; there is no god but He. He is the Knower of the unseen and the visible; He is the All-Merciful, the All-Compassionate. He is God; there is no god but He. He is the King, the All-Holy, the All-Peace, the Guardian of the Faith, the All-Preserver, the All-Mighty, the All-Compeller, the All-Sublime. Glory be to God, above that they associate. He is God, the Creator, the Maker, and the Shaper. To Him belongs the Names Most Beautiful. All that is in the heavens and the earth magnifies Him; He is the Almighty, the All-Wise. (59:22-24)

There is no god but He, the Living, the Everlasting. Slumber seizes Him not, nor sleeps. To Him belongs all that is in the heavens and the earth. Who is there that shall intercede with Him save by His leave? He knows what lies before them, and what is after them, and they comprehend not anything of His knowledge save such as He wills. His throne comprises the heavens and earth. The preserving of them oppresses Him not; He is the All-High, the All-Glorious. (2:255)

People of the Book, go not beyond the bounds in your religion, and say not as to God but the truth. The Messiah, Jesus, son of Mary, was only the Messenger of God, and His Word that He committed to Mary, and a Spirit from Him. So believe in God and His Messengers, and say not "Three". Refrain; better it is for you. God is only one God. Glory be to Him – (He is) above having a son. (4:171)

Prophethood in Islam

Prophethood is not unknown to heavenly revealed religions, such as Judaism and Christianity. In Islam, however, it has a special status and significance. According to Islam,

Allah created man for a noble purpose; to worship Him and lead a virtuous life based on His teachings and guidance. How would man know his role and the purpose of his existence unless he received clear and practical instructions of what Allah wants him to do? Here comes the need for prophethood. Thus Allah has chosen from every nation at least one prophet to convey His Message to people.

One might ask, how were the prophets chosen and who were entitled to this great honor? Prophethood is Allah's blessing and favor that He may bestow on whom He wills. However, from surveying the various messengers throughout history, three features of a prophet may be recognized:

1. He is the best in his community morally and intellectually. This is necessary because a prophet's life serves as a role model for his followers. His personality should attract people to accept his message rather than drive them away by his imperfect character. After receiving the message, he is infallible. That is, he would not commit any sin. He might make some minor mistakes, which are usually corrected by revelation.
2. He is supported by miracles to prove that he is not an imposter. Those miracles are granted by the power and permission of God and are usually in the field in which his people excel and are recognized as superior. We might illustrate this by quoting the major miracles of the three prophets of the major world religions, Judaism, Christianity and Islam.

   Moses' contemporaries were excellent in magic, so his major miracle was to defeat the best magicians of Egypt of his day. Jesus' contemporaries were recognized as skilled physicians, therefore, his miracles were to raise the dead and cure incurable diseases. The Arabs, the contemporaries of the Prophet Muhammad (PBUH), were known for their eloquence and magnificent poetry. So Prophet Muhammad's major miracle was the *Qur'an*, the equivalent of which the whole legion of Arab poets and orators could not produce, despite the repeated challenge from the *Qur'an* itself. Again, Muhammad's miracle has something special about it. All previous miracles were limited by time and place; that is, they were shown to specific people at a specific time. Not so with the miracle of Prophet Muhammad (PBUH), the *Qur'an*. It is a universal and everlasting miracle. Previous generations witnessed it and future generations will witness its miraculous nature in terms of its style, content and spiritual uplifting. These can still be tested and will thereby prove the divine origin of the *Qur'an*.

3. Every prophet states clearly that what he receives is not his own, but from God for the wellbeing of mankind. He also confirms what was revealed before him and what may be revealed after him. A prophet does this to show that he is simply conveying the message that is entrusted to him by the One True God of all people in all ages. So the message is one in essence and for the same purpose. Therefore, it should not deviate from what was revealed before him or what might come after him.

Prophets are necessary for conveying God's instructions and guidance to mankind. We have no way of knowing why we were created. What will happen to us after death? Is there any life after death? Are we accountable for our actions? These and so many other questions about God, angels, paradise, hell, and more, cannot be answered without direct revelation from the Creator and Knower of the unseen. Those answers must be authentic and must be brought by individuals whom we trust and respect. That is why messengers are the elite of their societies in terms of moral conduct and intellectual ability.

Hence, the slanderous Biblical stories about some of the great prophets are not accepted by Muslims. For example, Lot is reported to have committed incestuous fornication while drunk. David is alleged to have sent one of his leaders to his death in order to marry his wife. Prophets, to Muslims, are greater than what these stories indicate. These stories cannot be true from the Islamic point of view. The prophets are also miraculously supported by God and instructed by Him to affirm the continuity of the message. The content of the prophets' message to mankind can be summarized as follows:

a. Clear concept of God: His attributes, His creation, what should and should not be ascribed to Him.

b. Clear idea about the unseen world, the angels, jinn (spirits), Paradise and Hell.

c. Why God has created us, what He wants from us and what rewards and punishments are for obedience and disobedience.

d. How to run our societies according to His will. That is, clear instructions and laws that, when applied correctly and honestly, will result in a smoothly functioning, harmonious society.

It is clear from the above discussion that there is no substitute for prophets. Even today with the advancement of science, the only authentic source of information about the supernatural world is revelation. Guidance can be obtained neither from science nor from mystic experience. The first is too materialistic and limited; the second is too subjective and frequently misleading.

Now one might ask: How many prophets has God sent to humanity? We do not know for sure. Some Muslim scholars have suggested 240,000 prophets. We are only sure of what is clearly mentioned in the *Qur'an*, that God has sent a messenger to every nation. That is because it is one of God's principles that He will never call a people to account unless He has made clear to them what to do and what not to do. The *Qur'an* mentions the names of 25 prophets and indicates that there have been others who were not mentioned to Prophet Muhammad (PBUH). These 25 include Noah, Abraham, Moses, Jesus, and Muhammad (Peace be upon them all). These five are the greatest among God's messengers. They are called 'the resolute' prophets.

An outstanding aspect of the Islamic belief in prophethood is that Muslims believe in and respect all the messengers of God with no exceptions. All the prophets came from the same One God, for the same purpose: to lead mankind to God. Hence, belief in them all is essential and logical; accepting some and rejecting others has to be based on misconceptions of the prophet's role or on a racial bias. The Muslims are the only people in the world who consider the belief in all the prophets an article of faith. Thus the Jews reject Jesus and Muhammad (peace be upon them), and the Christians reject Muhammad (PBUH). The Muslims accept them all as messengers of God who brought guidance to mankind. However, the revelations which those prophets before Muhammad (PBUH) brought from God have been tampered with in one way or another.

The belief in all the prophets of God is enjoined upon the Muslims in the *Qur'an*:

> *Say (O Muslims):* We believe in Allah and that which is revealed to us and that which was revealed to Abraham and Ishmael, and Isaac and Jacob, and their children, and that which Moses and Jesus received and that the prophets received from their Lord. We make no distinction between any of them and unto Him we have surrendered. (2:136)

The *Qur'an* continues in the following verses to instruct the Muslims that this is the true and impartial belief. If other nations believe in the same, they are following in the right track. If they do not, they must be following their own whims and biases and God will take care of them. Thus we read:

> And if they believe in what you believe, then they are rightly guided. But if they turn away, then they are in disunity, and Allah will suffice you against them. He is the Hearer, the Knower. This is God's religion and who is better than God in religion? (2:137-138)

There are, at least, two important points related to prophethood that needs to be clarified. These points concern the roles of Jesus and Muhammad (peace be upon them) as prophets, who are usually misunderstood.

The Qur'anic account of Jesus emphatically rejects the concept of his 'divinity' and 'divine sonship' and presents him as one of the great prophets of God. The *Qur'an* makes it clear that the birth of Jesus without a father does not make him the son of God and mentions, in this respect, Adam, who was created by God without a father or mother.

Truly, the likeness of Jesus, in God's sight, is as Adam's likeness; He created him of dust, them said He unto him "Be", and he was. (3:59)

Like other prophets, Jesus also performed miracles. For example, he raised the dead and cured the blind and lepers, but while showing these miracles, he always made it clear that it was all from God. Actually, the misconceptions about the personality and mission of Jesus (PBUH) found a way among his followers because the Divine message he preached was not recorded during his presence in the world. Rather, it was recorded after a lapse of about one hundred years. According to the Qur'an, he was sent to the children of Israel; he confirmed the validity of the Torah, which was revealed to Moses (PBUH), and he also brought the glad tidings of a final messenger after him.

And when Jesus son of Mary said, "Children of Israel" I am indeed the messenger to you, confirming the Torah that is before me, and giving good tidings of a Messenger who shall come after me, whose name shall be the *praised one*. (61:6)

(The "*praised one*" is the translation of "Ahmad", which is Prophet Muhammad's name.)

However, the majority of the Jews rejected his ministry. They plotted against his life and in their opinion, crucified him. But the *Qur'an* refutes this opinion and says that they neither killed him nor crucified him; rather, he was raised up to God. There is a verse in the *Qur'an* which implies that Jesus will come back and all the Christians and Jews will believe in him before he dies. This is also supported by authentic sayings of the Prophet Muhammad (PBUH).

The last prophet of God, Muhammad, was born in Arabia in the sixth century C.E. Up to the age of forty, people of Makkah knew him only as a man of excellent character and cultured manners and called him Al-Ameen (the trustworthy). He also did not know that he was soon to be made a prophet and receiver of revelation from God. He called the idolaters of Makkah to worship the one and only God and accept him (Muhammad, PBUH) as His prophet. The revelation that he received was preserved in his lifetime in the memory of his companions and was also recorded on pieces of palm leaf, leather, etc. Thus the *Qur'an* that is found today is the same that was revealed to him, not a syllable of it has been altered, as God Himself has guaranteed its preservation. This *Quran* claims to be the book of guidance for all of humanity for all times, and mentions Muhammad (PBUH) as the last Prophet of God.

Life after Death

The question of whether or not there is life after death does not fall under the field of science, because science is only concerned with the classification and analysis of recorded data. Moreover, man has been busy with scientific enquiries and research, in the modern sense of the term, only for the last few centuries, while he has been familiar with the idea of life after death since time immemorial. All the prophets of God called their people to worship God and to believe in life after death. They laid so much emphasis on the belief in life after death that even a slight doubt in it meant denying God and made all other beliefs meaningless. The very fact that all the prophets of God have dealt with this metaphysical question so confidently and uniformly – the gap between their ages being thousands of years – goes to prove that the source of their knowledge of life after death, as proclaimed by them all, was the same: Divine revelation.

We also know that these prophets of God were greatly opposed by their people, mainly on the issue of life after death, as their people thought it impossible. But in spite of that opposition, the prophets won many sincere followers. The question arises, what made those followers forsake the established beliefs, traditions and customs of their forefathers, regardless of the risk of being totally alienated from their own community? The simple answer is that they made use of their faculties of mind and heart and realized the truth.

Did they realize the truth through experiencing it? Not so, as the perceptual experience of life after death is impossible. Actually, God has given man, besides perceptual consciousness, rational, aesthetic and moral consciousness too. It is this consciousness that guides man regarding realities that cannot be verified through sensory data. That is why all the prophets of God, while calling people to believe in God and the life hereafter, appealed to the aesthetic, moral and rational sides of man. For example, when the idolaters of Makkah denied even the possibility of life after death, the *Qur'an* exposed the weakness of their stand by advancing very logical and rational arguments in support of it.

And he has coined for us a similitude, and has forgotten the fact of his creation, saying; Who will revive these bones when they have rotted away? Say, He will revive them who produced them at the first, for He is the Knower of every creation, who has appointed for you fire from the green tree, and behold! You kindle from it. Is it not He who created the heavens and the earth, able to create the like of them? Yes, and He is indeed the Supreme Creator, the All-Knowing. (36:78-81)

At another occasion, the *Quran* very clearly says that the disbelievers have no sound basis for their denial of life after death. It is based on pure conjecture. They say, 'There is nothing but our present life; we die, and we live, and nothing but Time destroys us.' Of that they have no knowledge; they merely conjecture. And when our revelations are recited to them, their only argument is that they say, 'Bring us our father, if you speak truly.' (45:24-25)

Surely God will raise all the dead but God has His own plan of things. A day will come when the whole universe will be destroyed and then again the dead will be resurrected to stand before God. That day will be the beginning of the life that will never end, and that Day, every person will be rewarded by God according to his good and evil deeds. The explanation that the *Quran* gives about the necessity of life after death is what the moral consciousness of man demands.

Actually, if there is no life after death, the very belief in God becomes irrelevant, or even if one believes in God, that would be an unjust and indifferent God, having once created man only to be unconcerned with his fate.

Surely, God is just. He will punish the tyrants whose crimes are beyond count, having killed hundreds of innocent persons, created great corruption in the society, enslaved numerous persons to serve their whims, and so forth. Man, having a very short span of life in this world, and this physical world, also, not being eternal, punishments or rewards equal to the evil or noble deeds of persons are not possible here. The Quran very emphatically states that the Day of Judgment must come and God will decide about the fate of each soul according to his or her record of deeds, Those who disbelieve say: The Hour will never come unto us. Say, Nay, by my Lord, but it is coming unto you surely. (He is) the Knower of the Unseen. Not an atom's weight, or less than that or greater, escapes Him in the heavens or in the earth, but it is in a clear Record. That He may reward those who believe and do good works. For them is pardon and a rich provision. But those who strive against our revelations, challenging (Us), theirs will be a painful doom of wrath. (34:3-5)

The Day of Resurrection will be the Day when God's attributes of Justice and Mercy will be in full manifestation. God will shower His mercy on those who suffered for His sake in the worldly life, believing that an eternal bliss was awaiting them. But those who abused the bounties of God, caring nothing for the life to come, will be in the most miserable state. Drawing a comparison between them the *Qur'an* says:

Is he, then, to whom we have promised a goodly promise the fulfillment of which he will meet, like the one whom We have provided with the good things of this life, and then on the Day of Resurrection he will be of those who will be brought arraigned before God? (28:61)

The *Qur'an* also states that this worldly life is a preparation for the eternal life after death. But those who deny it become slaves of their passions and desires, and make fun of virtuous and God-conscious persons. Such people realize their folly only at the time of their death and wish in vain to be given a further chance in the world. Their miserable state at the time of death and the horror of the Day of Judgment, and the eternal bliss guaranteed to the sincere believers are very beautifully mentioned in the following verses of the *Qur'an.*

Until, when death comes unto one of them, he says, 'My Lord, send me back, that I may do right in that which I have left behind!' But nay! It is but a word that he speaks; and behind them is a barrier until the day when they are raised. And when the Trumpet is blown there will be no kinship among them that day, nor will they ask of another. Then those whose scales are heavy, they are successful. And those whose scales are light are those who lose their souls, in hell abiding, the fire burns their faces and they are glum therein. (23:99-104)

The belief in life after death not only guarantees success in the Hereafter, but also makes this world full of peace and happiness by making individuals most responsible and dutiful in their activities.

Think of the people of Arabia. Gambling, wine, tribal feuds, plundering and murdering were their main traits when they had no belief in a life hereafter. But as soon as they accepted the belief in One God and life after death, they became the most disciplined nation of the world. They gave up their vices, helped each other in hours of need, and settled all their disputes on the basis of justice and equality. Similarly, the denial of life after death has its consequences not only in the Hereafter, but also in this world. When a nation as a whole denies it, all kinds of evils and corruptions become rampant in that society and ultimately it is destroyed. The *Qur'an* mentions the terrible end of 'Aad, Thamud and the Pharaoh in some detail:

(The tribes of) Thamud and 'Aad disbelieved in the judgment to come. As for Thamud, they were destroyed by the lightning, and as for 'Aad, they were destroyed by a fierce roaring wind, which he imposed on them for seven long nights and eight long days, so that you might see the people laid prostrate in it as if they were the stumps of fallen down palm trees.

Now do you see remnant of them? Pharaoh likewise and those before him and the subverted cities committed errors and those before him, and they rebelled against the Messenger of their Lord, and He seized them with a surpassing grip. Lo, when the waters rose, we bore you in the running ship that we might make it a reminder for you and for heeding ears to hold.

So when the Trumpet is blown with a single blast and the earth and the mountains are lifted up and crushed with a single blow, then on that day, the Terror shall come to pass, and the heaven shall be split, for upon that day it shall be very frail.

Then as for him who is given his book in his right hand, he shall say 'Here, take and read my book! Certainly I thought that I should encounter my reckoning.' So he shall be in a pleasing life in a lofty garden, its clusters nigh to gather. Eat and drink with wholesome appetite for what you did long ago, in the days gone by.

But as for him who is given his book in his left hand, he shall say: 'Would that I had not been given my book and known my reckoning! Would it have been the end! My wealth has not availed me, my authority is gone from me.' (69:4-29)

Thus, there are very convincing reasons to believe in life after death.

First, all the prophets of God have called their people to believe in it.

Secondly, whenever a human society is built on the basis of this belief, it has been the most ideal and peaceful society, free of social and moral evils. Thirdly, history bears witness that whenever this belief is rejected collectively by a group of people in spite of the repeated warning of the Prophet, the group as a whole has been punished by God, even in this world. Fourthly, moral, aesthetic and rational facilities of man endorse the possibility of life after death. Fifthly, God's attributes of Justice and Mercy have no meaning if there is no life after death.

Concept of Worship in Islam

The concept of worship in Islam is misunderstood by many people, including some Muslims. Worship is commonly taken to mean performing ritualistic acts such as prayers, fasting, charity, etc.

This limited understanding of worship is only one part of the meaning of worship in Islam. That is why the traditional definition of worship in Islam is a comprehensive definition that includes almost everything in any individual's activities. The definition goes something like this: "Worship is an all inclusive term for all that God loves of external and internal sayings and actions of a person." In other words, worship is everything one says or does for the pleasure of Allah. This, of course, includes rituals as well as beliefs, social activities, and personal contributions to the welfare of one's fellow human beings.

Islam looks at the individual as a whole. He is required to submit himself completely to Allah, as the *Quran* instructed the Prophet Muhammad to do:

Say (O Muhammad) my prayer, my sacrifice, my life and my death belong to Allah; He has no partner and I am ordered to be among those who submit (Muslims). (6:162-163)

The natural result of this submission is that all of one's activities should conform to the instructions of the one to whom the person is submitting. Islam, being a way of life, requires that its followers model their life according to its teachings in every aspect, religious or otherwise. This might sound strange to some people who think of religion as a personal relationship between the individual and God, having no impact on one's activities and outside rituals.

As a matter of fact Islam does not think much of mere

rituals when they are performed mechanically and have no influence on one's inner life. The *Quran* addresses the believers and their neighbors from among the People of the Book who were arguing with them about the change of the direction of the Qibla (the direction in which Muslims pray) in the following verse:

It is not righteousness that you turn your faces toward the East or the West, but righteous is he who believes in Allah and the Last Day and the angels and the Book and the prophets, and gives his beloved money to his relatives and the orphans and the needy and for the ransoming of captives; and who observes prayer and pays the poor-due; and those who fulfill their promises when they have made one; and the patient in poverty and affliction and the steadfast in time of war. It is those who have proved truthful and it is those who are the God-fearing. (2:177)

The deeds in the above verse are the deeds of righteousness and they are only a part of worship. The Prophet (PBUH) told us about faith, which is the basis of worship, that it "is made up of sixty and some branches: the highest of which is the belief in the Oneness of Allah (that is, there is no god but Allah) and the lowest in the scale of worship is removing obstacles and dirt from people's way."

Decent work is considered in Islam a type of worship. The Prophet (PBUH) said: "Whoever finds himself at the nightfall tired of his work, God will forgive his sins." Seeking knowledge is one of the highest types of worship. The Prophet (PBUH) told his companions that "seeking knowledge is a (religious) duty on every Muslim." In another saying he said: "Seeking knowledge for one hour is better than praying for seventy years." Social courtesy and cooperation are part of worship when done for the sake of Allah as the Prophet told us: "Receiving your friend with a smile is a type of charity, helping a person to load his animal is a charity and putting some water in your neighbor's bucket is a charity."

It is worth noting that even performing one's duties is considered a sort of worship. The Prophet (PBUH) told us that whatever one spends for his family is a type of charity; he will be rewarded for it if he acquires it through legal means. Kindness to the members of one's family is an act of worship as when one puts a piece of food in his spouse's mouth. Not only are this, but even the acts we enjoy doing very much considered worship when they are performed according to the instructions of the Prophet (PBUH). He told his companions that they will be rewarded even for having sexual intercourse with their wives. The companions were astonished and asked, "How are we going to be rewarded for doing something we enjoy very much?" The Prophet (PBUH) asked them, "Suppose you satisfy your desires illegally; don't you think you will be punished for that?" They replied, "Yes." "So," he said, "by satisfying it legally with your wives, you are rewarded for it." This means they are acts of worship.

Thus, Islam does not consider sex a dirty thing that one should avoid. It is dirty and a sin only when it is satisfied outside marital life. It is clear, from the previous discussion that the concept of worship in Islam is a comprehensive concept that includes all the positive activities of the individual. This, of course, is in agreement with the all-inclusive nature of Islam as a way of life. It regulates human life on all levels: individual, social, economic, political and spiritual. That is why Islam provides guidance in the smallest details of one's life on all these levels. Thus, following these details is following Islamic instructions in that specific area. It is a very encouraging element when one realizes that all his activities are considered by God as acts of worship. This should lead the individual to seek Allah's pleasure in his actions and always try to do them in the best possible manner, whether he is observed by his superiors or is alone. There is always the permanent supervisor, who knows everything: Allah.

Discussing the non-ritual worship in Islam first does not mean underevaluating the importance of the ritual worship but if actually, ritual worship, if performed in true spirit, elevates man morally and spiritually and enables him to carry on his activities in all walks of life according to the Guidance of God. Among ritual worships, *Salah* (ritual prayer) occupies the key position for two reasons. Firstly, it is the distinctive mark of a believer. Secondly, it prevents an individual from all sorts of abominations and vices by providing him chances of direct communion with his Creator five times a day, wherein he renews his covenant with God and seeks His guidance again and again: *"You alone we worship and to you alone we turn for help. Guide us to the straight path."* (1:5-6). Actually, *Salah* is the first practical manifestation of Faith and also the foremost of the basic conditions for the success of the believers:

Successful indeed are the believers who are humble in their prayers. (23:1-2)

The same fact has been emphasized by the Prophet Muhammad (PBUH) in a different way. He says:

"Those who offer their Salah with great care and punctuality will find it a light, a proof of their Faith and cause of their salvation on the Day of Judgment."

After *Salah, Zakah* (poor-due) is an important pillar of Islam. In the Qur'an, *Salah* and *Zakah* have been mentioned together many times. Like *Salah, Zakah* is a manifestation of faith that affirms that God is the sole owner of everything in the universe. What men possess is a trust in their hands to discharge as God has laid down:

Believe in Allah and His messenger and spend of that over which He has made you trustees. (57:7)

In this respect, *Zakah* is an act of devotion that, like prayer, brings the believer nearer to his Lord.

Apart from this, *Zakah* is a means of redistribution of wealth in a way that makes a contribution to social stability, providing a means of survival for those who have not, and reminding those who are wealthy that what they have is a trust from God. By purging the soul of the rich from selfishness, and the soul of the poor from resentment against society, *Zakah* blocks the channels leading to class hatred and makes it possible for the springs of brotherhood and solidarity to gush forth. Such stability is not merely based on the personal generous feelings of the rich: it stands on a firmly based right of the destitute which, if denied by those holding the wealth, would be exacted by force, if necessary.

Siyam (fasting during the daylight hours of the month of Ramadan) is another pillar of Islam. The main function of fasting is to make the Muslim pure from "within" as other aspects of Shariah (Islamic law) make him pure from "without." By such purity he responds to what is true and good and shuns what is false and evil. This is what we can perceive in the Qur'anic verse:

O you who believe, fasting is prescribed for you as it was prescribed for those before you, that you may gain piety. (2:183)

In an authentic tradition, the Prophet (PBUH) reported Allah as saying: "He suspends eating, drinking and gratification of his sexual passion for my sake."

Thus his reward is going to be according to God's great bounty.

Fasting, then, awakens the conscience of the individual and gives it scope for exercise in a joint experience for all society at the same time, thus adding further strength to each individual. Moreover, fasting offers a compulsory rest to the overworked human machine for the duration of one month. Similarly, fasting reminds an individual of those who are deprived of life's necessities throughout the year or throughout life. It makes him realize the suffering of others, the less fortunate brothers in Islam, and thus promotes in him a sense of sympathy and kindness to them.

Lastly, we come to *Al-Hajj* (pilgrimage to the House of God in Makkah). This very important pillar of Islam manifests a unique unity, dispelling all kinds of differences. Muslims from all corners of the world, wearing the same dress, respond to the call of Hajj in one voice and language: *LABBAIK ALLAHUMMA LABBAIK* (Here I am at your service, O Lord!). In Hajj there is an exercise of strict self-discipline and control where not only sacred things are revered, but even the life of plants and birds is made inviolable so that everything lives in safety:

And he that venerates the sacred things of God, it shall be better for him with his Lord. (22:30)

And he that venerates the way marks of God, it surely is from devotion of the heart. (22:32)

Pilgrimage gives an opportunity to all Muslims from all groups, classes, organizations, and governments from all over the Muslim world to meet annually in a great congress. The time and venue of this congress have been set by their One God. Invitation to attend is open to every Muslim. No one has the power to bar anyone. Every Muslim who attends is guaranteed full safety and freedom as long as he himself does not violate its safety.

Thus, worship in Islam, whether ritual or non-ritual, trains the individual in such a way that he loves his Creator most and thereby gains an unyielding will and spirit to wipe out all evil and oppression from human society and make the word of God dominant in the world.

Ramadan and Fasting

Fasting the Ninth Month of the Islamic Lunar Calendar

Ramadan, the ninth month of the Islamic lunar calendar, may be 29 or 30 days long. An Islamic month begins with the sighting of the new crescent in the western horizon, immediately after sunset. Muslims look toward the western horizon for the new moon on the 29th day of Sha'ban, the eighth month. If the new moon is sighted, Ramadan has begun with the sunset but fasting begins with the next dawn. If the new moon is not sighted on this 29th day, Muslims complete 30 days of Sha'ban and Ramadan begins the following day.

The Significance of Ramadan and Fasting

Allah says in the Qur'an: O you who believe! Fasting is prescribed for you, even as it was prescribed for those before you, that you may attain God-consciousness. (2:183)

In the month of Ramadan the Qur'an was revealed, a

book of guidance with proofs of guidance distinguishing right from wrong. Therefore whoever of you is present in that month let him fast. But who is ill or on a journey shall fast a similar number of days later on. Allah desires your wellbeing, not your discomfort. He desires you to fast the whole month so that you may magnify Him and render thanks to Him for giving you His guidance. (2:185)

Accordingly, the month of Ramadan is called the month of the Quran. Therefore, Muslims have tradition of reciting Quran frequently in this month.

Sawm or Fasting

Sawm means a fast that begins with dawn and ends with sunset. Muslims rise before dawn, eat *Sahur* (predawn meal) and drink liquids for the preparation of *sawm*. Eating and drinking stops at dawn. During the day no eating, drinking or sexual activity is allowed. In addition, a Muslim must adhere to the moral code of Islam very strictly as failure violates the requirements of fasting. Fasting in the month of Ramadan is one of the deeds of worship required of all Muslims who have attained puberty. Women who are having their menstrual period or who have not fully recovered from childbirth postpone the fast until they are completely out of their special conditions.

In addition, those who are ill or in travel may choose to postpone their fast. Muslims fast because Allah has commanded them to do so. However, they may also think about the benefits of fasting which may include developing control over hunger, thirst and sexual urges, training to be a good moral person and testing sincerity to the Creator. During the fast, Muslims may conduct their business as usual. However, in the Muslim countries working hours are shortened by a couple of hours a day and the hours are changed to make the work comfortable.

The fast is broken immediately after sunset usually by eating dates and drinking water or juice. However, any lawful food or drink may be used to break the fast. This is followed by the *Maghrib salah* (after sunset prayer) which is followed by a complete meal. After a brief rest, Muslims go to the mosque to offer the *'Isha salah* (night prayer) and then a special night prayer, called *taraweeh.*

Taraweeh

This nightly congregational *salah* (prayer) is performed after the *'Isha salah*. Traditionally a *Hafiz*, the person who has memorized the whole *Quran* (in Arabic), leads the prayer. He recites the *Quran* in small portions, in proper sequence, every night and completes the recitation of the whole *Quran* before the end of the month of Ramadan. Every Muslim who attends such prayers regularly gets the opportunity of listening to the whole Qur'an in a month. If a *Hafiz* of the Qur'an is not available, the Muslim who has memorized the most in a group leads the prayer and recites according to his ability.

In the absence of a *Hafiz* some Muslims hold the Qur'an in the hand during their *salah* and read from it. Many Islamic scholars cite the *sunnah* (way) of the Prophet(S) that he always prayed during the night alone in his apartment whether it was Ramadan or not and same was the habit of many of his great companions.

Ramadan Generosity

The month of Ramadan brings many blessings multiplied manifold for those who do good. During this month people are more generous, more cordial, friendlier and more ready than other times of the year to do good work. The poor and the needy receive food, clothing and money from the well-to-do in the community. Many people go to the mosque in the neighborhood for fast-breaking and meals. People in the neighborhood send fruit, food and drinks to the mosque – the atmosphere is that of a friendly pot luck dinner every evening of the month.

Well-known philanthropists of the Muslim community find themselves surrounded by the needy people and Islamic workers for donations. *Zakat*, a wealth purifying tax, and donations are given at this time of the year since many

Muslims wish to take the opportunity of multiplied rewards from Allah.

Laylat al-Qadr

This is the night of the *Qadr*. The term *Al-Qadr* has been frequently translated as "the power". A better translation may be "the value" or "the decree" because Allah says the value of this night is better than one thousand months, a lifetime of over eighty-three years. Allah sends His decrees in this night. This is the night when the *Quran* was revealed. Allah says in the *Quran:*

We have indeed revealed this (the *Quran*) in the Night of Value (or Measure). And what will explain to you what the Night of Value is? The Night of Value is better than a thousand months. Therein come down angels and the Spirit (the angel Gabriel) by Allah's permission with all decrees. (That night is) Peace until the rising of the dawn. (97:1-5)

The Night of Value is a gift to mankind from Allah. However, it is not clear which night is *Laylat al-Qadr*. Some reports by companions of the Prophet(s) elude it to be the 27th night of the month of Ramadan, but many more sayings point to any of the odd date nights during the last third of the month of Ramadan. According to authentic teachings of the Prophet Muhammad(s), Muslims are advised to spend the 21st, 23rd, 25th, 27th and 29th nights of Ramadan in worship and doing good works to assure finding *Laylat al-Qadr*. A portion of the Muslims stay up all night in prayers and good works, however, the Prophet(s) and his companions used to sleep at least one-third of the night.

In Muslim countries, the 27th of Ramadan is a holiday to enable people to rest during the day after all night of worship. Schools are closed from the 27th of Ramadan through the 2nd of Shawwal (5 to 6 days) to combine *Laylat al-Qadr* and *'Eid al-Fitr* observances.

I'tekaf *or Seclusion*

The practice of the Prophet Muhammad(s) was to spend the last ten days and nights of Ramadan in the *masjid* (mosque). Following his practice, it is considered a community duty that some people go in *I'tekaf* (seclusion) in a neighborhood masjid.

The people in *I'tekaf* spend their time in various forms of *dhikr* (remembrance of Allah), such as doing extra *salah*, recitation and study of the Qur'an, study of the Hadith, repetition of some phrases of praise and glory to Allah, exhorting each other to be good through obeying Allah and His Messenger(s). Since people in *I'tekaf* are not permitted to go outside the masjid except for emergencies, they sleep in the masjid and use available facilities of the masjid.

The food for the people in *I'tekaf* is provided either by their own families or people in the community. *I'tekaf* is terminated, generally, at the declaration of sighting of the moon or the end of the month of Ramadan. For busy people a shorter version of *I'tekaf* is allowed, sucsh as one night, one day or a few days.

Sadaqat al-Fitr

In general, any material help extended to the poor, needy and to those who ask and deserve is called *Sadaqah. Sadaqat al-Fitr,* which is also called *Zakat al-Fitr,* is the obligatory material help extended to the poor of the society before the 'Eid prayers, preferably to be given early enough for the poor to prepare for the celebration. In North America, the estimated amount is $5 to $8 to be given on behalf of each member of the donor's family, including infants.

'Eid al-Fitr

The end of the fasting month is celebrated on the first of Shawwal, the 10th month, which follows Ramadan. Traditionally, on the 29th of Ramadan after sunset, people go out in the open looking for a new crescent in the western horizon where the sun sets and if the crescent is sighted, the end of Ramadan and 'Eid are declared. If the crescent is not sighted, Ramadan is extended by one day. On the day of 'Eid, people take a bath or shower in the early morning, eat breakfast, wear their best clothes, apply perfume and proceed to the place of 'Eid congregation while pronouncing *takbeerat*, saying, "Allah is the Greatest, there is no deity but Allah and all praise belongs to Allah."

Muslims pronounce *takbeerat* in their homes, in the street and at the place of congregation while waiting for the leader, the *Imam*. It was the practice of the Prophet Muhammad(s) to hold 'Eid prayer congregations in open grounds. Following the practice of the Prophet(s) Muslims are advised to hold 'Eid prayers in open grounds. In the Muslim countries with warm climate there are designated 'Eid prayer grounds. However, in North America Muslims rent halls at convention centers or major hotels.

The Imam rises at the appointed time, leads the prayers and delivers a *khutbah* (sermon). At the end of the sermon, people supplicate, greet, embrace and congratulate each other for the successful completion of Ramadan and ask Allah for the acceptance of their efforts in His obedience. During the day, people visit each other and children may receive gifts. In some countries, people go for picnics and other gatherings. In addition, special 'Eid celebrations may be arranged at work or in social settings. Essentially, 'Eid is a day of thanks to Allah, and also a gathering of family and friends.

'Umrah or Minor Hajj in Ramadan

There is a report from Prophet Muhammad(s) saying that performing 'Umrah in the month of Ramadan is equal to performing a major or complete Hajj. Hajj is a pilgrimage to Makkah. Hajj is the enactment of some of the trials and tribulations of Prophet Abraham (A), his wife Hajirah (Hagar) and his oldest son, Isma'il (A) (Ishmael). Hajj includes the sacrifice of Ishmael, represented by the sacrifice of an animal, such as a ram, goat, sheep, cow or a camel. Complete Hajj lasts for five days but 'Umrah is completed in a couple of hours. 'Umrah is only a small part of the Hajj. An animal sacrifice may be offered at the completion of 'Umrah. 'Umrah may be performed anytime during the year but it has special significance in Ramadan. Hajj is performed only during the

8th and 13th days of Dhul Hijjah, the twelfth month of the Islamic calendar.

Seven Basic Beliefs and Basic Practices

The approach to the presentation of Islamic beliefs and practices depends upon the addressee's religion and culture. A reference point of commonalty or contrast is useful. For example, the Christians believe in the "original sin"; the connotation is that a human being has the stigma of being born as a sinner and is dirty filthy by nature. What has a newborn done to be a sinner or to be a filthy person? Contrast this with the Islamic teaching that every human being is born in nature, meaning good with no stigma of any kind and, if left alone without any brain washing will do no wrong. Such a person has a natural ability to distinguish between right and wrong and his tendency is to do right. In the society which raises a person brain washed, many times when he reaches puberty he is all confused – good has become bad and bad has become good under the influence of the society. He was not dirty by birth but the society has made him dirty in beliefs and practices.

Purification

When clothes get dirty, they are washed; when the body gets dirty, a bath or a shower is in order. Similarly, when beliefs and practices have become dirty, a purification job is in order and this purification is the entry into Islam through the door of witnessing or *shahadah*. Once a person has entered Islam he is purified as a newborn and has a second chance to start over again. His past sins are washed away while keeping his good works as assets.

Analogy of a Building

There are two aspects of purification:

a. Physical, and

b. Spiritual.

Physical purification consists of purifying the body,

clothes and environment. Spiritual purification consists of purifying beliefs and practices (works or deeds). The analogy of Islam is that of a building. A building has its foundation, pillars, roof, walls and other components. The foundation of a building is underground and not visible; similarly, the foundation of Islam consists of beliefs and remains invisible.

The pillars, walls, roof and other parts of a building are visible. Similarly, what a Muslim says and does is visible and becomes the pillars, roof and walls of Islam. Frequently, Muslims talk about the five pillars of Islam without thinking that five pillars cannot stand without a foundation and only pillars standing on the ground are not called a building. It is, therefore, necessary that Islam be presented in its totality not just five pillars. Five pillars are a necessary but small part of a Muslim's life.

Beliefs as the Foundation of Islam

As the foundation of a building consists of many components, such as, steel, cement, rocks, etc., the foundation of Islam consists of seven components.

1. *Allah, the Only True God:* Nothing is made without its planner and maker. Similarly, this universe, the earth and life on it, did not happen by itself - the first cause is the Creator, Allah or the God. Allah is the Creator of life and death, hence He is free of death and is Ever Living or Eternal. He created males and females for procreation; hence He is free of gender. Whatever He created He knows in its minutest detail, hence He is All-Knowing. Similarly, He is All-Seeing, All-Hearing, Most Compassionate, Most Merciful, Forgiving, Just; He has many attributes or good names – Muslims are told that He has ninety-nine names. All of His names are not abstract words but they have relevance in every Muslim's life. He created everything and humankind for a purpose: to serve Him. The God, in Islam, is the bedrock of the foundation of Islam.
2. *Prophets and Messengers:* Only Allah can tell the purpose of the creation of humankind which He does through

his chosen human beings called prophets and messengers. Islam recognizes many prophets of the Bible, such as, Noah, Abraham, Moses, Jesus and many in between them. Muhammad Ibn Abd-Allah Ibn Abd-al Muttalib was the last prophet-messenger of Allah who lived fourteen centuries ago. He received guidance from Allah, gave its meaning in words and deeds, thus becoming the role model for humankind.

3. *The Guidance from Allah:* When one accepts a new job he is given a job description and someone shows him how to do various tasks. Similarly, Allah gives the job description in His revelations and the Prophet shows the meaning and implementation of what and how. All the prophets of the Bible fulfilled their duties and the last prophet, Muhammad, did also. He left behind the Word of Allah, the Qur'an, and his teachings, Hadith, were collected by his companions. The Qur'an and the Hadith are the textual sources of Islamic teachings and will remain so as long as there is life on earth. Allah Himself has taken the responsibility for their preservation.
4. *The Angels:* Another creation of Allah, scattered all over the universe doing the work for Him, is angels. Human beings have been given very little knowledge about angels. One much honored angel, Gabriel or Jibrail, brought Allah's guidance to the prophets. Along with other angels mentioned in the Qur'an there are two angels with each human being writing his deeds?
5. *The Last Day:* Allah has created everything with a preset life span. Everything and everyone, from the moment of creation, are running towards its destruction or death. Modern sciences have arrived at the same conclusion. Science tells us that the solar system is middle-aged; when sun arrives at the moment of its death that will be the end of its planets including the earth. Similarly, the whole universe has its life span and there will be a Big Crush, the opposite of the Big Bang.

   The last day for each human being is the day of his/her death, as there is a last day for life on earth. On the last day of the earth, there will be earthquakes, mountains will either be rendered to sand or will float in space like carded wool, water of the oceans will either be sucked into the earth or will boil away and the valleys thus created will be filled with earth or rocks. The earth will become smooth without mountains or valleys with no life on it. However, this is not the end of human beings. There is life hereafter or the after life.

6. *The Life Hereafter:* Allah is Just but there is much injustice on earth. Murderers are getting away with murders, embezzlers are getting away with their loot, dictators are getting away with their oppression and injustices, and other criminals are getting away with their crimes. Are they really getting away with their crimes? No, it only appears that way. Everyone will be accountable for his deeds to Allah on the Day of Judgment and will receive reward or punishment. The life of the earth is the life of trials, not the place of real reward or punishment. This leads to the reality of Life Hereafter. After destruction of life on earth Allah will command human beings to come back to life with body and soul, their resurrection. Resurrection is followed by the judgment by Allah. No judgment is complete without reward for good doers and punishment for evil livers. The reward is the life of paradise and punishment is the life of hell. Both are believed to be eternal.
7. *Al Qadr (Measure, Destiny, Decree):* People are created as males and females, short or tall, black, white, brown, yellow, smart or not so smart, with appointed parents, having a given time and place of birth and death and so on. All this is decreed by Allah. However, human beings have choices and enjoy limited freedom. The result of their activities depends upon their level of knowledge, level of effort and permission of Allah to succeed. Since human beings do not have perfect knowledge, sometimes they succeed and other times they fail in their pursuits. The admission that only Allah has perfect knowledge and human knowledge is imperfect and practical implications of this admission is *Qadr*.

The Building of Islam Above Ground

The visible part of a building is whatever exists above ground built on a stable foundation. Similarly, a Muslim's life, his talk and his activities must represent his beliefs. They are summarized below.

Five Rites (Acts) of Worship

The term worship has two aspects:

a. Love for Allah more than the love for anyone or anything in life, including the love of one's own life. It simply means that one is willing to give up anyone or anything for the love for Allah.

b. Obedience of Allah and His Messenger for the love of them. If one looks for worldly benefits in obedience of Allah or desires to avoid worldly harm by obeying, then it is for business not for the love of Allah. Five rites of worship are given below.

1. *Shahadah, Witnessing:* If one believes in the seven aspects of beliefs and is willing to live his life accordingly, he declares his intention voluntarily and publicly or at least in front of two or more witnesses. Such declaration consists of pronouncing, *"La Ilaha illa-Allah wa Muhammadur-Rasool-Allah"* meaning there is no deity but Allah and Muhammad is His Messenger. This pronouncement has the connotation that my Creator, Provider and Sustainer Lord is Allah and I have been brought to this world by Allah to serve Him for which I will be accountable on the Day of Judgment. The Messenger of Allah, Muhammad(s), brought the guidance from Allah, delivered to me and became a role model for me; therefore, I am going to live by the Qur'an and *Sunnah* (the way of the Messenger of Allah, Muhammad(s)).
2. *Salah, Prescribed Prayers:* Once a person takes *shahadah,* he is a Muslim and is required to perform the five daily prescribed prayers. In prayers a person addresses Allah directly without any intermediary or intercessor. Islam is the only religion in the world which has removed all

kinds of intermediaries and intercessors between man and Allah.

3. *Zakah, Wealth Cleansing Tax:* The basic principle is that Allah is the owner of heavens and the earth, therefore, He is my owner and everything in my possession belongs to Him. I am only a trustee of Allah for anything in my possession. I must do whatever Allah requires me to do. Allah demands that when a certain amount of money is in one's possession for a year, a small percentage (typically 2.5%) must be spent for Allah's causes. In general, collection of *Zakah* is spent to help the poor and needy and other Islamic causes.
4. *Sawm, Fasting in the Month of Ramadan:* Ramadan is the ninth month of Islamic lunar calendar. During this month Muslims are required to fast from dawn to dusk, meaning not to eat, drink, smoke or indulge in sex. After sunset all lawful food, drink and sex are allowed. However, one must implement the moral code of Islam very strictly because non-adherence has double jeopardy, namely, violating the moral code and nullification of the fast. The fast is a test of one's sincerity to Allah.
5. *Hajj, Pilgrimage to Makkah:* A Muslim must perform Hajj once in a life time provided expenses can be met without borrowing or owing any money to anyone, health is good and the way is safe. Hajj is the recreation of some of the trials and tribulations of Prophets Abraham and Ishmael, and Hagar, the wife of Abraham, with a few additional rituals. The Hajj lasts for five days from the 8th to 12th of Dhul Hijjah. Approximately two million people perform Hajj every year.

Significance of the Pillars

The above mentioned five rites of worship are also called the five pillars of Islam. Pillars are supporters of roofs and walls. If the pillars fall down there is no building left. Similarly, if a Muslim is not doing his five daily salah, this pillar is absent from his building of Islam and part of the building is destroyed. He may claim to be a Muslim but in practice he is a hypocrite. The same analogy is applied to other pillars.

Excellence in Knowledge and Conduct

A good believing and practicing Muslim is a role model for the people and the Muslim Ummah is the role model for all other societies. A Muslim scientist must be the best among his peers, a doctor must be the best, a car mechanic must be the best and so on. A role model must excel in all aspects of his life, that is, in knowledge, profession, on the job, in his moral character and honoring other people's rights. Most importantly he must excel in his service to his Lord, Allah.

Islamic Moral Code, Enjoining Good and Forbidding Evil

Islam requires Muslims to be righteous, truthful, fulfill their promises, be courteous, gentle in disagreements, have humility, keep the trust and keep all other well known virtues. Naturally, Islam condemns the immoral and criminal acts of lying, cheating, backbiting, slandering, breaking promises, breaching the trust, arrogance, haughtiness, and all other well known vices. It is not enough to stay away from vices and adopt all virtues but he has a duty to promote the same good in the society and do everything possible to stop evil and vice.

Fulfill the Duty to Others

There are mutual rights and duties. However, Allah will not ask on the Day of Judgment if you have received all your rights but He will ask if you have done all your duties. Human duties fall under four categories:

1. *Duty to Allah:* The first and foremost duty is to Allah. There are three duties to Allah,
    a. Not to associate partners with Him,
    b. Not to worship anyone but Allah, and
    c. Not to depend upon anyone for help but Allah.
2. *Duty to Other Human Beings:* Whenever there is interaction with another person there are mutual rights and duties. One person's rights are other person's duties. There are duties to parents, spouse, children, relatives, neighbors,

buyers, sellers, ruler, ruled, boss, and subordinates and so on.

3. *Community Duty:* There is a duty to defend the family, the country and the community as a whole. In addition there are people who cannot provide for themselves, such as, the poor, orphans, widows, handicapped, refugees and others whom a single person cannot support fully but the community as a whole can. Every Muslim should be a part of such a support system. Every human being has five basic rights, namely, food, clothing, shelter, education and health maintenance; every Muslim should be part of the system providing basic rights to all those who cannot provide for themselves.
4. *Duty to Manage the Earth:* Allah has appointed man Khalifah on the earth, meaning that man is a trustee or manager of the earth for the owner, Allah. Humankind, in general, and Muslims, in particular, has the duty to see that the resources of the earth are not abused: air and water are not polluted, animals are not killed for fun or for greedy people, and trees are not cut down unnecessarily and so on. Use resources of the earth but do not abuse them.

Lawful (Halal) and Unlawful (Haram)

This is a part of Islamic Shari'ah, civil and criminal law. Every Muslim is not going to be an Islamic lawyer or a judge, but he should know about a few unlawful things. The basic principle is that everything is lawful except those things which are explicitly unlawful. A few things are doubtful therefore it is advisable to avoid them. The unlawful things fall under four categories.

1. *Food and Drink:* There are a number of things which have been forbidden as food and drink, such as, flesh of swine, blood, anything offered in the name of anyone other than Allah, flesh of dead animals, carnivorous animals, birds of prey, all intoxicants including alcoholic liquor and drugs of abuse and anything poisonous to humans.
2. *Sources of Income:* Any business involving production,

distribution or sale of unlawful food or drinks is unlawful. In addition, all trades of exploitation or taking others rights away are unlawful, such as, prostitution, gambling, usury and interest, stealing, robbery, embezzlement, monopolizing and hoarding to raise prices and others.

3. *Spending the Wealth:* It has been mentioned that all wealth is owned by Allah and human beings are trustees for whatever they possess. It is, therefore, necessary that Allah's wealth not be spent wherever Allah does not desire it to be spent. A few examples of such unlawful areas are already given above. One person's spending is another person's source of income. Additional unlawful areas are spending money on unlawful food and drinks to serve others.
4. *Sexual Relations:* A simple principle is no sex without marriage. An engagement is a social custom not a religious rite. A person closest in blood relation lawful to marry is a first cousin. There is no permission for homosexuality or such "marriages" in Islam.

Conveying the Message of Islam

A duty of every Muslim, male and female, individually and collectively, is to present Islam to the non-Muslims. A Muslim, by the Grace and Mercy of Allah, may go to paradise but a non-Muslim has no such chance. At least, a person must convey the message of Islam to his loved ones, giving them a chance to save themselves from the hell fire.

Implementation of the Rule of Allah

Every aspect of a Muslim's life should be guided by Allah, including personal, family, social, economic and political life. None of the aspects of human life are outside the domain of Allah.

In summary, there are seven essential components of beliefs and seven essentials of good works required of every sane adult Muslim, male and female. The Qur'an and Hadith are essentially explanations of beliefs (*Iman*) and good works

(*'Amal-us-Salihat*) and learning them in detail could be a life long pursuit.

The Creator and Lord of the Universe

Allah is the name of the true One God in the Arabic language. In the Hebrew language His name is Eloh, Elohim for respect. It is well known that when a word is borrowed from one language to another it's spelling and pronunciation is often altered. It is, therefore, reasonable to say that Eloh and Allah are names of the same Deity of Abraham believed by the three monotheistic religions of Judaism, Christianity and Islam. Islam is the most rigorously monotheistic religion among the three dedicated to the worship of Allah, never seen by a human eye.

Who is Allah? The translation of verses from the Qur'an is given to answer this question. References of the verses are given in brackets, the number before the colon represents the Surah (chapter) and the following number represents the verse number.

Allah, the One Only

"Proclaim: Allah is one. Allah is Eternal. He neither begets nor was begotten." (112:1-4)

"Nothing is like unto Him." (42:11)

"If there were therein Gods besides Allah, then verily both (the heavens and the earth) would have collapsed into disorder and chaos. Glorified be Allah, the Lord of the Throne, transcendent beyond all they ascribe unto Him." (21:22)

"Sight can never reach Him; His sight reaches all things." (6:103)

"And proclaim: Praise be to Allah, Who has not taken unto Himself a son, and Who has no partner in the Sovereignty, nor has He (need for) any protecting friend through dependence. (17:111)

"Allah! There is no God save Him." (3:2, 2:255)

"Is there any God beside Allah? Nay, but they are folk who ascribe equals (unto Him)." (27:60).

"Is there any God beside Allah? Nay, but most of them know not." (27:61)

Attributes of Allah

Muslims talk about ninety-nine attributes of Allah; a few are given in the following verses of the Qur'an.

"And He is the Mighty, the Wise. His is the Sovereignty of the heavens and the earth; He gives life and He gives death; and He is able to do all things. He is the First and the Last, and the Outward and the Inward; and He is the Knower of all things." (57:1-3)

"Allah is He, other than Whom there is no deity. He knows (all things) both secret and open; He, Most Gracious, Most Merciful. Allah is He, other than Whom there is no deity; the Sovereign, the Holy One, the Source of Peace (and Perfection), the Guardian of Faith, the Preserver of Safety, the Exalted in Might, the Irresistible, the Supreme: Glory to Allah! (High is He) above the partners they attribute to Him. He is Allah the Creator, the Evolver, the Bestower of Forms (and Colors). To Him belong the Most Beautiful Names: Whatever are the heavens and on earth, do declare His Praise and Glory; and He is exalted in Might, the Wise." (59:22-24)

"Allah! There is no God save Him, the Alive, the Eternal. Neither slumber nor sleep overtakes Him. Unto Him belongs whatsoever is in the heavens and whatsoever is in the earth. Who is he that intercedes with Him saving by His permission? He knows that which is in front of them and that which is behind them, while they encompass nothing of His knowledge save what He will. His throne includes the heavens and the earth, and He is never weary of preserving them. He is the Sublime, the Tremendous." (2:255)

"The Originator of the heavens and the earth!" (6:101)

"The Beneficent, the Merciful: Owner of the Day of Judgment." (1:3-4)

"Say: Call upon Allah, or call upon Ar-Rahman: by whatever name you call upon Him, (it is well): For to Him belong the Most Beautiful Names." (17:110)

"And you seek the Grace of Allah: for Allah is Oft-Forgiving, Most Merciful." (73:20)

"The revelation of this Book is from Allah, Exalted in Power, Full of Knowledge, Who forgives sin, accepts repentance, is strict in punishment, and has a long reach (in all things). There is no god but He: to Him is the Final Goal." (40:2-3)

Allah the Creator

"Have not those who disbelieve known that the heavens and the earth were of one piece, then we parted them, and we made every living thing from water? Will they not then believe?" (21:30)

[*In this verse 'we' belongs to imperial language, not of plurality. In the Qur'an, Allah uses 'I', 'Me' 'we' and 'Us' for Himself.*]

"And He it is who created the night and the day, and the sun and the moon. They float each in an orbit... And from among His signs are the night and the day, and the sun and the moon. Prostrate neither to the sun nor to the moon, but prostrate to Allah who created them, if you (really) worship Him." (21:33, 41:37)

"He has created man: He has imparted unto him articulate thought and speech. [At His behest] the sun and the moon run their appointed courses; the stars and the trees prostrate themselves [before Him]. And the skies have He raised high, and has devised [for all things] a measure, so that you [too, O men,] might never transgress the measure [of what is right]: weigh, therefore, [your deeds] with equity, and cut not the measure short!" (55:3-9)

"It is Allah who created everything in the best of form...It is He Who created and perfected all things." (32:7, 87:2)

"It is Allah Who created life and death that you may prove yourself worthy in your deeds." (67:2)

"Such is Allah, your Lord. There is no god except Him, the Creator of all things, so serve Him. And He takes care of all things." (6:102)

"He is the Cleaver of the daybreak, and He has appointed the night for stillness, and the sun and the moon to run their appointed courses: [all] this is laid down by the Will of the Almighty, the All-Knowing. (6:96)

"Allah is He who created seven heavens and of the earth a similar number. Through the midst of them (all) descends His command: that you may know that Allah has power over all things, and that Allah comprehends all things in (His) knowledge." (65:12)

"He it is who has made the sun a [source of] radiant light and the moon shining [surface], and has determined for it phases so that you might know how to compute the years and to measure [time]. None of this has Allah created without [an inner] truth. Clearly does He spell out these messages unto people of [innate] knowledge?" (10:5)

"Allah has indeed made all things in heaven and earth subservient to humankind; it is all from Him. Lo! Herein verily are portents for people who reflect." (45:13)

Allah, the Sustainer, the Cherisher, the Lord (Al-Rabb)

"All praise is due to Allah Alone, the Lord [the Sustainer, the Cherisher] of the worlds." (1:2)

"Everything we have created and prescribed for its measure, its character and destiny...No creature creeps on earth but Allah provides for it its sustenance. He knows its purpose and destiny. For it is He Who prescribed them in His eternal order...The sun rises and sets traversing its orbit exactly as the Almighty, the All Knowing has ordained. And the moon passes regularly through its phases, returning to its original thin crescent form. Neither sun nor moon overtakes the other; neither night nor day deviates from their preordained courses. Each move in the orbit Allah has ordained for it. (54:49, 11:6, 36:38-40)

In the Qur'an, the name Allah is used more than 2,600 times and His attribute, Al-Rabb (the Lord, the Cherisher, the Sustainer), has been used over 1,000 times.

Allah Revealed the Truth - Option Given

"We revealed to you the Book in truth, that you may proclaim it to the world. Whoever decides to be guided by its guidance and so does to his own credit? Whoever rejects its guidance so does to his own discredit and you are not a warder over them." (39:41)

"Let there be no compulsion [or coercion] in religion: Truth stands out clear from error; whoever rejects evil and believes in Allah has grasped the most trustworthy handhold that never breaks. And Allah hears and knows all things." (2:256)

"And say: The Truth [has now come] from your Lord: let, then him who wills, believe in it, and let him who wills, reject it." (18:29)

"And if your Lord willed, all who are in the earth would have believed together. Would you [Muhammad] compel men until they are believers?" (10:99)

"No person is responsible for the guilt of another. To every person belongs the merit or demerit of what he had wrought... Allah does not charge a person with more than he can bear. Therefore, to everyone belongs the credit or discredit which he had personally earned." (53:38-39, 2:286)

"Whoever guides himself by our revelation does so to his own credit. Whoever goes astray does so to his own peril? Nobody will be responsible for another's deeds, and we will not judge but after a messenger sent [to proclaim and warn] ... Whoever does good will have that good reckoned for him. Whoever does evil will have that evil marked against him? Your Lord commits no injustice to His servants." (17:15, 41:46)

"Say: You are not accountable for our crimes; nor are we

for the evil you do... On the Day of Judgment, no person will of any avail to another, neither for good nor for ill. Those who committed injustice will be assigned to the Fire which they denied." (34:25, 42)

"Say: Are those who know equal with those who know not? But only men of understanding will pay heed." (39:9)

"There is not an animal in the earth or a flying creature flying on two wings, but they are community like unto you. We have neglected nothing in the Book. Then unto their Lord they will be gathered." (6:38)

"Allah has made what is in the heavens and on the earth subservient to you... And He has made subservient to you the sun and the moon, predetermined in their orbits, and the day and the night... It is Allah Who made you His trustees on earth... Can you not see that Allah made all that is on earth subservient to you?" (14:33, 31:29, 35:39, 22:65)

Allah was the God-in-Chief of the Pagan Arabs

"If indeed you ask them (the pagan Arabs) who has created the heavens and the earth and subjected the sun and the moon (to His Law), they will certainly reply, 'Allah'... And if indeed you ask them who it is that sends down rain from the sky, and gives life therewith to the earth after its death, they will certainly reply, 'Allah!'" (29:61, 63; similar message is found in 31:25; 39:38; 43:9)

"And those unto whom they (the pagan Arabs) call instead of Him (Allah) possess no power of intercession ... And if you ask them who created them (gods of the pagans and pagans themselves), they will surely say, 'Allah!'" (43:86, 87)

Fabrications against Islam

In 1990, one of the most anti-Islam demagogues, named Robert Morey, published an anti-Islam book in which he claimed that Allah is the name of the moon-god; therefore, Islam is another old pagan religion. The claim that Allah is the moon god did not exist before the publication of Robert

Morey's book in 1990; apparently he is the originator of this idea. Allah is the name of the originator of the Universe who has a variety of names in various languages. "Moon-god" has existed in many animist societies but it is Morey who combined two into one and the same deity. Others, like Jack Chic of Chick Publications of California and a few additional Islam-haters have picked up the Morey fabrication of moon-god, and are publishing tracts, brochures, flyers and comic books distributing them by the millions all over the world.

These Islam-haters subscribe to the Nazi belief that if a lie is spoken loud enough and spoken repeatedly, it will be believed. Thus, Robert Morey, Jack Chick and others like them are disciples of the Nazis and are not ashamed of using the scare tactics of McCarthyism. Muslim leaders have met both of them and asked for the proof of their allegations; they had none but refused to cease their propaganda of lies and deception. For documentary evidence of Robert Morey's fabrication of "Allah, the moon-god", see on Internet "Islamic Awareness" by Shabbir Ally. Any intelligent reader, however much he may be ignorant of Islam, can see from the above quoted sixty plus verses of the *Quran* that the moon is one of the creations of Allah. The moon is a tiny part of Allah's universe.

Arab Christians and Arab Jews believe in Allah

Arabs include Christians and Jews who speak Arabic language as their mother tongue. In the Arabic language Bible the name "Allah" is written wherever "God" appears in the English language. The Arabic language Bible printed in the U.S. uses the name, Allah, on the first page of Genesis. Does this mean that the Christians also believe in "Allah, the moon-god" of Robert Morey and Jack Chic?

An Appeal

The reader of this brochure is requested to distribute this brochure to the widest possible audiences. Photocopies may be made and distributed to American people. You may obtain printed copies of this brochure and other brochures about

Islam from the III&E for a small donation. Islam-haters are trying to widen the gap between the Muslims and their non-Muslim American brethren. The goal of anti-Islam demagogues is to create hate against the Muslim minority in the non-Muslim majority of America. Would you, as a decent human being allow it happen? The reader of this brochure is requested to bridge the gap between fellow Americans of different faiths by participating in the education of the American people about the correct faith of the Muslims.

The Authenticity of the *Quran*

The importance of this question cannot be underestimated. Scriptures form the bedrock of a religion's teachings and typically compel people to follow them on the assumption that they are of divine origin. However, with so many competing claims, it is no longer sufficient to rely on mere assumption alone to feel confident that a religious scripture ought to be trusted as Truth. If being a "Muslim" means "one who surrenders to the will of Allah", then every Muslim should know that it really is the will of Allah that one is surrendering to.

To answer the question, we first need to establish that the Qur'an we have today is the same Qur'an as revealed to the Prophet Muhammad (p) and that no corruption has taken place in the transmission of that message. In other words, we initially need to prove the fact that the Qur'an has survived history, perfectly preserved. Secondly, we need to establish who the author of the Qur'an really is. This may be done by eliminating all possible authors that are unacceptable to reason. That is, we may be certain of the definite author by eliminating all unlikely authors. This two-step process is outlined below:

The Recording and Perfect Preservation of the Quran

The Glorious Qur'an, the Muslims' religious Scripture, was revealed in Arabic to the Prophet Muhammad (p) through the angel Gabriel. The revelation occurred piecemeal, over a period of twenty-three years, sometimes in brief verses and sometimes in longer chapters.

The Qur'an (lit. a "reading" or "recitation") is distinct from the recorded sayings and deeds (Sunnah) of the Prophet Muhammad (p), which are instead preserved in a separate set of literature collectively called the "*Ahadith*" (lit. "News"; "report"; or "narration").

Upon receiving revelation, the Prophet (p) engaged himself in the duty of conveying the message to his Companions through reciting the exact words he heard in their exact order. This is evident in his inclusion of even the words of Allah which were directed specifically to him, for example: "*Qul*" ("*Say* [to the people, O Muhammad]"). The Qur'an's rhythmic style and eloquent expression make it easy to memorize. Indeed, Allah describes this as one of its essential qualities for preservation and remembrance (Q.44:58; 54:17, 22, 32, 40), particularly in an Arab society which prided itself on orations of lengthy pieces of poetry. Michael Zwettler notes that "in ancient times, when writing was scarcely used, memory and oral transmission was exercised and strengthened to a degree now almost unknown". Large portions of the revelation were thus easily memorized by a large number of people in the community of the Prophet (p).

The Prophet (p) encouraged his Companions to learn each verse that was revealed and transmit it to others. The Qur'an was also required to be recited regularly as an act of worship, especially during the daily meditative prayers (*salat*). Through these means, many repeatedly heard passages from the revelation recited to them, memorized them and used them in prayer. The entire Qur'an was memorized verbatim (word for word) by some of the Prophet's Companions. Among them were Zaid ibn Thabit, Ubayy ibn Ka'b, Mu'adh ibn Jabal, and Abu Zaid.

Furthermore, the sequence or order of the Qur'an was arranged by the Prophet (p) himself and was also well-known to the Companions. Each Ramadan, the Prophet (p) would repeat after the angel Gabriel (reciting) the entire Qur'an in its exact order as far as it had been revealed, while in the presence of a number of his Companions. In the year of his death, he recited it twice. Thereby, the order of verses in each chapter and the order of the chapters became reinforced in the memories of each of the Companions present. As the Companions spread out to various provinces with different populations, they took their recitations with them in order to instruct others. In this way, the same Qur'an became widely retained in the memories of many people across vast and diverse areas of land.

Indeed, memorization of the Qur'an emerged into a continuous tradition across the centuries, with centers/ schools for memorization being established across the Muslim world. The Qur'an is perhaps the only book, religious or secular, that has been memorized completely by millions of people. Leading orientalist Kenneth Cragg reflects that "this phenomenon of Qur'anic recital means that the text has traversed the centuries in an unbroken living sequence of devotion. It cannot, therefore, be handled as an antiquarian thing, or as a historical document out of a distant past. The fact of hifz (Qur'anic memorization) has made the Qur'an a present possession through the entire lapse of Muslim time and given it a human currency in every generation, never allowing its relegation to a bare authority for reference alone".

The entire Qur'an was however also recorded in writing at the time of revelation from the Prophet's dictation by some of his literate companions, the most prominent of them being Zaid ibn Thabit. Others among his noble scribes were Ubayy ibn Ka'b, Ibn Mas'ud, Mu'awiya ibn Abi-Sufyan, Khalid ibn Waleed and Zubayr ibn Awwam. The verses were recorded on leather, parchment, scapulae (shoulder bones of animals) and the stalks of date palms.

The codification of the Qur'an (i.e. into a 'book form') was done soon after the Battle of Yamama (11AH/633CE), after the Prophet's death, during the Caliphate of Abu Bakr. Many companions became martyrs at that battle and it was feared that unless a written copy of the entire revelation was produced, large parts of the Qur'an might be lost with the death of those who had memorized it.

Therefore, at the suggestion of Umar to collect the Qur'an in the form of writing, Zaid ibn Thabit was requested by Abu Bakr to head a committee which would gather together the scattered recordings of the Qur'an and prepare a suhuf - loose sheets which bore the entire revelation on them. To safeguard the compilation from errors, the committee accepted only material which had been written down in the presence of the Prophet (p) himself, and which could be verified by at least two reliable witnesses who had actually heard the Prophet (p) recite the passage in question.

Once completed and unanimously approved of by the Prophet's Companions, these sheets were kept with the Caliph Abu Bakr (d. 13AH/634CE), then passed on to the Caliph Umar (13-23AH/634-644CE), and then Umar's daughter and the Prophet's widow, Hafsa. Although the Qur'an was initially revealed in the Qurayshi dialect of Arabic to the Prophet (p), it was also later revealed in seven different Arabian dialects to aid the understanding of those belonging to non-Quraysh tribes. At the time of the third Caliph Uthman (23AH-35AH/644-656CE), however, a companion named Hudhayfah ibn Al-Yaman observed that the people of the regions of present-day Syria and Iraq had begun disputing over various pronunciations of some of the words of the Qur'an, while new Muslims in provinces outside Arabia were unsure which dialect should be learned.

Urged by Hudhayfah to take heed of how the *Ahl al-Kitab* (People of the Book) had differed among them regarding Allah's Word, Uthman perceived the danger of divisions, disunity and corruption arising on the basis of different readings/dialects of the Qur'an which were earlier on approved by the Prophet (p). He therefore requested Hafsa to send him the manuscript of the Qur'an which was in her safekeeping, and ordered the production of several bounded copies of it (*masaahif*, sg. *mushaf*) using the Quraysh dialect (i.e. the dialect of the Prophet himself and in which the Qur'an had commenced being revealed in). This task was entrusted to the Companions Zaid ibn Thabit, Abdullah ibn Az-Zubair, Sa'id ibn As-'As, and Abdur Rahman ibn Harith ibn Hisham.

Upon completion (in 25AH/646CE), Uthman returned the original manuscript to Hafsa and sent the copies to the major Islamic provinces to replace other materials that were in circulation. He also ordered that all other extracts or copies of the Qur'an which differed from that undoubted "official" copy (including incomplete manuscripts and those with additional personal notes) be burnt so that the Qur'an would not suffer the same fate of alterations, uncertainty of authenticity and contradictory versions which characterized prior religious scriptures. This action of Uthman was unanimously approved of by the Prophet's Companions, as evidenced in the accounts of Zaid, Mus'ab, and Ali that the Companions had gathered in large numbers to witness the burning, with no-one speaking out against it. Their accounts also reveal that many had openly declared their support for Uthman at the time, and how pleased they were with the measures he had taken.

It was therefore not the "Original" Qur'an that was burnt, nor a fabricated story to discredit Uthman in the eyes of the community, as some critics of Islam allege. The story of how the Qur'an came to be preserved as described above is drawn entirely from authentic Ahadith. Some orientalist critics, however, claim that the narrations in Hadith collections cannot be trusted due to their being recorded by "Muslim sources". These orientalists ignore the fact that news and social history have always been uncovered through eye-witness reports, and that early Muslim scholars have developed some of the most rigorous criteria to scrutinize such reports for authenticity. The majority of what we know of the life of the Prophet (p) and his Companions are from *mutawaatir* reports (reported by many different reliable narrators, who all independently verify the same account).

This continuing and dynamic science (now over thirteen centuries old) has produced highly accurate (albeit not perfect) reports of Muslim history. Through this science, thousands of scholars have repeatedly analyzed the Ahadith collections in order to identify and filter out any fabrications. The accusation that most Muslim scholarship has been based on forgery would necessarily implicate that all the geographically scattered scholars of the first four centuries of Hadith collection, who belonged to varied and competing schools of thought, collaborated together in a mutual conspiracy – an idea which neither appeals to reason nor the fact that such scholars were renowned for their piety and integrity of character.

A number of orientalists (such as Ignaz Goldziher) have been attached to the theory that certain variations in some of the reports make the entire story of the Qur'an's codification dubious. Yet other scholars have pointed out that these differences are often reconcilable due to context of each narration (contexts which, incidentally, are also recorded in Ahadith collections), and the time of narration (some referring to earlier instances, such as prior to the completion of the entire Qur'an). Muslim scholars also note that the number of memorizers was great for any given portion of the Qur'an and therefore if any error had been made in Uthman's codification, someone would have pointed it out. Furthermore, the majority of the reports indicate that the text of Uthman's codification is *mutawaatir* – i.e. transmitted and agreed upon by many people – while other variant readings were only used by a sole companion or occasionally two or three.

Jeffrey Lang points out that orientalists often base their conclusions on mere speculation or fragmentary data which also stem from the same Hadith collections that they criticize. In line with Edward Said's comments on the underlying biases of Western scholarship, he also remarks that the bulk of orientalist analysis has been so predisposed to write off discrepancies in the body of early Muslim literature as evidence of Hadith fabrications that it often overlooks clear evidence that easily explains otherwise. An example of this is the frequent criticism that Ahadith were forged in the second and third century after Hijrah to support jurists' legal rulings.

Azami explains that such accusations often relied on a faulty comparison of legal and hadith literature when in fact they are two distinct fields. One involves narrating and verifying Ahadith, the other involves deriving legal opinions and discussions from such Ahadith. Inferences about one science cannot validly be made by studying the development of another. The theory that all Ahadith about the collection of the Qur'an were forged in the second and third century has been further refuted by proof that much of the Ahadith were actually written down in the first century.

In an excellent attempt at objective analysis of Western criticism of Hadith traditions, Jeffrey Lang concludes those Muslim scholars' deductions of history hold ground more solidly with the available evidence than their orientalist counterparts'. Orientalist theories are further addressed and refuted in the works of Ali, Azami, Abbott, Siddiqi, and Abdul Ghafar.

Despite such defective theories, many orientalists themselves have admitted like Gibb that "It seems reasonably well established that no material changes were introduced and that the original form of Mohammed's discourses were preserved with scrupulous precision". John Burton, at the end of his substantial work on the Qur'an's compilation, says with reference to criticisms made of different readings narrated in Ahadith that "No major differences of doctrines can be constructed on the basis of the parallel readings based on the Uthmanic consonantal outline, yet ascribed to mushafs other than his. All the rival readings unquestionably represent one and the same text. They are substantially agreed in what they transmit..." He further states that the Qur'an as we have it today is "the text which has come down to us in the form in which it was organized and approved by the Prophet.... What we have today in our hands is the mushaf of Muhammad."

Kenneth Cragg describes the transmission of the Qur'an from the time of revelation to today as occurring in "an unbroken living sequence of devotion". Schwally concurs that "As far as the various pieces of revelation are concerned, we may be confident that their text has been generally transmitted exactly as it was found in the Prophet's legacy". The historical credibility of the Qur'an is further established by the fact that one of the copies sent out by the Caliph Uthman is still in existence today. It lies in the Museum of the City of Tashkent in Uzbekistan, Central Asia. A facsimile of the mushaf in Tashkent is available at the Columbia University Library in the USA. This copy is proof that the text of the Qur'an we have in circulation today is identical with that of the time of the Prophet and his companions.

A copy of the mushaf sent to Syria (duplicated before a fire in 1310AH/1892CE destroyed the Jaami' Masjid where it was housed) also exists in the Topkapi Museum in Istanbul, and an early manuscript on gazelle parchment exists in Dar al-Kutub as-Sultaniyyah in Egypt. More ancient manuscripts from all periods of Islamic history found in the Library of Congress in Washington, the Chester Beatty Museum in Dublin (Ireland) and the London Museum have been compared with those in Tashkent, Turkey and Egypt, with results confirming that there have not been any changes in the text from its original time of writing.

The Institute for Koranforschung, for example, in the University of Munich (Germany), collected over 42,000 complete or incomplete ancient copies of the Qur'an. After around fifty years of research, they reported that there was no variance between the various copies, except the occasional mistakes of the copyist which could easily be ascertained. This Institute was unfortunately destroyed by bombs during WWII.

Thus, due to the efforts of the early companions, with Allah's assistance, the Qur'an as we have it today is recited in the same manner as it was revealed. This makes it the only religious scripture that is still completely retained and understood in its original language. Indeed, as Sir William Muir states, "There is probably no other book in the world which has remained twelve centuries [now fourteen] with so pure a text".

The evidence above confirms Allah's promise in the Qur'an: *"Verily, We have revealed the Reminder, and verily we shall preserve it."* (Q.15:9). The Qur'an has been preserved in both oral and written form in a way no other book has, and with each form providing a check and balance for the authenticity of the other. But though it is proven that the text of the Qur'an has remained intact till today, how are we sure that that words actually originated from God and not some other source? This takes us to look at the authenticity, authority, or source of the Qur'an.

Source or Authority of the Qur'an

Concerning the authorship of the Qur'an, Muslims believe that it was revealed verbatim (ie. word for word) by God, to Muhammad (p). Non-Muslims, however, who do not support this view can have no differences with Muslims concerning the fact that the Qur'an was at least first witnessed to be uttered by Muhammad (p), a Makkan Arab in the 7th century CE and, as proved above, there have been no changes to the records of his utterances since then.

Muslims' claim of "internal evidence" for the divine authorship of the Qur'an, i.e. from statements to that effect in the Qur'an itself (e.g. Q.4:82; 6:19; 6:92; 27:6; 45:2, etc.), is understandably looked upon with skepticism, as nearly anyone can quote passages from his or her scripture that claim the scripture in question is revelation from God. We are therefore forced by reason and objectivity to look elsewhere for "external evidence" of the Qur'an's divine source or authority.

The simple proposed structure for the presentation of this "external evidence" is an elimination process, where we get to the answer of the question – "Who is the author of the Qur'an?" – by eliminating all alternative answers to this question which are definitely implausible. In other words, the definite or (at least) most probable author or source of the Qur'an is identified by eliminating unacceptable alternative candidates.

There are various contradictory views and opinions held by some non-Muslims as to the source of the Qur'an. The following list of "possible" authors reflects the main theories.

1. Muhammad (p)
2. Some other Arab poet(s), scholars, etc.
3. Some non-Arab scholars, or poets or religious personalities
4. Monks or Rabbis (i.e. from the Bible or Judeo-Christian sources)
5. Satan (or other deceitful "spirits" or "aliens", etc.)
6. God

We may now proceed to examine from a closer study of the Qur'an and history how plausible these theories are.

Muhammad: Unlettered and Uneducated

The fact that Muhammad could neither read nor write (Q.29:48) is well known and uncontested by even his non-Muslim contemporaries and present day historians. He had no schooling or teacher of any kind. He had never been known to compose oral poetry or prose. The Qur'an, with its all-embracing laws and freedom from all inconsistencies, has its greatness acknowledged even by non-Muslim scholars. Its contents treat social, economic, political and religious legislation, history, views of the universe, living things, thought, human transactions, war, peace, marriage, worship, business, and everything relating to life - with no contradicting principles.

The Qur'an has never been edited or revised as it was never in need of any revision or correction. How were such vast subject areas expounded upon with such precision by a 7th century Arab with no formal education or even the ability to read what scant material there may have been in his environment on such topics? Where and when has history ever produced an illiterate and uneducated author of such a scripture?

Muhammad's known Integrity

Muhammad's sincerity, truthfulness and integrity were so well known that he was even nicknamed "*Al-Ameen*" (The

Trustworthy) by his pre-Islamic community. Not a single lie is recorded against him, and many modern Western orientalists have themselves admitted that contrary to any deliberate deception, that the Prophet (p) had a profoundly sincere conviction that it was revealed to him by God Himself is undeniable.

If his integrity had been in question, and he was supposed to have been motivated by the desire for personal glory to produce the Qur'an, why then would he disclaim authorship and instead claim it was from God, especially when the pagan Makkans had conceded that no one could produce such a scripture (Q.2:23-24, 17:88, etc.), but only marvel at it?

His enemies even offered him kingship over Makka and any riches he desired if only he would stop reciting. If it was true that he desired his personal glory and leadership, why would he decline the offer when it was presented to him and instead prefer a life of humility, simplicity, persecution, sanctions, and even hostile attack by those who felt threatened by the Message of One God?

In addition, how reasonable is it to believe that unlettered Muhammad (p) would author the Qur'an for personal benefit and then within the Qur'an correct and reprove himself? For example:

"He frowned and turned away when the blind man came to him..." (Q.80:1-2),

"...And you did fear men, though God is more deserving that you should fear Him" (Q.33:37).

See also Q.18:23-24, etc. Why would he embarrass himself when he could simply omit or favorably modify such verses in the Qur'an? They were certainly not to his advantage if his goals were power and prestige. The existence of such verses only proves that Muhammad (p) was indeed a truthful and sincere Messenger of God!

The Style of the Quran

There is a world of difference between the style of the

Qur'an and Muhammad's own style as recorded in the books of Ahadith. The differences between the two in every respect – style and contents – are immediately evident. The sayings of Muhammad (Ahadith) are conversational, oratorical, and expository, of a kind the Arabs were already familiar with. By contrast, the style of the Qur'an is authoritative ("*We created the heavens and the earth...*"; "*Say...*") and challenging ("*... had it (the Qur'an) been from any other than God, they would have found therein much discrepancies*" (Q.4:82;, "*... Say then: "Bring a chapter like it and call, if you can, on other than God...*" (Q.10:38); "*... then bring a chapter like unto it... and if you can not — for surely you cannot, then...*" (Q.2:23-24)).

Which fallible human being would write a book and challenge humanity to find discrepancies in it, as does the author of the Qur'an (Q.4:82)? Would any sensible student after writing an exam paper add a note to the lecturer saying "Read my answers with care and find any discrepancies or mistakes in it if you can!"? The style of the Qur'an is simply that of the All-Knowing Creator.

Furthermore, the Qur'an is a literary masterpiece of Arabic which was and remains unrivaled in its eloquence. Its rhythmic style, rhyme, near-haunting depth of expression, majesty, and "inimitable symphony, the very sounds of which move men to tears and ecstasy", shook the foundations of a society which had prided itself on its oratory skills. Contests were held every year in Makka for who could recite the longest and most eloquent pieces from memory. When the Qur'an was revealed, all such contests were brought to a halt, as there was no more competition.

Like the miracle of Moses' stick turning into a real snake which outdid the ability of all the Pharaoh's magicians at a time when the Egyptians were noted for their mastery of sorcery and magic, and the miracle of Jesus' healing of the blind and bringing the dead back to life which outdid the ability of all the doctors at a time when the Jews were noted for their mastery of medicine, the Qur'an was the Prophet Muhammad's own miracle. How could such magnificent and unrivaled expressions emanate from a man who, for 40 years, was never known for any such ability?

The Qur'an and the Bible

The mere existence of similarities between any two books is insufficient to prove that one must have been copied from the other. Both could have drawn information from a third common source, thus accounting for some similarities between them. This, in fact, is the argument of the Qur'an that Allah is the Source of all authentic revelation (Q.4:47).

Some scholars have noted that the only Christians the Prophet (p) is recorded as having been personally introduced to prior to his mission did not spend long enough time with him to teach him of their scripture, and no other historical record mentions anyone who taught the Prophet from among the Jews and Christians. Furthermore, the Arabs of his time were very eager to discredit him. Hence, if there was any secret teacher, he would most likely have been exposed by them then.

Furthermore, could the Qur'an have been copied from the Bible if they exhibit serious creedal differences? Regarding doctrines such as the concepts of God and prophethood, sin and forgiveness, the Qur'an differs significantly with the Bible. The Qur'an in fact addresses Jews and Christians directly when correcting what it states are corruptions in their own scriptures. Interestingly, Qur'anic revelations of doctrinal problems with Christianity were sent largely in the Makkan period, prior to the Prophet's migration to Madina, where he would have encountered many more Jewish and Christian scholars.

Even in the case of narration common to both scriptures, vital discrepancies can be observed. For example, the Qur'an, unlike the Bible:

- Does not blame women for the mistake committed by Adam and Eve (peace be upon them) in disobeying God in the Garden of Eden. (Compare Genesis 3:12-17 with Q.91:7-8 and 2:35-37);

- emphasizes that Adam and Eve repented to God (Q.7:23) and were forgiven by Him (Q.2:37);
- Mentions that the eventual dwelling of Adam and Eve on Earth was already part of God's plan even before He created them (Q.2:30), and not a sort of punishment (Genesis 3:17-19).

Other significant variations can be seen in the stories of Solomon, Abraham, Ishmael and Isaac, Lot, Noah, Moses and Jesus (peace be upon them).

The Qur'an also mentions a good amount of historical information about which the Bible is completely silent. From which portion of the Bible were the following copied?

- The stories of the people of 'AD and Thamud, and their Prophets, Hud (p) and Saleh (p).
- The dialogue between Prophet Noah (p) and his son before the flood (Q.11:42-43).
- The dialogue between Abraham (p) and his father (Q.6:74), as well as between he and a king (Q.2:258), and between he and his people (Q.22:70-102; 29:16-18; 37:83-98; 21:57).
- The mention of the city of Iram (Q.89:7).
- The Pharaoh of the Exodus having drowned, with his body preserved as a sign for people of future generations (Q.10:90-92).
- Jesus's miracles of speaking from the cradle (Q.3:46), and his producing (by God's will) a bird from clay (Q.3:49), etc.

Qur'anic Teachings about Satan and about Morality

Some claim that the Qur'an was the work of the devil. Let us examine how much sense (or nonsense) this allegation makes. If he authored or inspired the Qur'an, why would Satan curse himself and call himself the worst enemy of man (Q.35:6; 36:60)? Why would Satan command that before reciting the Qur'an, one must first say "I seek refuge in God from Satan the accursed" (Q.16:98)? How could Satan so vehemently condemn himself? Is it really acceptable to common sense to hold the view that Satan would ask people to do good, to be moral and virtuous, to worship none but God, to not follow Satan or his whispers, and to avoid and struggle against evil?

To hold such a view is clearly repugnant to reason, as Satan has only undermined himself through this means if he is the author. Even the Bible attests: "And if Satan has risen up against himself and is divided, he cannot stand, but is coming to an end." (Mark 3:26). This argument applies to any "Satanic forces", be they "evil spirits", "deceitful aliens", etc.

The Qur'an's Factual Contents and Scientific Information

Within the *Quran* are recorded facts about ancient times that were unknown to Muhammad's contemporaries and even to historians in the first half of the 20th century. In scores of verses, we also find references to scientific wonders, some only recently discovered or confirmed, regarding the universe, biology, embryology, astronomy, physics, geography, meteorology, medicine, history, oceanography, etc. Below are some examples of modern scientific discoveries mentioned in the *Quran*?

The Lost City of Iram (Qur'an 89:7): The existence of the city of Iram was unknown to any historian in the world prior to the excavation in Syria (in 1973) at the site of the ancient city of Ebla where clay tablets found there confirmed that the people of Ebla used to do business with the people of Iram. Details of this can be found in the National Geographic magazine of December, 1978. So unknown was the city of Iram until recently that even some Muslim commentators, out of embarrassment or feeling apologetic for their religion, have commented on this mention of the city in the Qur'an as being perhaps figurative, saying that Iram was possibly a man and not a city! How did the author of the Qur'an know of the existence of the city of Iram (Q.89:7) when no one else knew it?

Worker bees being female (Qur'an 16:68): A subtle yet

extraordinary precision in describing a natural phenomenon occurs in Q.16:68: *"And your Lord inspired the bee, (saying), 'Take for yourself dwellings in hills, on trees and in what they (mankind) build.'"* The imperative "take" above is the translation of the Arabic word *"ittakhidhi"*, which is a feminine form (for Arabic verbs, unlike English ones, differentiate between the sexes). In Arabic, the female form is used when all those it refers to are female, whereas the masculine is used when a group contains at least one male. Therefore the Qur'an is in fact saying: "Take for you, you female bees, dwellings..."

A swarm of bees comprises three types: a queen, the worker bees that collect honey and build the hive, and the male drones, whose sole purpose is to impregnate the queen and are then killed off by the worker bees. These worker bees are all females with underdeveloped sex organs. Thus the phrasing of this command in the Qur'an is in perfect correspondence with the fact that male bees do not participate in the construction of the hive or "dwelling", which is the sole work of the females.

Mountains as "stakes" and stabilizers: In his coauthored book entitled *"Earth"*, Professor Emeritus Frank Press says that mountains have underlying roots. These roots are deeply embedded in the ground; thus, mountains have a shape like a stake.

This is just how the Qur'an has described mountains. The Creator is recorded in the Qur'an (78:6-7) as saying: *"Have we not made the earth as a resting place (for you), and the mountains as (its) stakes?"*

Modern earth sciences have shown that mountains have deep roots underground, and that these roots can reach several times their elevations above the surface of the ground. So the most suitable word to describe mountains on the basis of this information is the word "stake", since most of a properly set (tent) stake is hidden underground. How did the author of the Qur'an know such a precise description when the theory of mountains having deep roots was introduced only in the latter half of the nineteenth century?

Mountains also play an important role in stabilizing the crust of the earth. They hinder the shaking of the earth. The author of the Qur'an states: *"And He has set firm mountains in the earth so that it could not shake with you..."* (Q.16:15) Likewise, the modern theory of plate tectonics holds that mountains work as stabilizers of the rapidly spinning earth. This knowledge about the role of mountains just began to be understood in the late 1960's.

The spherical shape of the Earth: In several places (Q.7:54; 36:37; 31:29), the Qur'an directs us to consider the alternation of night and day as another sign from the Almighty. For example, the verse 39:5 states: *"...He wraps the night around the day and He wraps the day around the night."* The Arabic verb *"kawwara"* means "to coil or wrap around" and has the connotation of wrapping or winding something around a spherical object, such as winding a strand of yarn around its ball, or a turban cloth around a person's head.

From the perspective of the planet Earth, this is exactly what takes place in that a half sphere of night followed by a half sphere of day is continually being wound around its surface. An observer from space, looking at Earth from a distance, would see in fact what appears to be the winding of day and night around the planet in a circular motion. When observing from a stationary angle, the light of the day appears to merge into the night and vice versa. This is due to the earth's rotation and the sun's relatively stationary position in relation to the earth. The Qur'an's use of words in this description is thus remarkable.

The expanding universe (Qur'an 51:47): By studying the galactic spectrum, scientists have recently established that the universe is expanding. In the Qur'an (51:47), we read: *"The firmament, We have built it with power. Verily, we are expanding it."* The word *"samaa'a"* means firmament or heaven in the sense of the extraterrestrial world, and the word *"musi'un"* is the present plural participle of the verb *"awsa'a"*, which means "to widen, to extend, to expand." This fact is confirmed in Stephen Hawking's classic book "A Brief History of Time".

The "Big Bang" (Qur'an 21:30)

In Qur'an 21:30 we read:

"Have not those who disbelieve seen that the heavens and the earth were fused (ratq) and then we broke them apart (fataqa), and We made every living thing out of water. Will they then not believe?"

Scientists have postulated for a long time now that the universe was originally a single primary mass of nearly infinite density that subsequently split into multiple fragments after a tremendous explosion, called the "Big Bang." It has also been established that all living cells consist mostly of water, which is the essential element for the existence of life as we know it. The word "maa'a" is commonly translated as "water" but refers to both water in the sky and in the sea and in fact any sort of liquid. The verse above therefore is in agreement with scientific observations.

Jeffrey Lang also notes that "the more interesting observation is that this challenge to unbelievers was proclaimed in the seventh century. We may ask ourselves: Which unbelievers are being addressed here? For the contemporaries of Muhammad, this revelation had many compelling aspects, but this question could not have made much sense to them unless there was some ancient, and presently unknown, Arabian mythology to which they could relate it. Was it then meant to be understood by people of a much later era who would be familiar with modern scientific findings?"

That at one point in time, the whole universe was nothing but a cloud of "smoke" (Q.41:11)

The description of the Qur'an of the universe as having been shaped out of a cloud of smoke: "*And He who turned [His design] to the skies when it had been smoke...*" (Q.41:11) is now an undisputed principle of modern cosmology. The term "smoke" is most befitting to explain the opaque, highly dense and hot gaseous composition that existed prior to the universe's expansion. New stars are in fact still forming, as astronomers explain, from the remnants of that primary "smoke". It is virtually inconceivable that a person of seventh century Arabia could have known such information about the beginnings of the universe.

The Qur'anic description of the development of the human embryo:

The Qur'an (23:12-14) describes the development of the embryo at a microscopic level inside the womb in the following manner: *"Man We did fashion from a quintessence of clay. Then we placed him as (a drop of) seminal fluid in a place of rest firmly fixed. Then we fashioned the seminal fluid into a leech-like thing that clings* (the word "alaq" is sometimes incorrectly translated as a bloodclot). *Then we fashioned that leech-like thing that clings into a chewed-like lump. Then we fashioned the chewed-like lump into bones and we clothed the bones with flesh. Then we developed out of it another creature. So hallowed be Allah, the Best of Artisans"*; Q.96:1-2: *"...who fashioned man from a leech-like thing that clings"*; and Q.22:5: *"We fashioned you out of dust, then out of a drop of fluid, then out of a leech-like thing that clings, then out of a morsel of flesh - partly formed and partly unformed..."* The incredible accuracy of these descriptions of the various stages of embryonic development are confirmed in Keith Moore and T.V.N. Presaud's 5th edition textbook "The Developing Human" and others.

These are just a few of the numerous scientific revelations in the Qur'an. Readers who are interested in further examples, are referred to *"The Bible, the Qur'an and Science"* by Maurice Bucaille, *"Struggling to Surrender"* p.33-38, by Jeffery Lang, *"The Qur'anic Phenomenon"* by Malik Bennabi, *"The Developing Human"*, 3rd edition, by Keith L. Moore, *"A Brief Illustrated Guide to Understanding Islam"*, by I. A. Ibrahim, *"The Sources of the Qur'an"* by Hamza Mustapha Njozi, *"The Basis of Muslim Beliefs"* and *"The Amazing Qur'an"* by Gary Miller, etc.

How many well trained modern scientists and geniuses with the aid of hitech equipment, satellites, telescopes, microscopes and computers were required to discover the above facts, and over what time span? Is it even conceivable that any human being over 1,400 years ago could have produced a scripture with such information in it, let alone a person who had never been educated?

Although the inability of man to encompass all the mysteries and complexity of creation is mentioned in the Qur'an (67:3-4), the revelation nevertheless seems to point to various natural phenomena as if urging human beings to enquire and verify what is said – again, with such an attitude of confidence that one can only assume the author is indeed challenging our disbelief. To be generous to the skeptic, perhaps one or two of the scientific revelations were the result of nothing more than a good guess or coincidence, but how probable could it have been that they all were?

Comparing Qur'anic statements that deal with the physical universe with certain scientific notions leads us to discover profound similarities. But, more notably, as Dr. Maurice Bucaille observes, the Qur'an is distinguished from all other works of antiquity that describe or attempt to explain the workings of nature in that it avoids mistaken concepts. For in the Qur'an, many subjects are referred to that have a bearing on modern knowledge without a single statement that contradicts what has been established by present-day science.

Dr. Bucaille goes as far as to conclude his study with the following remark: "In view of the level of knowledge in Muhammad's day, it is inconceivable that many statements in the Qur'an which are connected with science could have been the work of a man. It is, moreover, perfectly legitimate, not only to regard the Qur'an as an expression of Revelation, but also to award it a very special place, on account of the guarantee of authenticity it provides and the presence in it of scientific statements which, when studied today, appear as a challenge to explanation in human terms."

In examining the possible source of the *Quran* we have covered the following points:

- Muhammad's being unlettered,
- Muhammad's integrity,

- The Style of the Qur'an,
- Discrepancies between the Qur'an and the Bible,
- Qur'anic teachings about Satan and about morality, and
- The Qur'an's factual contents and scientific information.

These points were presented to aid us in our "elimination process" of unacceptable sources or authors of the Qur'an, as follows:

Muhammad (p): We might start by eliminating Muhammad (p) from the list of possible authors of the Qur'an. There is just no way could he have authored the Qur'an in view of points 1, 2, 3, 5 and 6 presented above.

Other Arab Poet(s), Scholar(s), etc. can also eliminate any other Arab from the list of possible authors in view of points 2, 3 and 6 (at least).

Some non-Arab: The reasons for the elimination of any Arab from the list also eliminate any non-Arab scholar, poet or religious personality.

Christian Monks or Jewish Rabbis (i.e. Judeo-Christian sources): This alternative source of the Qur'an is unreasonable in view of points 1, 2, 3, 4 and 6.

Satan (or other deceitful spirits or aliens, or anyone on his side, etc.): This option is also unacceptable in view of the points discussed, especially under 5.

God (i.e. Allah): In the absence of any more acceptable alternative as source and author of the Qur'an, one is more or less forced by reason to accept the Qur'an for what it claims to be – revelation from God through His Prophet Muhammad (p). This position seems reasonable not just because it is the only option that cannot be objectively eliminated, but because it is only reasonable to expect that a book with such qualities and contents would come from man's Creator and Guide. Of all the possible sources of the Qur'an, it is also only the last alternative – God – who even claims in the Qur'an itself to be the author of the scripture.

The position, therefore, which holds that Allah is the

author of the Qur'an still stands, and the challenge (or falsification test, Q.4:82) remains open to anyone to disprove the Qur'an's claim to being revelation from Allah. Having undertaken this task ourselves, the Muslim's contention that the Qur'an is the Word of God appears not just a product of blind faith but, in fact, a product of very sound and reasoned judgment in light of all the available evidence. Indeed, after having assessed the evidence, it would be blind faith to contend otherwise!

Islam and Muslims

The name of this religion is Islam, the Arabic root of which is "Silm" or "Salam", both meaning peace. The name of this religion is Islam, the Arabic root of which is "Silm" or "Salam", both meaning peace. "Salam" may also mean greeting one another with peace. One of the beautiful names of God is that He is The Peace, but this Divine Name also means more than that: it means submission to the One God, and living in peace with the Creator. It means living in peace with one's self, with other people, and with the natural environment. A Muslim is supposed to live in peace and harmony with all these segments. Hence, a Muslim is any person anywhere in the world whose obedience, allegiance, and loyalty are to God, the Lord of the Universe, and to the innate harmony of His Creation. Thus, Islam is a total system of living.

Muslims and Arabs

The followers of Islam are called Muslims. Muslims are not to be confused with Arabs. Muslims may be Arabs, Turks, Persians, Indians, Pakistanis, Malaysians, Indonesians, Europeans, Africans, Americans, Chinese, Russians, or other nationalities. An Arab could be a Muslim, a Christian, a Jew, or an atheist. Any person who adopts the Arabic language is called an Arab. However, the language of the Qur'an (the Revealed Book of Islam) is also Arabic. Muslims all over the world try to learn Arabic so that they may be able to read the Qur'an and understand its meaning. Although personal supplications can be in any language, Muslims pray their five required daily prayers in the language of the Qur'an, namely Arabic, which is also, and perhaps not by coincidence, one of the most stable, sophisticated, and beautiful languages in modern history.

Thus, whereas some religions have their liturgical languages (such as the Catholics used to have Latin), the Muslims are blessed with more than that. The Muslims have a Revelatory Language, the unchanged and incorruptible language in which the Qur'an was actually received. The Prophet Muhammad was confronted and entranced by the Angel Gabriel off and on over a period of years in both Makkah and Madinah, and all of these segments of the Qur'an were immediately dictated to his Companions. Yet, even though there are more than a billion Muslims in the world, there are only about two hundred million Arabs, of whom about ten percent are not Muslim. Thus, Arab Muslims constitute only about twenty percent of the Muslim population of the world.

Allah, the One and Only God

Although Allah is the name of the One and Only God, we may call Him by ninety-nine other beautiful names, such as: The Gracious, The Merciful, The Beneficent, The Creator, The All-Knowing, The All-Wise, The Lord of the Universe, The First, The Last, and others. He is the Creator of all human beings. He is the God for the Christians, the Jews, the Muslims, the Buddhists, the Hindus, the atheists, and others. Muslims put their trust entirely in Allah, and they seek only His help and only His guidance.

Muhammad

Muhammad was chosen by God to deliver His Message of Peace, namely Islam. Muhammad was born in 570 C.E. (Christian or Common Era), in Makkah in Arabia. He was entrusted with the Message of Islam when he was at the age of forty years. The revelation that he received is called the Qur'an, while the message is called Islam. Muhammad is considered to be the summation and the culmination of all the prophets and messengers that came before him. He purified the previous messages from adulteration and completed the Message of God for all humanity. He was also entrusted with the power of explaining, interpreting, and living the teachings of the Qur'an. When asked why he did not perform miracles as other prophets before him were said to have done, he replied that the Qur'an was his miracle.

The Sources of Islam

The legal sources of Islam are the Qur'an and the Hadith. The Qur'an contains the exact words of God - its authenticity, originality, and totality is intact. The Hadith are reports by Companions of Muhammad of indisputable integrity of the sayings, deeds, and explanations of the Prophet Muhammad. The Prophet's sayings and deeds themselves are called "Sunnah". Those related to explication of verses of the Qur'an are considered binding upon all Muslims. Those Hadith related to Prophet Muhammad's dress and personal behavior as an Arab is considered optional. However, the "Seerah", or writings of followers of Muhammad about his life and actions, provide examples of daily living for Muslims.

The Islamic Creed

Muslims, or those who wish to convert to Islam, must agree to and hold the following beliefs as inviolable:

1. *Oneness of God:* He is One and the Only One. He is not two-in-one or three-in-one. This means that Islam rejects the idea of a trinity, a son of God, or any man-god. By implication, people are created equal in front of the Law of God. There is no superiority for one race over another. However, God has created the races with different ethnic cultures, colors, languages, beliefs, and skills, so as to interest and inspire one another. The Qur'anic teaching is that the different races are meant to be complementary, not confrontational. The concept is global, not tribal. If there is superiority among mankind, it is only God Who knows what it really is. It is only God Who knows which men or women are among the truly pious or the truly righteous.

2. *The Revealed Books*: Christians, Jews, and Muslims are all "People of the Book". All have received teachings revealed directly from God, and perhaps others before them have received revealed Books as well, even though their books may have been lost or fragmented. The Qur'an, being the only fully authentic and unchanged of the revealed Books, is considered the final treasure given to mankind. Further advice is not needed, only deeper understanding of divine advice already given in the Qur'an, as well as earlier books. Muslims are required to believe in and respect all revealed Books that have descended to mankind throughout its history.

   God promised in the Qur'an to protect its contents until the end of history, and evidence of that protection can be found in the thousands and thousands of children, as well as devout adults, who can recite the entire Qur'an by memory, from cover to cover, as well as the millions who can and do recite portions of it every day of their lives.

3. *The Prophets of God:* Muslims believe that God sent different messengers throughout the history of mankind. All came with the same message and the same teachings. It was the people who misunderstood and misinterpreted them. Muslims believe in, among others, Adam, Noah, Abraham, Isaac, Ismail, Jacob, Moses, David, Jesus, and Muhammad. The Prophets of Christianity and Judaism are indeed the Prophets of Islam. Even the Buddha may have been a prophet whose original teachings were lost or corrupted, since the Qur'an states that many prophets unknown to modern history also brought revealed Books and teachings. The Hindu Vedas may have been fragments of the Book brought by Abraham (Brahmanism).

4. *Angels:* Muslims believe that there are unseen creatures such as angels created by God for special missions in the universe. At the end of every prayer, Muslims give the greeting of "Peace" to the angels which accompany them over each shoulder - to the right, the Recording Angel for our good deeds; to the left, the Recording Angel for

our sins. The Qur'an was revealed and taught to Prophet Muhammad through the agency of the Angel Gabriel. The Prophet tells many stories in his Hadith about angels appearing in the world.

5. *The Day of Judgement:* Muslims believe that there is a Day of Judgement when all people of the world throughout the history of mankind till the last day of life on earth, are to be brought for accounting, reward, and punishment. The Prophet enjoined all Muslims to hold the reality of this day in awe and trepidation, and to manage all their earthly affairs with the inevitability of this day in mind. To that end, the following Islamic rituals and actions have been given by God to the Prophet, and thence to all the Muslims, to protect and sharpen Muslims' remembrance of the Last Day.

Islamic Practices

Whereas the Islamic creed shares much with other world religions, the true Muslim distinguishes himself from the followers of these other religions by means of diligent study and practice of the following rituals and practices, known as the Five pillars of Islam:

1. *Witnessed Profession of Faith ("Shahada"):* The verbal commitment and pledge that there is only One God and that Muhammad is the Messenger of God, is considered to be the Creed of Islam. In addition to anyone who is born to Muslim parents, anyone who utters the words of this creed before two sane, adult Muslim witnesses has become Muslim all the rest of his life, both in this world and the next.
2. *Prayer ("Salat"):* In further witness thereto, children and Muslim converts eight years of age and up are required to learn the distinctive Islamic way of approaching the One God by means of the Muslim Prayer, or "Salat", as revealed to Prophet Muhammad on his miraculous Ascension to the Throne of Allah, which began from the famous golden "Dome of the Rock" in Jerusalem. This Dome is not really a mosque, as is often supposed. It is

rather a shrine to the Prophet's Ascension. However, it is sometimes also referred to as the "Mosque of Omar", because it was built by the Caliph Omar to mark and protect the large rock within it, from which the Prophet's journey to Heaven traditionally began. The third holiest mosque in Islam is nearby, the "Aqsa Mosque" at the other end of the Temple Mount in Jerusalem.

Although children and new Muslims are given any amount of time to learn their "Salat" properly, it is an absolute requirement for anyone who calls himself Muslim. It generally becomes second nature, something like the act of respiration, for those of sincere dedication to Islam. The absence of "Salat" may create various hazards for Muslims who think they can ignore this bedrock of Muslim worship with impunity. "Salat" contains many benefits and secrets for the worshipper, psychological as well as spiritual.

3. *Fasting ("Saum"):* Every ninth month of the Muslim lunar calendar is Ramadan, and the Qur'an orders all Muslims of sound mind and body to fast from dawn until sunset all the days of the month. No drinking, eating, or marital relations are permitted. In addition, harsh words, acts of anger, and various other emotional indulgences are also not permitted. As with "Salat", this Ramadan fast holds many secrets and benefits. Many Muslim converts come to Islam after practicing this fast and experiencing the proofs and benefits thereof.
4. *Purifying Tax ("Zakat"):* The distinction between pure and impure financial gain is important in Islam, and in order to protect oneself against the temptations of undeserved or impure gain, every Muslim must pay a given percentage of his wealth to the poor or other rightful beneficiaries before the end of every Ramadan month. There have been eras in Islamic history when the "Zakat" system solved all the problems of poverty and hardship within Muslim communities.
5. *Pilgrimage ("Hajj"):* The performance of pilgrimage to Makkah is required once in a lifetime if means are

available. "Hajj" is partly in memory of the trials and tribulations of Prophet Abraham, his wife Hagar, and their eldest son Prophet Ismail. A successful "Hajj" may not be performed on credit. It is sometimes taught that a reasonably successful Ramadan fast must precede the "Hajj", which is then considered a response to an invitation from Allah, the Most High, to visit His Holy House on earth. The realty of heaven, hell, prayers of supplication, and forgiveness of one's sins, are all often experienced by sincere "Hajjis".

Other Related Aspects

Following from the beliefs and practices mentioned above, Muslims gain personal conviction that people are born free of sin. It is only after they commit sins that they are to be charged for their mistakes. No one is responsible for or can take responsibility for the sins of others. However, the door of forgiveness through true repentence is always open, provided it is accompanied by sincere remorse.

Muslims believe that Islam is a total and a complete way of life. It encompasses all aspects of life. As such, the teachings of Islam do not separate religion from politics. As a matter of fact, both private and public life are considered under the obedience of Allah through His teachings. Hence, economic and social transactions, as well as educational and political systems, are also part of this obedience. However, early Islamic polities did not call themselves, or refer to, an "Islamic State". All states must be Islamic in values and beliefs, whether or not they refer to themselves as "Islamic". Admittedly, many modern states do not yet reach this standard, though they may be full of Muslims.

Islamic practices and celebrations are based on the lunar calendar. However, most Muslim countries use the Gregorian solar calendar for business or economic purposes. Central to Islamic culture, however, is the "Hijra", or migration of the Prophet and all Muslims from Makkah to Madinah in the year 623 C.E. This "Hijra" enshrines each Muslim's individual effort to free himself from the bonds or dangers of the non-

Muslim elements of the culture into which he or she may have been born. Therefore, only the "Hijra", or lunar calendar, truly expresses distinctively Muslim culture, and should hang in every Muslim home on earth.

The two main celebrations marked by the "Hijra" or lunar calendar, are the Idul Fitra, which follows Ramadan and celebrates whatever degree of inner revelation we may have attained by virtue of our diligent fasting; and the Idul Adha, which follows the Pilgrimage Season and celebrates our gratitude for the performance of a successful "Hajj" by ourselves or those Muslims who were able that year, by means of sacrificing dedicated animals to feed the poor.

Charity at the end of Ramadan is economic, charity at the end of Hajj season is by feeding the poor. As for the Islamic diet, only animals slaughtered in the name of the One God should be eaten by Muslims, although some jurists allow western meat to be eaten since western Christians are still considered "People of the Book". A further consideration, however, is that "zabiha" slaughter must also involve draining of the blood, so that most western meat suppliers cannot be considered fully "zabiha". Muslims are also restricted from consuming pork, alcohol, or any dangerous or addictive drug.

The Muslim place of worship is called a Mosque or Masjid. The three most holy places of worship in the world for Muslims are: Mosque of Ka'aba in Makkah, Mosque of the Prophet Muhammad in Madinah, and Masjid Aqsa, adjacent to Dome of the Rock in Jerusalem. A Muslim may pray anywhere in the world, whether in a Mosque, a house, an office, or outside. The whole world is a place of worship. Muslims may pray individually anywhere, though it is preferable to pray in congregation.

The special day for Muslims is Friday. It is considered sacred and it is said that the Day of Judgement will take place on Friday. A leader ("Imam") gives a sermon ("Khutba") and leads the congregational prayer. However, in contrast to the Jewish and Christian "Sabbath" days (Saturday and Sunday),

Muslims are allowed to return to their economic activities immediately after the Friday prayers.

Although differing in days of congregational worship, Muslims, Christians, and Jews are all called "People of the Book" in the Qur'an and they are advised to work together for common terms, to worship the One God, and to cooperate in solving the many problems in society. Modern European Jewish Zionism is considered a political maneuver that is totally distinct from Judaism as a monotheistic religious entity, with whom Muslims have no quarrel. Proof of the peaceful relations between Muslims and Jews can be found in the many Jews who fled the Catholic Inquisition in Spain and were welcomed by the Muslims. These Jews settled in the heart of the Islamic Caliphate. They enjoyed positions of power and authority.

6

World Religion

Christianity and its Belief System

The history of Christianity goes back into Jewish ancestry and revolves around the 300 prophecies in the Old Testament which reveals the upcoming of a Jewish Messiah who would be a Savior of humanity. Around 2000 years ago this prophecy was fulfilled by the birth of Jesus from the Virgin Mary in the town of Bethlehem in the land of Israel. He brought a hope of delight to the poor and rejected ones. The New Testament book of Luke (1:26-38) and Matthew (1:18-25) explains the virgin birth of Jesus. The birth of Jesus Christ also claimed a revolution and the revival of the teachings of Judaism. In the beginning Christianity was considered as a sect of Judaism. As Jesus said, "Do not think that I have come to abolish the Law or the Prophets; I have not come to abolish them but to fulfill them." (Matthew 5:17). But later on, the teachings of Jesus established the foundation of Christianity. The concept of salvation and eternal peace blessed the gloomy hearts.

Just as the message of Jesus started to spread among the people, he was betrayed by one of his disciples Judas Iscariot for 30 pieces of silver. He was held responsible for treason and blasphemy. He was viciously beaten up and crucified at Golgotha before suffering on the cross for about 6 hours. The following Sunday, when the loyal Mary Magdalene and the other Mary went to his tomb, they were astonished to see that the tomb was empty. The book of Matthew explains the resurrection of Jesus, "The angel said to the women, do not be afraid, for I know that you are looking for Jesus, who was crucified. He is not here; he has risen, just as he said. Come and see the place where he lay." (Matthew 28:5-7)

In spite of the ban on Christianity in Rome during the second century, it kept on growing. In third century, the Emperor Constantine stopped the harassment and encouraged the growth of Christianity. The differences between the Greek East and Latin West churches began to grow with time on the issues of use of icons, nature of Holy Spirit and day of Easter celebration. As time progressed, Christianity divided into three major branches. The Roman Catholic branch of Christianity is the successor of the church established in Rome soon after Christ's death. It traces its spiritual history to the early disciples of Jesus. The Pope, or spiritual leader, traces his office's lineage back to St. Peter, the first Pope, one of Jesus' disciples. Roman Catholicism was originally predominately practiced in Ireland, Poland, France and Spain.

During the fourth century, the Roman Catholic Church split and the Eastern Orthodox branch was formed. The split was primarily a political one due to the division of the Roman Empire into western and eastern components. The two churches became officially separate in 1054. Orthodox churches are largely national, each associated with a particular country. Orthodoxy is common in Russia, Greece, Romania, Bulgaria, the Ukraine, and Armenia.

The Protestant branch split from Roman Catholicism during the Reformation, a sixteenth and seventeenth century series of church reforms in doctrine and practice. This movement challenged the authority of the Pope, and became popular in Scandinavia, England, and the Netherlands. Protestantism eventually divided into many denominations which arose in response to disputes over doctrine, theology, or religious practice. Some of the large denominations today are Lutherans, Methodists and Baptists.

Christian Denominations

For the first thousand years of Christian history, there were no "denominations" within the Christian church as there are today. Various offshoot groups certainly existed, but they were considered "heresies" and not part of the Christian church. Most were small and, until the 16th century, were never very influential. From the beginnings of Christianity through the middle Ages, there was only one the catholic ("universal") church. Basically, if you did not belong to the Church, you were not considered a Christian.

The first division within Christendom came in 1054 with the "Great Schism" between the Western Church and the Eastern Church. From that point forward, there were two large branches of Christianity, which came to be known as the Catholic Church (in the West) and the Orthodox Church (in the East).

Protestant Reformation

The Reformation was famously sparked when Martin Luther posted his *95 Theses* in 1517, but "Protestantism" as a movement officially began in 1529. That year marked the publication of the *Protestation*, directed at the imperial government. The authors, German princes who wanted the freedom to choose the faith of their territory, protested that "in matters which concern God's honor and salvation and the eternal life of our souls, everyone must stand and give account before God for himself."

With its emphasis on individual interpretation of scripture and a measure of religious freedom, the Reformation marked not only a break between Protestantism and Catholicism, but the beginning of denominationalism as we know it today. This historical perspective is perhaps the best way to make sense of the initially astounding variety of Christian denominations.

Those who remained within the fold of Roman Catholicism argued that central regulation of doctrine is necessary to prevent confusion and division within the church and corruption of its beliefs. Those who broke from the church, on the other hand, insisted that it was precisely this policy of control that had already led to corruption of the true faith. They demanded that believers be allowed to read the scriptures for themselves (it was previously available only in Latin) and act in accordance with their conscience. This issue of religious authority continues to be a fundamental difference in perspective between Catholic and Orthodox Christians on one hand, and Protestant Christians on the other.

As the Reformation developed in Germany, various groups in other parts of Europe also began to break away from the Catholic Church. Reformed Christianity developed in Switzerland based on the teachings of Ulrich Zwingli and John Calvin. When it spread to Scotland under John Knox, the Reformed faith became Presbyterianism. Switzerland was also the birthplace of the Anabaptists, spiritual ancestors of today's Amish, Mennonites, Quakers, and Baptists. Anglicanism was established in 1534 when England's King Henry VIII broke from the authority of the Pope, and became Episcopalianism in America. Methodism, based on the teachings of John Wesley, also has its roots in Anglicanism.

Catholicism as a Denomination

For the first thousand years of Christianity there was no "Roman Catholicism" as we know it today, simply because there was no Eastern Orthodoxy or Protestantism to distinguish it. There was only the "one, holy, catholic church" affirmed by the early creeds, which was the body of Christian believers all over the world, united by common traditions, beliefs, church structure and worship (catholic simply means "universal"). Thus, throughout the middle Ages, if you were a Christian, you belonged to the Catholic Church. Any Christianity other than the Catholic Church was a heresy, not a denomination.

Today, however, Roman Catholicism is not the only accepted Christian church. Thus to be a Roman Catholic means to be a certain kind of Christian: one with unique beliefs, practices and traditions that are distinct from those of other Christians. Nevertheless, the Catholic Church continues to maintain that it alone has carried on the true tradition of the apostolic church and has traditionally regarded dissenting groups as heresies, not alternatives (Martin Luther was swiftly excommunicated). However, the recent Second Vatican Council declared all baptized Christians to be "in a certain, although imperfect, communion with the Catholic Church."

Although it did not begin at a specific point in history like the Protestant denominations, in its long history Roman Catholicism has evolved into a distinctive branch of Christianity with beliefs, practices and organization that differ from both Protestantism and Orthodoxy.

Roman Catholicism is by far the largest Christian group. With more than one billion adherents, Catholics constitute about half of the world's Christians. Catholicism is the majority religion of Italy, Spain, and nearly all Latin American countries. In 2001, about 24 percent of Americans identified themselves as Catholic, making Catholicism the largest Christian denomination in America (if the Protestant denominations are counted individually). The next largest denomination, Baptist, was claimed by 16 percent of Americans. Yet if Protestants are considered as one group, Catholics remain a minority among America's Christians.

Roman Catholicism traces its history to the apostles, especially the Apostle Peter. St. Peter is considered the first pope, and every pope since him is regarded as his spiritual successor. This gives the leader of the church spiritual authority and provides a means for resolving disputes that could divide the church. Through trials like persecution, heresy, and the Reformation, the notion that the church leadership represents the continuation of an unbroken line from the apostles and their teachings ("apostolic succession") has contributed to the survival of Christianity.

However, the idea of the "pope" did not exist from the beginning of the church. It was not until several centuries after Christ that the church began to develop into the "Roman Catholic Church" as we think of it today, with its particular doctrines, practices, and hierarchical system of authority. Thus Catholics and non-Catholics alike are able to claim they are most faithful to the message of the apostles and the early church.

From the Catholic perspective, the early church is faithfully continued in the developments of later centuries, while non-Catholics tend to regard the church as having corrupted the original message of Christianity. In the years of persecution prior to the Emperor's conversion, the church was focused primarily on survival. There were prominent church leaders whose authority was recognized - primarily those who had known the apostles - but no central authority.

But with the conversion of Emperor Constantine in 318 AD, the church began to adopt a governmental structure mirroring that of the Empire, in which geographical provinces were ruled by bishops based in the major city of the area. Soon, the bishops of major cities in the empire emerged as preeminent, including the bishops of Jerusalem, Alexandria, Antioch, Rome, and Constantinople. It was natural that Rome would eventually become the most important of these. It was not only the capital of the empire, but the city in which the apostles Peter and Paul were believed to have been martyred.

The Roman bishop Leo I (440-461) is considered the first pope by historians, as he was the first to claim ultimate authority over all of Christendom. In his writings one can find all the traditional arguments for papal authority, most notably that which asserts Christ had designated Peter and his successors the "rock" on which the church would be built.

Leo's claims were strengthened greatly by his own impressive career as Bishop of Rome. In 445 he earned the express support of Emperor Valentian, who said the Bishop of Rome was the law for all. In 451, he called the important Council of Chalcedon, which put to rest Christological issues that had been plaguing the church. In 452, he impressively saved Rome from Attila the Hun. It is said that the Pope met the warrior at the gates and somehow persuaded him to spare the city.

Legend has it that Attila saw Peter and Paul marching along with Leo to defend their city. In 455 he was not as successful with Vandal invaders, but led negotiations with them and succeeded in preventing the burning of Rome (it was, however, plundered).

Catholic Beliefs

Roman Catholic beliefs do not differ drastically from those of the other major branches of Christianity - Greek Orthodoxy and Protestantism. All three main branches hold to the doctrine of the Trinity, the divinity of Christ, the inspiration of the Bible, and so on. But on more minor doctrinal points, there are clear Catholic distinctives in belief.

Distinctive Roman Catholic beliefs include the special authority of the pope, the ability of saints to intercede on behalf of believers, the concept of Purgatory as a place of afterlife purification before entering Heaven, and the doctrine of transubstantiation - that is, that the bread used in the Eucharist becomes the true body of Christ when blessed by a priest.

Distinctive Catholic Practices

With the possible exception of some Anglican churches, the Catholic liturgy tends to be more formal and ritualized than its Protestant counterparts. Services follow a prescribed liturgy and priests wear more elaborate vestments than most Protestant ministers. Catholics usually celebrate the Eucharist more often than do Protestants, usually weekly. In Catholicism, the Eucharist is called the Mass. Catholics observe seven sacraments, which are religious rituals believed to be commanded by God and effective in conferring grace on the believer.

There are several Catholic monastic orders, the most well known being the Jesuits, Dominicans, Fransciscans, and

Augustinians. Catholic monks and nuns take vows of poverty, chastity and obedience and devote themselves to a simple life focused on worshipping God. Unlike their counterparts in both Protestant and Orthodox churches, Catholic priests take vows of celibacy. This practice is rooted in the papacy's early connections with monasticism, but has become controversial in recent years in part as a result of child abuse scandals. Other distinctive Catholic practices include veneration of saints, use of the crucifix, and the use of rosary beads in prayer.

Eastern Orthodoxy

The denomination now known as Orthodox Christianity, Eastern Orthodoxy, or the Orthodox Church began as the eastern half of Christendom, the site of the former Byzantine Empire. Today, the highest concentration of Orthodox Christians remains in the former Byzantine Empire (Greece, Turkey, and nearby countries) and in Russia. But Orthodoxy is found throughout the world, and approximately 225 million people are Orthodox Christians.

Eastern Orthodoxy arose as a distinct branch of Christianity after the 11th-century "Great Schism" between Eastern and Western Christendom. The separation was not sudden. For centuries there had been significant religious, cultural, and political differences between the Eastern and Western churches. Religiously, they had different views on topics such as the use of images (icons), the nature of the Holy Spirit, and the date on which Easter should be celebrated.

Culturally, the Greek East has always tended to be more philosophical, abstract and mystical in its thinking, whereas the Latin West tends toward a more pragmatic and legal-minded approach. (According to an old saying, "the Greeks built metaphysical systems; the Romans built roads.")

The political aspects of the split date back to the Emperor Constantine, who moved the capital of the Roman Empire from Rome to Constantinople. Upon his death, the empire was divided between his two sons, one of whom ruled the western half of the empire from Rome while the other ruled the eastern region from Constantinople.

These various factors finally came to a head in 1054 AD, when Pope Leo IX excommunicated the patriarch of Constantinople (the leader of the Eastern Church). In response, the patriarch anathematized (condemned) the Pope, and the Christian church has been divided into West ("Roman Catholic") and East ("Greek Orthodox") ever since. A glimmer of hope for reconciliation came at the onset of the Crusades later that century, when the West came to the aid of the East against the Turks. But especially after the Fourth Crusade (1200-1204), in which crusaders sacked and occupied Constantinople, the only result was an increase in hostility between the two churches.

However, attempts at reconciliation have been renewed in recent years. In 1964, the Second Vatican Council issued this statement praising its Eastern counterparts:

The Catholic Church values highly the institutions of the Eastern Churches, their liturgical rites, ecclesiastical traditions, and their ordering of Christian life. For in those churches, which are distinguished by their venerable antiquity, there is clearly evident the tradition which has come from the Apostles through the Fathers and which is part of the divinely revealed, undivided heritage of the Universal Church.

On December 7, 1965, the mutual excommunication of 1054 was officially removed by Pope Paul VI and Patriarch Athenagoras.

Organisation and Religious Authority

The Orthodox Church is organized into several regional, autocephalous (governed by their own head bishops) churches. The Patriarch of Constantinople has the honor of primacy, but does not carry the same authority as the Pope does in Catholicism. Major Orthodox churches include the Greek Orthodox Church, the Russian Orthodox Church, the Romanian Orthodox Church, the Bulgarian Orthodox

Church, the Church of Alexandria, the Church of Jerusalem, and the Orthodox Church in America.

The religious authority for Orthodox Christianity is not the Pope as in Catholicism, nor the individual Christian with his Bible as in Protestantism, but the scriptures as interpreted by the seven ecumenical councils of the church. Orthodoxy also relies heavily on the writings of early Greek fathers such as Gregory of Nyssa, John Chrysostom and St. Basil the Great. Although some Orthodox confessions of faith were produced in the 17th century as counterparts to those of the Reformation, these are regarded as having only historical significance.

Distinctive Orthodox Beliefs

As in all of Christianity, doctrine is important in Eastern Orthodoxy. Orthodox Christians attach great importance to the Bible, the conclusions of the Seven Ecumenical Councils, and right ("orthodox") belief. However, the Eastern Churches approach religious truth differently than the Western Churches. For Orthodox Christians, truth must be experienced personally. There is less focus on the exact definition of religious truth and more on the practical and personal experience of truth in the life of the individual and the church. Precise theological definition, when it occurs, is for the purpose of excluding error.

This emphasis on personal experience of truth flows into Orthodox theology, which has a rich heritage. Especially in the first millenium of Christian history, the Eastern Church produced significant theological and philosophical thought. In the Western churches, both Catholic and Protestant, sin, grace, and salvation are seen primarily in legal terms. God gave humans freedom, they misused it and broke God's commandments, and now deserve punishment. God's grace results in forgiveness of the transgression and freedom from bondage and punishment.

The Eastern churches see the matter in a different way. For Orthodox theologians, humans were created in the image of God and made to participate fully in the divine life. The full communion with God that Adam and Eve enjoyed meant complete freedom and true humanity, for humans are most human when they are completely united with God. The result of sin, then, was a blurring of the image of God and a barrier between God and man. The situation in which mankind has been ever since is an unnatural, less human state, which ends in the most unnatural aspect: death. Salvation, then, is a process not of justification or legal pardon, but of reestablishing man's communion with God. This process of repairing the unity of human and divine is sometimes called "deification." This term does not mean that humans become gods but that humans join fully with God's divine life.

The Eastern Orthodox view of the Trinity also differs somewhat from that of the Christian West. In its Christology, Orthodoxy tends to emphasize the divine, preexistent nature of Christ, whereas the West focuses more on his human nature. However, both East and West affirm Christ's full humanity and full divinity as defined by the ecumenical councils. In fact, Christ's humanity is also central to the Orthodox faith, in the doctrine that the divine became human so that humanity might be raised up to the divine life.

The process of being reunited to God, made possible by Christ, is accomplished by the Holy Spirit. The Spirit plays a central role in Orthodox worship: the liturgy usually begins with a prayer to the Spirit and invocations made prior to sacraments are addressed to the Spirit. It is in the view of the Holy Spirit that Orthodox theology differs from Western theology, and although the difference might now seem rather techinical and abstract, it was a major contributor to the parting of East from West in the 11th century. This dispute is known as the Filioque Controversy, as it centers on the Latin word *filioque* ("and from the Son"), which was added to the Nicene Creed in Spain in the 6th century.

The original creed proclaimed only that the Holy Spirit "proceeds from the Father." The purpose of the addition was to reaffirm the divinity of the Son, but Eastern theologians objected both to the unilateral editing of a creed produced by an ecumenical council and to the edit itself. For Eastern Christians, both the Spirit and the Son have their origin in the Father.

Protestant Christianity

In a 2002 study conducted by the Pew Research Council, 53 percent of Americans identified themselves as Protestant Christians. There are approximately 500 million Protestants in the world. "Protestantism" is less a denomination than a general branch of Christianity encompassing numerous denominations and a wide theological spectrum ranges from conservative to liberal. Protestantism originated in the 16th century Reformation, and most modern Protestant denominations can trace their heritage to one of the major movements that sprung up in the 16th century. Presbyterians are indebted to John Calvin and Reformed theology, as well as to John Knox and the Church of Scotland. Anglicans and Episcopalians trace their heritage to the Church of England that resulted from King Henry VIII's break from the authority of Rome.

Evangelicalism (and to a slightly lesser degree, Methodism) is indebted to Pietism, a 17th century Protestant movement emphasizing a holy life, individual study of the scriptures, and better training of ministers. Protestant denominations differ in the degree to which they reject Catholic belief and practice. Some churches, such as Anglicans and Lutherans, tend to resemble Catholicism in their formal liturgy, while others, like Baptists and Presbyterians, retain very little of the liturgy and tradition associated with the Catholic church.

In common with Catholic and Orthodox Christians, Protestants adhere to the authority of the Bible and the doctrines of the early creeds. Protestants are distinguished by their emphasis on the doctrines of "justification by grace alone through faith, the priesthood of all believers, and the supremacy of Holy Scripture in matters of faith and order." Most Protestant churches recognize only two sacraments directly commanded by the Lord - baptism and communion - as opposed to the seven sacraments accepted by the Catholic Church.

Anglicanism and Episcopalianism

The Anglican Communion is an organization of autonomous national churches connected with the Church of England, which has its roots in the 16th century Reformation. Anglicanism or Episcopalianism is the general form of doctrine, worship and structure based on the tradition of the Church of England, which extends beyond membership in the Anglican Communion.

Anglicanism is characterized by a *via media* (middle way) between Catholicism and Protestantism. Anglicans are not subject to the Pope and are Protestant in most areas of doctrine, but Anglicans also retain many Catholic forms of worship, including a hierarchy based on bishops (which is the meaning of the world "episcopalian").

The churches of the Anglican Communion have their historical roots in the English Reformation, when King Henry VIII (r. 1509-1547) wished to obtain a divorce that the pope would not grant. Through the Act of Supremacy of 1534, the king made himself the "supreme head" of the Church of England in place of the Pope.

After this dramatic move, King Henry dissolved England's monasteries, destroyed Catholic shrines, and ordered the Great Bible (in English) to be placed in all churches. However, Henry allowed few doctrinal changes and very little changed in the religious life of the common English worshipper. Under Henry VIII, and the Church of England remained almost fully Catholic with the exception of loyalty to Rome.

A power struggle between English Protestants and Catholics ensued during the reigns of Edward VI and Mary I. Under King Edward, Archbishop of Canterbury Thomas Cranmer contributed a great deal to the Protestant movement, including the first two versions of the Book of Common Prayer (1549 and 1552) and the 42 Articles (1553). After the ascension of the Catholic "Bloody Mary" to the throne in 1553, England was restored to Catholicism, much of the reforming work under Kings Henry and Edward was undone, and Thomas Cranmer was burned at the stake.

Protestantism finally emerged victorious under Queen Elizabeth I (r. 1558-1603). It was under Elizabeth that "Anglicanism" took shape, established on the notion of a *via media* between Catholicism and Protestantism (specifically Reformed Protestantism). Elizabeth appointed Protestant bishops, but reintroduced a crucifix in her chapel, tried to insist on traditional clerical vestments, and made other attempts to satisfy conservative opinion. The 42 Articles were reduced to 39 and the Book of Common Prayer was reissued. The 39 Articles and the Book of Common Prayer, which together expressed the faith and practice of the Church of England, were sufficiently vague to allow for a variety of interpretations along the Catholic-Protestant spectrum.

After Elizabeth, Calvinist influences were dominant for a time, but High Churchmen regained control of the Church of England in the Restoration of 1660. In the latter 17th and early 18th centuries, Anglicanism was characterized by its emphases on reason, simple devotional religion and moral living. After about 1690, the controversy quieted down and the Church of England settled into the form that still characterizes it today.

Evangelicalism arose in 18th century in part as a reaction against the lack of spiritual fervor and enthusiasm in the Church. This had a balancing effect on Anglicanism (and there remains a strong evangelical group within the Church of England), but evangelicals also went beyond the bounds of the traditional Anglican outlook and many, like John Wesley's Methodists, broke away from the Church of England.

Another important development in the history of Anglicanism, the Oxford movement, began in 1833. Also known as the Catholic Revival, this movement sought to restore the sacraments, rituals and outward forms of Catholicism to the Church of England. By the mid-20th century, many of the practices advocated by this group had been incorporated. Also in the 19th century, the Church of England found room for the new German biblical criticism and liberal theology. Scholarship is still highly regarded in Anglicanism, and Anglican scholars have generally been free to adopt views ranging from conservative to radical while remaining in the Anglican fold.

Anglicanism expanded along with the British Empire, creating a network of autonomous churches that were loyal to the faith and forms of the Church of England. After the American Revolution, Anglicans in the U.S. called themselves Episcopalians (the name reflecting the role of the episcopate, or bishops) to distinguish themselves from the British crown and the Church of England. Today, the Episcopalian Church in the United States and many other Anglican churches in former British colonies are members of the Anglican Communion.

The 21st century has proven to be an important point in history for Anglicanism. The recent ordination of a gay bishop in America and the disapproving reaction from the Communion will have great implications for the question of how much variation can be tolerated within Anglicanism. And, as always, the Archbishop of Canterbury, the bishops and the priests in Anglican churches must decide how to react to the continuing influences of biblical criticism, liberal theology and modern ethical values.

Anglican/Episcopalian Beliefs and Practices

Anglicanism in general allows for significant freedom and diversity within the bounds of scripture, reason and tradition. This has led to considerable variation in doctrine and practice between Anglican churches in different provinces. For example, some Anglican churches ordain women to the priesthood while others do not, and some emphasize Protestant doctrines while others hold more to Catholic teachings.

This diversity has sometimes caused strain with regard to issues of authority and comprehensiveness of the Anglican

Communion, which is especially apparent after the recent ordination of a practicing homosexual bishop in North America, which most other Anglican churches do not agree with. Anglican rituals are expressed primarily in the *Book of Common Prayer,* a collection of liturgy developed by Thomas Cranmer in the 16 th century and periodically modified since then. However, the *Book of Common Prayer* is not held to be normative. Much diversity has recently developed in Anglican worship around the world, and many different Prayer Books have been issued. In general, Anglican worship tends to be Catholic or "High Church" in flavor, with prescribed rituals and readings, bishops and priests, vestments, saints' days and elaborately decorated churches.

The Amish

The Amish (sometimes called Amish Mennonites) are members of an Anabaptist Christian denomination who are especially known for their separation from society and rejection of most modern technology. The denomination originated in Switzerland, with the strict teachings of Jacob Amman that led to a split from other Mennonites in 1693.

The Amish are one of several denominations that developed out of the Radical Reformation in 16th-century Europe. The Anabaptists, as the radical reformers came to be called, differed from mainstream Protestants in their rejection of all church authority, belief that a church consists only of baptized believers and rejection of infant baptism. Anabaptist denominations include the Mennonites, Hutterites and the Amish. The Amish arose from a schism among Swiss Mennonites in 1693. Mennonite leader Jakob Amman (1656-1730) and his followers applied the Mennonite practice of shunning very strictly and condemned other Mennonites for not doing so. Amish communities sprang up in Switzerland, Alsace, Germany, Russia and Holland, but there are no Amish remaining in Europe today. Many immigrated to North America in the 19th and 20th centuries and those who stayed behind gradually assimilated with Mennonite groups.

Amish began immigrating to North America early in the 18th century, in large part to avoid religious persecution and compulsory military service. They first settled in eastern Pennsylvania, where a large settlement remains today. In 1850, there was a schism between the traditional Old Order Amish and the "New Order" Amish, who accept social change and technological innovation but retain most other Amish practices.

There are now about 200,000 Old Order Amish living in more than 200 settlements in the United States and Canada; the largest communities are in Pennsylvania, Ohio, Indiana, Iowa, Illinois, and Kansas, and others exist in Wisconsin, Missouri, and Minnesota.

Amish Texts

As conservative Protestants, the Amish value the Bible alone as the source of religious authority. But in most Amish homes a special place is reserved alongside the Bible for the *Martyr's Mirror*, a book chronicling Amish history and honoring the many Amish, Mennonites, and Anabaptists who died for their faith. *The Budget*, established in 1890, is the national newspaper serving the many Amish and Mennonite communities; it is published in Sugarcreek, Ohio.

Distinctive Beliefs of the Amish

Amish religious beliefs are virtually the same as that of the Mennonites and other religious reformers. They believe in the importance of individual Bible study and the necessity of living a life free of sin after adult baptism. The Amish are primarily set apart from other Mennonites in their great emphasis on the values of humility, family, community, and separation from the world.

Two key concepts for understanding Amish practices are their revulsion of *Hochmut* (pride, arrogance, haughtiness) and the high value they place on *Demut* (humility) and *Gelassenheit* (calmness, composure, placidity). This all translates into a reluctance to be forward, self-promoting, or to assert oneself in any way. The willingness to submit to the will of God, as expressed through group norms, is at odds with the individualism that is central to general American culture.

Religious Services

As in Mennonite communities, the Amish celebrate Holy Communion twice each year and practice foot washing. Persons are baptized when they are admitted to formal membership in the church, about the age of 17 to 20 years. Amish religious services are conducted in High German. Pennsylvania Dutch (which is not Dutch but a mixture of High German, various German dialects and English) is spoken at home and in daily discourse. Children learn English at school.

Religious services are held on a rotating basis in family homes and barns. A large wagon, filled with benches for the service and dishes and food for the meal that follows, will often be pulled to the host's property. The use of musical instruments is not permitted in an Amish church service or at any time, as it is considered wordly and vain. Singing, however, is important to Amish life, whether at work or at play, at home or in church. Selections from the *Ausband* (the Amish hymnal) are commonly sung. Group singing is always in unison and never harmonized.

Education

Amish children attend one-room schools run by the community and they attend school only through the eighth grade (this was deemed acceptable by a 1972 U.S. Supreme Court ruling). School classes are in English and focus on the basics of reading, writing, and math, along with Amish history, farming techniques and homemaking skills.

Rumspringa

Rumspringa ("running around") is the general Amish term for adolescence and the period leading up to serious courtship during which rules may be relaxed a little. As in non-Amish families, it is understood as a practical matter that there will likely be a certain amount of misbehavior during this period, but it is neither encouraged nor overlooked.

At the end of this period, Amish young adults are expected to find a spouse and be baptized. But in accordance with Anabaptist doctrine, this must be a free and personal decision. At this point, some young people choose not to join the church and instead live the rest of their lives in a different community or wider society. If a young man joins a Mennonite church or other less exacting religion, the Amish will often say "he got his hair cut." If a young person abandons the faith altogether, they say that person "went English."

Some communities will actively shun those who decide to leave the community, even those going to a different Amish congregation with different doctrines. Still other communities practice hardly any shunning, keeping close family and social contact with those who leave.

The Ordnung

Everyday life and customs in the Amish community are governed by an unwritten code of behavior called the *Ordnung*. The Ordnung began as a basic outline of Anabaptist faith in the 16th century, and since then, details and new rules have been added that help define what it means to be Amish. It now governs everything from clothing and child bearing to occupational activities and how the weekend is spent.

The enforcement of the rules depends on the bishop, who is charged with upholding Amish values. An Amish minister has explained of the Ordnung: A respected Ordnung generates peace, love, contentment, equality, and unity. It creates a desire for togetherness and fellowship. It binds marriages; it strengthens family ties to live together, to work together, and to worship together and to commune secluded from the world.

Shunning

Shunning (*Meidung*, "avoidance") was the practice that

set the Amish apart from the Mennonites several centuries ago, and it remains the fundamental way in which the community deals with disobedient members. Amish differ considerably from community to community in the severeness and strictness of the shunning, but in light of the closeness of the community and separation from the outside world, it is invariably a painful experience for the one shunned.

An Amish person may be shunned for a variety of offenses, ranging from major moral offenses to using improper technology. In accordance with the teachings of Jakob Amman, an Amish person in good standing may buy from, sell to, eat with or sleep with a shunned person, even if the person is one's spouse or close relative.

Electricity

The use of electricity is fervently avoided by Amish, because it is a prime connection to the world that could lead to temptations and worldly amenities detrimental to the community and family life. There are occasional exceptions to this general ban, such as adding electric flashers to buggies when required to drive legally and certain types of farm equipment such as milking equipment and electric fences to contain cattle. Bottle gas is often used to operate appliances, even barbecue grills, and gas-pressured lanterns and lamps might be used for indoor lighting. Amish buggies may also be equipped with such modern conveniences as heaters, windshield wipers, and upholstered seats. The New Order Amish permit the use of electricity, the owning of cars, and telephones in the home.

Clothing and Personal Appearance

The Amish are especially known for their distinctive self-made clothing, which is essentially that of 17th-century European peasants. The distinctive attire reflects the Amish resistance to change, respect for tradition and interpretation of biblical instructions against conforming to the ways of the world (e.g., Romans 12:2). Its plainness also reflects the great importance of humility in Amish communities.

Men and boys wear broad-brimmed black hats, dark-coloured suits, and straight-cut coats without lapels, broadfall pants, suspenders, solid-colored shirts and black socks and shoes. Their shirts may fasten with conventional buttons, but their coats and vests fasten with hooks and eyes. Men must grow beards after they marry but are forbidden to have mustaches.

Amish women and girls wear bonnets, long full dresses with capes over the shoulders, shawls, and black shoes and stockings; their capes and aprons are fastened with straight pins or snaps. Amish women never cut their hair, which is worn in a bun, and they are not allowed to wear jewelry of any kind.

Buggies, Product Sales and Photography

The Amish do not live in complete isolation and are often seen making regular trips into their local town for groceries. They reject the use of automobiles and use either bicycles or horse-drawn buggies instead. The buggies are box-like and usually black, but some are white, gray, or even yellow, and many groups can be distinguished by their chosen color of buggy. The Amish may also travel, for which they usually prefer to use buses. The Amish are excellent farmers and most communities are almost entirely self-supporting. However, some have to sell produce and crafts to outsiders in order to make a sufficient living.

Amish products are widely prized for their quality and craftsmanship. The Amish typically accept the photo-graphing of their way of life, but they forbid photos of themselves because they believe such things are graven images in violation of the Second Commandment. (For this same reason, the dolls of young Amish girls are traditionally faceless.) It also comes too close to vanity to allow one's portrait to be taken.

Politics and Government

The Amish are not involved in state or national politics, they do not vote, and they do not serve in the military. They also reject social security and most types of insurance. Instead, they pool their resources to help Amish families in need and will visit doctors, dentists, and opticians when necessary.

Recreation

The Amish may be reserved and humble, but they are not always solemn and enjoy common pastimes and games. Volleyball and softball are popular with many Amish families, but they are played strictly for enjoyment and not in a spirit of competition. Flower gardens, if kept simple, are also permissible. Once the daily chores are finished and the schoolwork completed, Amish families will often read or sing together in the evenings, before turning in early.

Organization

The Amish community is divided into church districts, autonomous congregations of about 75 baptized members. This small number is necessary because congregations meet in member's homes — there are no Amish churches. Each district has a bishop, two to four preachers, and an elder and is very independent; there are no Amish general conferences or cooperative agencies.

Baptists

The Baptists are one of the largest Protestant Free Church denominations. At the turn of the 21st century, there were about 43 million Baptists worldwide with about 33 million of those in the United States and 216,000 in Britain. There are over 850,000 Baptists in South America and 230,000 in Central America and the Caribbean. As indicated by their name, the primary Baptist distinctive is their practice of believer's baptism and corresponding rejection of infant baptism.

Most Baptists are evangelical in doctrine, but Baptist beliefs can vary due to the congregational governance system that gives autonomy to individual local Baptist churches. Historically, Baptists have played a key role in encouraging religious freedom and separation of church and state. In the United States, the two largest Baptist organizations are the

Southern Baptist Churches (SBC) and American Baptist Churches (ABC), with the former being the more conservative branch. Notable Baptists have included Martin Luther King, Jr., Charles Spurgeon, John Bunyan and Billy Graham.

Many Baptists trace their denomination's origins to the early church, a period when the church consisted of committed believers who were baptized upon confession of faith as adults. Baptist beginnings have also been traced to medieval sects who protested against prevailing baptismal theory and practice, and to the Anabaptists of the Continental Reformation, especially in Zurich. The Anabaptists (spiritual ancestors of the Mennonites, Amish, and Hutterites) share emphasized believer's baptism and religious freedom and were probably influential in the development of Baptist characteristics. However, some Anabaptists differed from the Baptists on many other issues such as pacifism and the communal sharing of material goods.

The origins of the Baptists are most commonly traced to John Smyth and the Separatists. In 1609, John Smyth, led a group of separatists to the Netherlands to start the General Baptist Church with an Arminian theology. In 1616, Henry Jacob led a group of Puritans in England with a Calvinist theology to form a congregational church that would eventually become the Particular Baptists in 1638 under John Spilsbury. Both groups had members who sailed to America as pilgrims to avoid religious persecution in England and Europe and who started Baptist churches in the early colonies. The Particular and General Baptists would disagree over Arminianism and Calvinism until the formation of the Baptist Union of Great Britain in the 1800s under Andrew Fuller and William Carey for the purpose of missions.

Baptist Churches were established in the American colonies from the mid-17th century. In 1639, Roger Williams founded a church on Baptist principles in Providence, Rhode Island, and this is usually regarded as the beginning of American Baptist history. Also established in the 17th century was a small group known as the Seventh Day Baptists, who required rest and worship on Saturday based on the fourth commandment. In the 18th century, many of the General Baptist Churches in England were influenced by the Unitarians and ultimately ceased to insist on believer's baptism. However, Dan Taylor (1738-1816) formed a "New Connection" in 1770 that maintained Baptist principles and later united with the Baptist mainstream. The Baptist Missionary Society was founded by Particular Baptists in 1792, which would have a profound impact on the future of the Baptists.

The Baptist revival in England inspired the Baptist Churches of America, leading to widespread missionary zeal and growth of the movement across America as the frontier extended. The Baptists became the largest religious group in many of the southern states; today, two-thirds of the members of Black Churches of the USA are Baptists.

In the 19th century, Baptist churches continued their rapid growth, and from their ranks came such great preachers as Charles Spurgeon, Robert Hall, Alexander Maclaren and John Clifford. In Britain, the Baptist Union was formed in 1813. Notable in its development was J.H. Shakespeare, who was secretary for over 25 years (1898-1924). The Baptist movement in Scotland was furthered by Archibald McLean (1733-1812), who strongly emphasized emulating the New Testament pattern in doctrine and practice. The "Scotch Baptists" were one of the sources of the Disciples of Christ movement.

In 1834, a Baptist church was formed in Hamburg under J.C. Oncken, and from there came an extensive Baptist movement in contentiental Europe and among Slavic-speaking people. Baptists were persecuted by Tsarist Russia and suffered from the restrictions on religious freedom under the Soviet regime, but their numbers have grown significantly in recent years (to about 548,000 in 1988). Baptists are the largest Protestant denomination in the countries of the former USSR. In the 20th century, Baptist missionaries have established churches throughout Asia, Africa and South America. In 1905, the Baptist World Alliance was formed for the purpose of international Baptist cooperation. Its headquarters is in McLean, Virginia.

Baptist Beliefs and Practices

Baptist churches tend to be evangelical in doctrine and Reformed in worship. However, Baptist churches do not have a central governing authority, so a wide range of beliefs can be seen between one Baptist church and another. Some Baptist churches use the following acronym as a summary of the common distinctives of Baptists:

- Biblical authority
- Autonomy of the local church
- Priesthood of the believer
- Two ordinances (Believer's Baptism and Communion)
- Individual soul liberty
- Separation of Church and State
- Two offices of the church (Pastor and Deacon)

These and other Baptist distinctives are explored briefly below.

Believer's Baptism

Believer's baptism is an ordinance performed after a person professes Jesus Christ as Lord and Savior and is symbolic of the cleansing or remission of their sins. In the Baptist denomination, baptism plays no role in salvation; it is rather an outward expression of the inward change that has already taken place. Baptists emphasize baptism by full immersion, which follows the method used by John the Baptist. This usually consists of lowering the candidate in water backwards, while a pastor recites the Trinitarian formula of Matthew 28:19. This mode of baptism is also preferred for its parallel imagery to the death, burial, and resurrection of Jesus. A few Baptist churches allow for baptism by sprinkling as an alternative method for the disabled or elderly, and most Baptist churches will recognize adult baptisms performed in other mainstream Christian churches. Baptism is seen as a public identification of the person with Christianity and that particular church and is often used as a criterion for membership in Baptist churches.

Most Anabaptist, Pentecostal, Restorationist and non-denominational churches share this understanding of baptism.

Congregational Governance

Congregationalist church governance gives autonomy to individual local churches in areas of policy, polity and doctrine. Baptist churches are not under the direct administrative control of any other body, such as a national council, or a leader such as a bishop or pope. Administration, leadership and doctrine are decided democratically by the lay members of each individual church, which accounts for the variation of beliefs from one Baptist church to another. John Wycliffe and Huldrych Zwingli were strong influences in the early development of the idea of congregationalism. In a manner typical of other congregationalists, many cooperative associations of Baptists have arisen.

Other congregationalist churches include Anabaptists, Pentecostal, Congregationalist Churches, the United Church of Christ and many non-denominational churches.

Separation of Church and State

Baptists have played an important role in the struggle for freedom of religion and separation of church and state in England, the United States, and other countries, including many who were imprisoned and even died for their faith. Some important figures in this struggle were John Smyth, Thomas Helwys, Edward Wightman, Leonard Busher, Roger Williams (who was a Baptist for a short period but became a seeker), John Clarke, Isaac Backus, and John Leland.

In 1612 John Smyth wrote, "the magistrate is not by virtue of his office to meddle with religion, or matters of conscience". That same year, Thomas Helwys wrote that the King of England could "comaund what of man he will, and wee are to obey it," but concerning the church — "with this Kingdom, our lord the King hath nothing to do." In 1614, Leonard Busher wrote what is believed to be the earliest Baptist treatise dealing exclusively with the subject of religious liberty.

Baptists were influential in the formation of the first civil government based on the separation of church and state in what is now Rhode Island. Anabaptists and Quakers also share a strong history in the development of separation of church and state.

The Danbury Baptist Association of Danbury, Connecticut sent a letter, dated October 7, 1801, to the newly elected President Thomas Jefferson, expressing concern over the lack in their state constitution of explicit protection of religious liberty, and against government establishment of religion. As a religious minority in Connecticut, the Danbury Baptists were concerned that a religious majority might "reproach their chief Magistrate... because he will not, dare not assume the prerogatives of Jehovah and make Laws to govern the Kingdom of Christ," thus establishing a state religion at the cost of the liberties of religious minorities. In their letter to the President, the Danbury Baptists also affirmed that "Our Sentiments are uniformly on the side of Religious Liberty — That Religion is at all times and places a matter between God and individuals — That no man ought to suffer in name, person, or effects on account of his religious Opinions - That the legitimate Power of civil government extends no further than to punish the man who works ill to his neighbor..."

Thomas Jefferson's response, dated January 1, 1802, concurs with the Danbury Baptists' views on religious liberty, and the accompanying separation of civil government from concerns of religious doctrine and practice. Quoting the First Amendment of the United States Constitution, he writes: "...I contemplate with sovereign reverence that act of the whole American people which declared that their legislature should 'make no law respecting an establishment of religion, or prohibiting the free exercise thereof,' thus building a wall of separation between Church and State."

While there is a general belief that the state should not decide what the church can believe and should not prohibit the practice of religion, Baptists do disagree among themselves as to the degree to which the church should influence the state and what exactly constitutes state prohibition of religion. These disagreements manifest themselves in issues such as whether the state should restrict gambling, the purchase of alcohol or abortion and whether the prohibition of state-sanctioned public prayer in public schools in the United States constitutes state interference in religion.

Baptist Lifestyle

Many conservative Baptists oppose gambling, alcohol, tobacco, and some prohibit dancing and movies. Especially in areas where Southern Baptists form a majority of the population, the denomination has been successful in imposing its values on the general population – "dry counties" in the South or the ban on music and dancing in the film *Footloose*) are examples.

Biblical Authority

Authority of the Scriptures or sola scriptura states that the Bible is the only authoritative source of God's truth and any view that cannot be directly tied to a scriptural reference is generally considered to be based on human traditions rather than God's leading. Each person is responsible before God for his or h er own understanding of the bible and is encouraged to work for their own salvation with fear and trembling.

Biblical inerrancy is also a common position held by Baptists in addition to literal interpretations of the bible and fundamentalist theologies. However, because of the variety allowed under congregational governance, many Baptist churches are neither literalist nor fundamentalist, although most do believe in biblical inerrancy. Even though it is only the Bible that is authoritative, Baptists also cite other works as illustrative of doctrine. One work which is commonly read by Baptists is the allegory Pilgrim's Progress by John Bunyan. This is a position shared by almost all post-Reformation Christian groups, with only a few exceptions (such as Quakers).

Priesthood of All Believers

The Baptist position of the priesthood of believers is one column that upholds their belief in religious liberty. Priesthood of all believers removes the hierarchical layers of priests, traditions and authority so that all Christians have equal access to God's revelation of truth through the careful study of the Bible. This is a position shared by all post-reformational Christian groups.

Justification by Faith

The doctrine of justification by faith states that it is by faith alone that we receive salvation and not through any works of our own. Baptists place a strong emphasis on the concept of salvation. Baptist theology teaches that humans have been contaminated by the sin of Adam and Eve's rebellion against God and that for this sin we are condemned to damnation. The theology holds that Christ died on the cross to give humans the promise of everlasting life, but that this requires that each individual accept Christ into his life and ask for forgiveness. Nevertheless, the Baptist view of soteriology runs the gamut from Calvinism to Arminianism. Justification by faith is a position shared by all post-reformational Christian groups.

Variations in Baptist Belief and Practice

Because of the congregational style of church governance on doctrine, doctrine often varies significantly between one Baptist church and another, especially in the following areas:

- Calvinism vs. Arminianism
- Nature of Law and Gospel

- Ordination of women
- Homosexuality
- Eschatology (end times)

Baptists generally believe in the literal Second Coming of Christ at which time God will sit in judgment and divide humanity between the saved and the lost (the Great White Throne judgment Book of Revelation 20:11) and Christ will sit in judgment of the believers (the Judgment Seat of Christ Second Epistle to the Corinthians 5:10), rewarding them for things done while alive. Amillennialism, dispensationalism, and historic premillennialism stand as the main eschatological views of Baptists, with views such as postmillennialism and preterism receiving only scant support.

Lutheranism

Lutheranism is one of the largest Protestant denominations today. According to the Lutheran World Federation, there are nearly 66 million Lutherans worldwide. Of these, 36 million live in Europe, 13 million in Africa, 8.4 million in North America, 7.3 million in Asia, and 1.1 million in Latin America.

Lutheranism was founded by Martin Luther, a German monk and professor who has been called the "Father of the Reformation." In 1517, he famously protested against the Catholic Church's sale of indulgences. In his sermons and writings, Luther stressed the doctrine of justification by faith alone and the authority of scripture alone. Lutheranism quickly spread throughout Germany and Scandanavia, and the Protestant movement in various forms could soon be found throughout Europe.

The Lutheran denomination is the oldest Protestant denomination. It was founded (not deliberately at first) by Martin Luther, the German monk and professor who famously posted *95 Theses* against the practice of indulgences in 1517. Luther saw contradictions between the Bible and current church practice as well as corruption and abuses within the

(Catholic) church, and initially hoped for reform, not schism. When that proved impossible, he continued to spread his teachings despite excommunication and threats to his life.

Martin Luther taught that salvation comes by the grace of God and faith in Christ alone, and the many rituals and works prescribed by the church were not only unnecessary, but a stumbling block to salvation. He rejected such traditions as the intermediary role of priests, priestly celibacy, the Latin Bible and liturgy, purgatory, and transubstantiation, and advocated for the scriptures to be available to the laity in their own language.

Despite his rejection of many aspects of medieval Catholicism, Luther did accept any aspects of church practice that did not contradict the scriptures. Some other Protestant groups, by contrast, rejected any Catholic tradition not explicitly commanded in the Bible. For this reason, Lutheran churches tend to have more of a Catholic "look and feel" than their more austere Presbyterian counterparts.

Those who followed Luther's teachings were called "Lutherans" by their opponents, and they accepted the name for themselves. Lutheranism spread throughout Germany and into Scandanavia (Norway, Sweden, Finland, Iceland, and Denmark). Today, Germany remains predominantly Lutheran, and Lutheranism is the official state church of Norway, Sweden, Denmark, and Iceland. Eighty-one percent of Finland's citizens are members of the Evangelical Lutheran Church of Finland.

In the 17th century, Lutherans from these countries began to migrate to the United States, bringing their language, culture, and Lutheran faith with them. As the number of Lutheran congregations grew, some began to join together to form "synods," or church bodies.

On January 1, 1988, three American synods, the American Lutheran Church, the Association of Evangelical Lutheran Churches and the Lutheran Church in America, merged to become the Evangelical Lutheran Church in America (ELCA).

In August 1997, the ELCA declared full communion with the United Church of Christ, the Reformed Church of America, and the Presbyterian Church-USA. The ELCA also decided that the differences between it and the Roman Catholic Church in matters of salvation had essentially been resolved.

Lutheran Beliefs

Lutheran beliefs are expressed in numerous historical Lutheran confessions, most of which were penned by Luther himself or early Lutheran leaders. These confessions have been collected into the Book of Concord, which is regarded as an authority for doctrine and practice by all Lutherans.

ELCA Lutherans view the Book of Concord as an important expression of the Lutheran faith, but not necessarily binding in its entirety for all modern Lutherans. LCMS Lutherans, on the other hand, "regard their doctrinal content as a true and binding exposition of Holy Scripture and as authoritative for all pastors, congregations and other rostered church workers."

The Book of Concord contains the following Lutheran texts:

- The Three Ecumenical Creeds
- The Augsburg Confession
- The Defense of the Augsburg Confession
- The Large Catechism
- The Small Catechism
- The Smalcald Articles
- Treatise on the Power and Primacy of the Pope
- The Epitome of the Formula of Concord
- The Solid Declaration of the Formula of Concord

The official statement of faith of the ELCA is as follows:

1. This church confesses the Triune God, Father, Son, and Holy Spirit. This church confesses Jesus Christ as Lord and Savior and the Gospel as the power of God for the salvation of all who believe:

- Jesus Christ is the Word of God incarnate, through whom everything was made and through whose life, death, and resurrection God fashions a new creation.
- The proclamation of God's message to us as both Law and Gospel is the Word of God, revealing judgment and mercy through word and deed, beginning with the Word in creation, continuing in the history of Israel, and centering in all its fullness in the person and work of Jesus Christ.
- The canonical Scriptures of the Old and New Testaments are the written Word of God. Inspired by God's Spirit speaking through their authors, they record and announce God's revelation centering in Jesus Christ. Through them God's Spirit speaks to us to create and sustain Christian faith and fellowship for service in the world.

2. This church accepts the canonical Scriptures of the Old and New Testaments as the inspired Word of God and the authoritative source and norm of its proclamation, faith, and life.
3. This church accepts the Apostles', Nicene, and Athanasian Creeds as true declarations of the faith of this church.
4. This church accepts the Unaltered Augsburg Confession as a true witness to the Gospel, acknowledging as one with it In faith and doctrine all churches that likewise accept the teachings of the Unaltered Augsburg Confession.
5. This church accepts the other confessional writings in the Book of Concord, namely, the Apology of the Augsburg Confession, the Smalcald Articles and the Treatise, the Small Catechism, the Large Catechism, and the Formula of Concord, as further valid interpretations of the faith of the Church.
6. This church confesses the Gospel, recorded in the Holy Scriptures and confessed in the ecumenical creeds and Lutheran confessional writings, as the power of God to create and sustain the Church for God's mission in the world.

Lutheran Practices

Lutherans practice infant baptism and the baptism of believing adults. In the Lutheran perspective, baptism is a sacrament that is commanded by God and "cleanses from sin, snatches us from the power of Satan, and gives us everlasting life." Some Lutheran churches ordain women to the ministry, while others do not. The LCMS does not, and offers a full explanation of this decision in its online document "What About the Ordination of Women?"

Social/Ethical Issues

Lutheran churches vary in their perspective on homosexuality and their response to homosexuals in the church. The Lutheran Church - Missouri Synod "believes that the Bible teaches that homosexual behavior is contrary to God's Word and will, and seeks to minister to those who are struggling with homosexual inclinations." The ELCA has not yet taken a defined stand on the issue, but has been conducting a study of the issue in recent years. Its current policy is to welcome homosexual persons to participate fully in its congregations and to encourage open conversations about the issue. The ELCA does not currently bless same-sex marriages nor ordain homosexuals to church positions.

Differences between ELCA and LCMS

The two largest Lutheran church bodies in America are the Evangelical Lutheran Church in America (ELCA), with about 5 million members in 2003, and the Lutheran Church - Missouri Synod (LCMS), which had about 2.5 million members in 2003. Other large Lutheran churches include the Wisconsin Evangelical Lutheran Synod (WELS) (413,839 members), the Association of Free Lutheran Congregations (36,400), and the Evangelical Lutheran Synod (ELS; 24,000).

The ELCA meets in assembly every two years, and elects a bishop to a six-year term. In 2001, the ELCA elected the Rev. Mark S. Hanson, who may be reelected in 2007. "In addition to fulfilling such roles as preacher, teacher and administrator of the sacraments, which traditionally belong to the office of bishop, the presiding bishop of this church serves as president and chief executive officer of the corporation and oversees the staff, budget, and overall administration of the church."

The Lutheran Church - Missouri Synod (LCMS) is more conservative than the Evangelical Lutheran Church in America (ELCA). The ELCA allows for the possibility of errors and cultural limitations in the Bible and interprets it using the methods of historical criticism. The ELCA ordains women and is tends to be open to the acceptance of homosexuality and abortion among its members. Similarly, although all Lutherans are guided by the 16th-century Lutheran confessions set out in the Book of Concord, the ELCA does not require its members to accept them in their entirety as normative standards for modern life. LCMS members, on the other hand, "accept without reservation all the confessions of the Evangelical Lutheran Church as a true and unadulterated statement and exposition of the Word of God, normative also for the church today."

Another important difference between the LCMS and the ELCA is in the area of ecumenism. The ELCA is a member of the Lutheran World Federation and the World Council of Churches, and has entered into full fellowship with non-Lutheran churches. This means that the ELCA accepts sacraments, such as ordination and communion, performed by churches other than the ELCA as valid. The LCMS, on the other hand, "believes that the Bible requires full agreement in doctrine before it is possible to join in altar and pulpit fellowship with other churches (Rom. 16:17)." The practical difference for a Lutheran churchgoer is that LCMS members and certain other Protestants may take communion in an ELCA congregation, but one must be an LCMS member to take communion in an LCMS congregation.

Christian Beliefs on Hell

"Some will not be redeemed. There is no doctrine which I would more willingly remove from Christianity than this if it lay in my power."

C.S. Lewis, *The Problem of Pain*

"Abandon hope, all ye who enter here!"

Inscription over the gates of hell, according to Dante

"It would be dreadful to suffer this fierceness and wrath of Almighty God for one moment; but you must suffer it for all eternity."

Jonathan Edwards, *Sinners in the Hands of an Angry God* (1741)

According to a 2004 Gallup Poll, 70% of Americans believe in hell. Belief in hell is highest among regular churchgoers: 92% of those who attend church weekly believe in hell, as do 74% of those who attend nearly weekly.

In Christian theology, hell is the place or state into which unrepentant sinners pass after this life. Hell is generally thought to be eternal, and to include both punishment (*poena sensus*) and separation from God (*poena damni*). Although not central to the Christian faith, the doctrine of hell has been a significant part of historical Christian theology throughout its history.

Hell was a strong incentive to lead a righteous life in the early church. It was the setting for Dante's literary masterpiece *The Inferno*. It was fear of hell and judgment that terrified Martin Luther before his spiritual enlightenment. The doctrine of hell was central to the Jonathan Edwards' famous sermon "Sinners in the Hands of An Angry God" and many others like it.

For some, however, especially since the Enlightenment, hell has also been a major stumbling block to acceptance of Christianity. Some Christian groups no longer believe in an eternal hell, or at least regard belief in it as unnecessary. This article will explore the doctrine of hell as it developed first in the sacred texts of Christianity and then in the hands of Christian theologians over the centuries. It concludes with a summary of modern Christian beliefs about hell, by way of quotes and excerpts from Christian groups.

The Word "Hell"

The word "hell" in English Bibles is used to translate the Hebrew word *Sheol* (and its Greek equivalent *Hades*) and the Greek word *Gehenna*. The English word derives from the Anglo-Saxon meaning "to conceal" or "to cover," which is similar to the meanings of Sheol and Hades. In the Old Testament, Sheol (which is also sometimes translated "grave" or "pit") denotes the underworld or the place of departed spirits. "The notion reflects an undeveloped and shadowy belief in the future life which was gradually superseded by the more defined beliefs of later Judaism."

Gehenna ("the Valley of Hinnom") is the Greek translation of a Hebrew word that seems to refer to an actual place on earth. The identity of Hinnom is not known for certain, but scholars have suggested an area southwest of Jerusalem near the Cedron. Gehenna is mentioned in Jos. 15:8 and 18:16, and in 2 Kings, it is described as a place of human sacrifice (16:3, 21:6) that was polluted (23:10-12). Jeremiah warned that one day would be renamed "Valley of Slaughter" (Jer. 7:32, 19:6). In later Jewish thought, Gehenna was a place of punishment for apostates and other great sinners (e.g., 1 Enoch 27:2, 90:26; 2 Esdras 7:36-38). A statement dating to 1200 AD that fires were continually kept burning in the Valley of Hinnom is generally regarded as reliable, although no earlier reference has yet been found.

Hell in the Old Testament

The idea of hell (as understood in Christianity) is virtually absent from the Old Testament, which has very little to say about the afterlife at all. A possible mention hell in the Old Testament is this prophecy about the end times:

- "Multitudes who sleep in the dust of the earth will awake: some to everlasting life, others to shame and everlasting contempt." (Daniel 12:2, NIV)
- Another notable passage that likely contributes to Christian imagery of hell is Isaiah 66:24, which also refers to the end times:

- "And they will go out and look upon the dead bodies of those who rebelled against me; their worm will not die, nor will their fire be quenched, and they will be loathsome to all mankind.

Other passages that speak of the afterlife seem to indicate extinction of the soul after death. Rabbis have generally the taught the existence of a hell-like place for the unrighteous, but many Jews, both historical and modern, do not believe in hell or an afterlife.

Hell in the New Testament

In the New Testament, the notion of hell is more clearly expressed, but still not in a systematic way. In many cases, "death" and "destruction" are the only mentioned penalties for rejecting God (e.g., Matthew 7:13, John 3:16, Acts 4:12, Romans 6:23, 2 Thessalonians 1:9, James 1:15). Also, as noted in the section above, the same terminology is often used in the New Testament that in the Jewish context may have suggested nothing more than physical death and destruction of the soul.

New Testament passages that have suggested eternal torment to Christians include the following:

- "Anyone who says, 'You fool!' will be in danger of the fire of hell." (Matthew 5:22, quoting Jesus)
- "And if your right hand causes you to sin, cut it off and throw it away. It is better for you to lose one part of your body than for your whole body to go into hell." (Matthew 5:29, quoting Jesus; see parallel passage in Mark 9:44, which adds, "where the fire never goes out.")
- "Do not be afraid of those who kill the body but cannot kill the soul. Rather, be afraid of the One who can destroy both soul and body in hell." (Matthew 10:28, quoting Jesus)
- "As the weeds are pulled up and burned in the fire, so it will be at the end of the age. The Son of Man will send out his angels, and they will weed out of his kingdom everything that causes sin and all who do evil. They will

throw them into the fiery furnace, where there will be weeping and gnashing of teeth." (Matthew 13:40-42, quoting Jesus)

- "Throw that worthless servant outside, into the darkness, where there will be weeping and gnashing of teeth." (Parable of the Talents, Matthew 25:30)
- "Then he [the King] will say to those on his left, 'Depart from me, you who are cursed, into the eternal fire prepared for the devil and his angels." (Parable of the Sheep and the Goats, Matthew 25:41)
- "The tongue also is a fire, a world of evil among the parts of the body. It corrupts the whole person, sets the whole course of his life on fire, and is itself set on fire by hell." (James 3:6)
- "The sea gave up the dead that were in it, and death and Hades gave up the dead that were in them, and each person was judged according to what he had done. Then death and Hades were thrown into the lake of fire. The lake of fire is the second death. If anyone's name was not found written in the book of life, he was thrown into the lake of fire." (Revelation 20:13-15)
- "The cowardly, the unbelieving, the vile...the idolaters and all liars - their place will be in the fiery lake of burning sulpher. This is the second death." (Revelation 21:8)

The Doctrine of Hell in the Church Fathers

In the church fathers (post-New-Testament Christian leaders and theologians), the doctrine of hell quickly becomes more well-defined as a place of eternal torment, which is generally seen as physical in nature:

- "The way of darkness is crooked, and it is full of cursing. It is the way of eternal death with punishment." (Pseudo-Barnabas, c. 70-130 AD)
- "You should fear what is truly death, which is reserved for those who will be condemned to the eternal fire. It will afflict those who are committed to it even to the end." (*Letter to Diognetus*, c. 125-200)

- "[The martyrs] despised all the torments of this world, redeeming themselves from eternal punishment by the suffering of a single hour.... For they kept before their view escape from that fire which is eternal and will never be quenched." (*Martyrdom of Polycarp,* c. 135)
- "Sinners will be consumed because they sinned and did not repent." (*Shepherd of Hermas,* c. 150)
- "Those who have not known God and do evil are condemned to death. However, those who have known God and have seen his mighty works, but still continue in evil, will be chastised doubly, and will die forever." (*Shepherd of Hermas,* c. 150)
- "We believe...that every man will suffer punishment in eternal fire according to the merits of his deed.... Sensation remains to all who have ever lived, and eternal punishment is laid up." (Justin Martyr, c. 160)
- "Hell [Gehenna] is a place where those who have lived wickedly are to be punished." (Justin Martyr, c. 160)
- "Some are sent to be punished unceasingly into judgment and condemnation of fire." (Justin Martyr, c. 160)
- "We who are now easily susceptible to death, will afterwards receive immortality with either enjoyment or with pain." (Tatian, c. 160)
- "We are persuaded that when we are removed from the present life we will live another life, better than the present one...or, if they fall with the rest, they will endure a worse life, one in fire. For God has not made us as sheep or beasts of burden, who are mere byproducts. For animals perish and are annihilated. On these grounds, it is not likely that we would wish to do evil." (Athenagoras, c. 175)
- "To the unbelieving and despisers...there will be anger and wrath, tribulation and anguish. At the end, everlasting fire will possess such men." (Theophilus, c. 180)
- "Eternal fire is prepared for sinners. The Lord has plainly declared this and the rest of the Scriptures demonstrate it." (Irenaeus, c. 180)

- "All souls are immortal, even those of the wicked. Yet, it would be better for them if they were not deathless. For they are punished with the endless vengeance of quenchless fire. Since they do not die, it is impossible for them to have an end put to their misery." (Clement of Alexandria, c. 195; from a post-Nicene manuscript fragment)
- "We [Christians] alone make a real effort to attain a blameless life. We do this under the influence of... the magnitude of the threatened torment. For it is not merely long-enduring; rather, it is everlasting." (Tertullian, c. 197)
- "Gehenna... is a reservoir of secret fire under the earth for purposes of punishment." (Tertullian, c. 197)
- "There is neither limit nor termination of these torments. There, the intelligent fire burns the limbs and restores them. It feeds on them and nourishes them.... However, no one except a profane man hesitates to believe that those who do not know God are deservedly tormented." (Mark Minucius Felix, c. 200)

However, some early church fathers, such as Origen of Alexandria and Gregory of Nyssa, questioned the eternality of hell and the literal interpretation of it as a fiery place.

Modern Christian Views of Hell

Modern Christian views of hell tend to emphasize its spiritual aspects over the notion of physical suffering or material fire. Hell is seen as a logical extension of the free will of mankind to reject God's gracious advances, even for eternity, and its punishment as a realization of one's mistake and the great remorse that would follow. Many modern Christians also question hell's eternality in favor of some form of universalism (all are saved in the end) or annihilationism (wicked souls are destroyed).

Following is a sampling of the positions of various Christian denominations on the issue of hell. It is impossible to describe the glory and splendor of heaven and the terror and torment of hell. Whether taken literally or figuratively, the meaning is the same: Hell is a place where one will experience total separation from God; heaven enjoys the total presence of God. Knowing that this is the horrible end awaiting the wicked, the Assemblies of God is strongly motivated to win the lost before it is too late. To die in mortal sin without repenting and accepting God's merciful love means remaining separated from him for ever by our own free choice. This state of definitive self-exclusion from communion with God and the blessed is called "hell."

The statement of Christ in Matthew 25, and elsewhere, are taken at face value. It is believed that after death each man must come before God in judgment and that he will be judged according to the deeds done while he lived (Hebrews 9:27). After judgment is pronounced he will spend eternity either in heaven or hell. We believe that glorious and everlasting life is assured to all who savingly believe in, and obediently follow, Jesus Christ our Lord; and that the finally impenitent shall suffer eternally in hell.

This hope for the final salvation of humanity and the eternal universal restitution of all things in heaven and on earth... is drawn from the unlimited promise of the Gospel and the magnitude of God's grace made known to the world through Christ. We believe in the bodily resurrection of the dead; of the believer to everlasting blessedness and joy with the Lord; of the unbeliever to judgment and everlasting conscious punishment. The moral progress of the soul, either for better or for worse, ends at the very moment of the separation of the body and soul; at that very moment the definite destiny of the soul in the everlasting life is decided.... The Orthodox Church believes that at this moment the soul of the dead person begins to enjoy... the life in Paradise or to undergo the life in Hell. There is no way of repentance, no way of escape, no reincarnation and no help from the outside world.

Arguments for an Eternal Hell

Among the common arguments advanced for the existence of an eternal hell are these:

1. Words and pictures in the New Testament imply finality.

2. The doctrine of hell has been believed for a long time by eminent theologians.
3. Offers of pardon are restricted to the present world.
4. The judgment occurs at the close of the redemptive era, and hence is final.
5. Character tends to final permanance.
6. The conscience expects and demands retribution in another life.
7. Arguments Against An Eternal Hell

Commonly presented arguments against the existence of an eternal hell include:

1. Words and pictures in the New Testament imply death and destruction (i.e., annihilation).
2. "Eternal punishment" can refer to results that are eternal, not an eternal process.
3. Vindictive justice is not compatible with the God of love and compassion revealed in the New Testament.
4. The punishment does not fit the crime (i.e. non-eternal sin and disbelief).
5. Hell contradicts the Christian assertion of the final victory of God over evil.

Beliefs of Jehovah's Witnesses

The religious beliefs of Jehovah's Witnesses are in many ways similar to those of mainstream Christians. For instance, Witnesses rely on the authority of the Bible, worship only one God, and trust in Jesus' death and resurrection for salvation. Some other beliefs of Jehovah's Witnesses differ from mainstream Christianity, most notably their rejection of the doctrine of the Trinity and the existence of Hell. Witnesses also have stronger apocalyptic expectations than most Christians - since the founding of the group, Witnesses have been expecting the imminent arrival of Armageddon and the end times. The following article summarizes the doctrines of Jehovah's Witnesses, noting where they agree and disagree with mainstream Christian doctrines.

Bible

In agreement with most conservative Christians, Jehovah's Witnesses affirm the full inspiration of the Bible by God and the preservation of its copies over the centuries. Witnesses see the Bible as a gift from God that tells humans about what God is like, how to cope with problems, and how to please God.

God

Jehovah's Witnesses believe in one God, the Creator of the universe and the God of the Hebrew and Christian scriptures. They stress the fact that God has revealed his personal name to humanity, which is Jehovah. Jehovah has a spirit body and lives in heaven, but sees all things. Jehovah's Witnesses reject the doctrine of the Trinity.

Jesus Christ

Jehovah's Witnesses disagree with the mainstream Christian belief that Jesus was "fully God, fully man." Witnesses teach that Jesus was not God, but rather God's first creation. Jesus existed in prehuman form as God's agent of creation and God's chief spokesman (the Word), and took on human form as the man Jesus by means of a virgin birth.

The purpose of Jesus' incarnation on earth was threefold in the view of Witnesses:

1. To teach the truth about God;
2. To provide a model of a perfect life for people to follow; and
3. To sacrifice his life to set humans free from sin and death. His crucifixion was not on a cross, but a single upright stake. After his death, God raised Jesus from the dead "as a spirit creature" and Jesus returned to his home in heaven. Jesus was not made King, however, until 1914.

Holy Spirit

In accordance with their rejection of the doctrine of the Trinity, Witnesses disagree with mainstream Christianity that the Holy Spirit is one of the three Persons in the Godhead. Instead, they believe the Holy Spirit to be "God's active force."

Human Nature

Like most Christians, Jehovah's Witnesses trace humanity's current situation to the sin of Adam and Eve in the Garden. The disobedience of the first couple caused death to enter the world, and as a result, all human beings get sick, age, and die. This is against God's plan, which was to make the entire Earth a paradise.

However, Witnesses do not emphasize the spiritual consequences of Adam's sin on humanity nor they teach that human free will has been damaged. Rather, Witnesses expect and encourage their members to strive to do God's will and remain pure in his eyes.

Meaning of Life and Salvation

For Jehovah's Witnesses, the purpose of life is to earn the right to participate in God's future Kingdom on earth, and to help others to do so. Witnesses therefore focus on living a moral, acceptable life before God and witnessing about their faith to others.

Witnesses believe that salvation was made possible through Christ's death, who made up for the sin of Adam. But eternal life comes not simply from faith in Jesus but from "learning about Jehovah and obeying his requirements," proving oneself to be God's loyal subject, and listening to the Kingdom message and acting on it.

After Life

Jehovah's witnesses deny the existence of hell. Instead, they hold that the souls of the wicked will be annihilated. The death that Adam brought into the world is spiritual as well as physical, and only those who gain entrance into the Kingdom of God will exist eternally. However, this division will not occur until Armageddon, when all people will be resurrected and given a chance to gain eternal life. In the meantime, "the dead are conscious of nothing."

Witnesses also have a slightly different view of heaven than mainstream Christianity. Based on their reading of prophetic books like Daniel and Revelation, Jehovah's Witnesses believe that only 144,000 people will go to heaven to rule with God and Jesus. The remainder of the righteous will enjoy paradise on earth - a restored Garden of Eden in which there is no sickness, old age, death or unhappiness.

End Times

A belief that is unique to Jehovah's Witnesses is that the eschatological events predicted in Revelation began in 1914. This is when God gave Jesus his Kingdom, and Jesus has been ruling from heaven ever since. At this time Jesus threw Satan and his demons out of heaven and down to earth, which is why, according to Witnesses, the world has been getting progressively worse since 1914.

Jehovah's Witnesses look forward to a theocracy, in which all human governments are abolished and God rules the entire earth himself. This is expected to occur soon. Although Witnesses once predicted specific dates for this event, they now state that "the Bible does not give a date for these events, but it provides evidence to show that we are living in 'the last days' of this troubled world.

As a Christian church, Seventh-day Adventists are a faith community rooted in the beliefs described by the Holy Scriptures. Adventists describe these beliefs in the following ways: God's greatest desire is for you to see a clear picture of His character. When you see Him clearly, you will find His love irresistible.

For many, "seeing God clearly" requires that they see God's face. However, how He looks is not the issue. Seeing and understanding His character is what's most important. The more clearly we understand Him, the more we will find His love irresistible. As we begin to experience His love, our own lives will begin to make more sense.

God most clearly reveals His character in three great events. The first is His creation of man and woman—and His giving them the freedom of choice. He created humans with the ability to choose to love Him or to hate Him! The death of Jesus Christ, God's only Son, on the cross as our substitute is the second great event. In that act He paid the penalty we deserve for our hateful choices toward God and His ways. Jesus' death guarantees forgiveness for those choices and allows us to spend eternity with Him. The third event confirms the first two and fills every heart with hope: Christ's tomb is empty. He is alive, living to fill us with His love.

Jesus' disciple John wrote that if everyone wrote all the stories they knew about Jesus, the whole world could not contain them. Our knowledge of God helps us understand His love, character, and grace. Experiencing that love begins a lifelong adventure in growth and service. This knowledge and experience powers our mission to tell the world about His love and His offer of salvation.

Scripture is a road map. The Bible is God's voice, speaking His love personally to you today.

The Bible speaks the Creator's directions to us, like a detailed road map that clearly shows the exit ramp directly into heaven. It is also much like an owner's manual for a life ready to be lived on the cutting edge of liberty.

Sometimes His voice speaks through stories, such as those of David and Goliath, Ruth and Boaz, Naaman's little servant girl, Christ on the cross, and fisherman Peter learning how to tend sheep. Some of these stories teach us how to handle the troubles we face each day. Others fill us with hope and peace. Each of them is like a personal letter from God to you.

Portions of Scripture are direct instructions and laws from God such as the Ten Commandments, recorded in Exodus 20. These tell us more about God and His expectations for us. When people asked Jesus to summarize these commands, He focused on the way God's love affects the way we live. "Love the Lord your God with all your heart, mind, and soul," He said. "And love your neighbor as you love yourself."

On other pages the Bible gives God's practical advice and

encouragement through parables, lists, promises, and warnings. Amazingly, though many different writers throughout thousands of years wrote the Bible, each page describes the same God in ways we can understand and apply in our lives today. This book is always His voice talking personally to anyone who is willing to read and hear.

God loves us even when we choose to reject His love. In those times He allows us to walk away into the life of our own choices. Yet He is still there, always ready to redeem us from the results of our decisions. Jesus is the one who never changes in a universe that always does. Jesus is Creator, Sustainer, Saviour, Friend, God's Son, and God Himself!

Everything in this world is always changing, even our desires, interests, skills, and body shapes. He's consistent. He's always the same. Sure, He's always surprising us and touching our lives in thousands of new and different ways, but His character is unchanging. He's God's Son, the Creator, our Saviour, and Friend.

Jesus has promised to be all of that, and more, for each of us. We can trust His promises because He is God. When the words of Colossians say "in Him all things hold together" (1:17, NIV) that includes everything in our lives. He keeps us whole when the enemy is trying to make us fall apart.

Seventh-day Adventists believe that Jesus is one of the three persons, called the Trinity, who make up our one God. The Bible describes Jesus, the Father, and the Holy Spirit as each being committed to our growth as Christians and to our salvation as their children. They made this salvation possible when Jesus came to Bethlehem as a human baby. He lived a life perfectly in accord with God's will and then died innocently for all of our sins. He was placed in a borrowed tomb, but He came back to life three days later. Now he is in heaven interceding with the Father for us, preparing for our deliverance from sin and death.

When everything may be falling apart, when you feel totally alone in the universe, Jesus is right there in the center of it all, offering personal peace and hope. Allow Him into your life. He immediately begins "remodeling" who you are and how you live. Jesus, in fact, is busily transforming. His followers into accurate representatives of God's character.

Look to Jesus, and you'll be looking into the understanding and loving face of God. God's vision for you is life as He lives it! God loves you, and wants to give you the highest quality of life imaginable. No, not a second-rate existence somewhere on earth, but the highest quality of life imaginable, here and in eternity with Him! That's what God wants us to have. The best!

This is why He provides church families where we can belong. This is why He gives each of us special gifts and talents, so we can live life fully. Amazingly, this is why He's concerned about what you're doing, when you're doing it, and how you relate to Him. God doesn't want anything to get in the way of our friendship.

He especially doesn't want us to get involved in anything damaging or hurtful. He's like a loving father or a good big brother. He's someone who loves you so much that He's always looking out for you.

When God designed you, He included special talents and skills that will help you become a uniquely valuable individual. These may be your ability to teach, your love for others, or your leadership skills. Still, whatever special gifts you have received, God has also provided all of the energy and wisdom necessary for you to use them well.

By the way, how God feels about death is part of the quality life He offers. For followers of Christ, death holds no fear. Remember, Jesus defeated death on Calvary and has given us freedom from death. Cemeteries, then, are filled with followers of God who are in the "peaceful pause before the resurrection." Yes, they are dead, but that death holds no power over their future. Jesus is coming to take them (and those of us who are still living) Home! Death is almost like a wintery promise of spring.

The Seventh-day Adventist faith in today and in the future comes from seeing this life "overflowing" with hope! Because love is the key aspect of His character, God is also deeply into gratitude. Before we even finish saying thank you, He's already busy sending more blessings.

In the heart of God is a place you can experience as home. God loves you, and wants to spend time with you personally, one on one, as two close friends. Because you and God are friends, you will spend time together as friends do. Each morning you'll share a hello and a hug and discuss how you can face the day's events together.

Throughout the day you'll talk with Him about how you feel. You'll laugh with Him at funny things and ache with Him over sadness and hurts. It's pleasant being God's friend, able to snuggle comfortably into the safety of your relationship. You can always trust Him to treat you well, because He loves you.

The seventh day (Saturday) is an extra-special part of the relationship. The Bible, from Genesis through Revelation, describes the seventh day as the one day God has set aside for focused fellowship with His people. God has named that day "Sabbath" and asked us to spend it with Him. "Remember the sabbath day," He says, "to keep it holy." The Sabbath is a whole day to deepen our friendship with the Creator of the universe! A day when we're together, Jesus with us and us with Jesus.

There's another great truth about friendship with God. It doesn't end in a cemetery; for God is planning a homecoming better than anything we can dream. A homecoming filled with angels, trumpets, Jesus, and resurrections. He's promised to bring His followers, those who have accepted the offer of His life-changing love, from this earth to His home, a place He calls heaven. A place where our friendship can go on growing forever, endlessly, joyfully!

- God keeps a family album and your picture is in it. God loves you and has a plan for your life.

God made you and has a very special plan for your life. It's a plan that will fill you with hope, love, peace, and activity and in fact, when Christ paid the penalty for the sin on the cross that gave Him the right to claim to be His. As a result, you can experience His love and priceless salvation freely and fully without limit.

By the way, pictures of everyone fill that album: Nepalese, Brazilians, Nigerians, Yupiks, and Germans, people of every nation, culture, background, gender, hair color, and foot size. In God's eyes all are equally "children of the King"!

Salvation? God cleans away all our sins and replaces them with His goodness. We don't have to be "good" for Him to accept us. Nevertheless, we must accept His promise and allow Him to clean out everything the enemy has left in us. Then we begin to experience the transforming power of His love. It's like a giant war: one side pulling us toward empty pleasure and destruction, and God urging us to accept His offer of peace and purpose.

Remember, Jesus has already won the war. He is victorious! We celebrate His victory in our lives when we participate in the Lord's Supper. This meal includes three symbols:

- Foot washing (which symbolizes our commitment to love others as Jesus loves us),
- bread ("This bread is my flesh," Jesus said, "which I will give for the life of the world," John 6:51, NIV), and
- wine or grape juice ("Whoever eats my flesh and drinks my blood has eternal life." John 6:54, NIV)

To help us understand how God can transform us into His children, Jesus modeled the process of baptism for us. Baptism symbolized dying to self and coming alive in Jesus. Seventh-day Adventists practice full immersion baptism because by being fully buried beneath the water we symbolize that God's grace fully fills us with His new life for the future. Through baptism we are truly born again in Jesus.

Eternal life, peace, purpose, forgiveness, transforming

grace, hope: Everything He promises is ours, because He's offering it and He's shown we can trust Him to do exactly as He promises. Accept His gifts, and you immediately become an active part of His family, and He joyfully becomes part of yours.

Fundamental Beliefs

Seventh-day Adventists accept the Bible as their only creed and hold certain fundamental beliefs to be the teaching of the Holy Scriptures. These beliefs, as set forth here, constitute the church's understanding and expression of the teaching of Scripture. Revision of these statements may be expected at a General Conference session when the church is led by the Holy Spirit to a fuller understanding of Bible truth or finds better language in which to express the teachings of God's Holy Word.

1. *Holy Scriptures:* The Holy Scriptures, Old and New Testaments, are the written Word of God, given by divine inspiration through holy men of God who spoke and wrote as they were moved by the Holy Spirit. In this Word, God has committed to man the knowledge necessary for salvation. The Holy Scriptures are the infallible revelation of His will. They are the standard of character, the test of experience, the authoritative revealer of doctrines, and the trustworthy record of God's acts in history.
2. *Trinity:* There is one God: Father, Son, and Holy Spirit, a unity of three coeternal Persons. God is immortal, all-powerful, all-knowing, above all, and ever present. He is infinite and beyond human comprehension, yet known through His self-revelation. He is forever worthy of worship, adoration, and service by the whole creation.
3. *Father:* God the eternal Father is the Creator, Source, Sustainer, and Sovereign of all creation. He is just and holy, merciful and gracious, slow to anger, and abounding in steadfast love and faithfulness. The qualities and powers exhibited in the Son and the Holy Spirit are also revelations of the Father.

4. *Son:* God the eternal Son became incarnate in Jesus Christ. Through Him all things were created, the character of God is revealed, the salvation of humanity is accomplished, and the world is judged. Forever truly God, He became also truly man, Jesus the Christ. He was conceived of the Holy Spirit and born of the virgin Mary. He lived and experienced temptation as a human being, but perfectly exemplified the righteousness and love of God. By His miracles He manifested God's power and was attested as God's promised Messiah. He suffered and died voluntarily on the cross for our sins and in our place, was raised from the dead, and ascended to minister in the heavenly sanctuary in our behalf. He will come again in glory for the final deliverance of His people and the restoration of all things.
5. *Holy Spirit:* God the eternal Spirit was active with the Father and the Son in Creation, incarnation, and redemption. He inspired the writers of Scripture. He filled Christ's life with power. He draws and convicts human beings; and those who respond He renews and transforms into the image of God. Sent by the Father and the Son to be always with His children, He extends spiritual gifts to the church, empowers it to bear witness to Christ, and in harmony with the Scriptures leads it into all truth.
6. *Creation:* God is Creator of all things, and has revealed in Scripture the authentic account of His creative activity. In six days the Lord made "the heaven and the earth" and all living things upon the earth, and rested on the seventh day of that first week. Thus He established the Sabbath as a perpetual memorial of His completed creative work. The first man and woman were made in the image of God as the crowning work of Creation, given dominion over the world, and charged with responsibility to care for it. When the world was finished it was ``very good," declaring the glory of God.
7. *Nature of Man:* Man and woman were made in the image of God with individuality, the power and freedom to

think and to do. Though created free beings, each is an indivisible unity of body, mind, and spirit, dependent upon God for life and breath and all else. When our first parents disobeyed God, they denied their dependence upon Him and fell from their high position under God. The image of God in them was marred and they became subject to death. Their descendants share this fallen nature and its consequences. They are born with weaknesses and tendencies to evil. But God in Christ reconciled the world to Him and by His Spirit restores in penitent mortals the image of their Maker. Created for the glory of God, they are called to love Him and one another, and to care for their environment.

8. *Great Controversy*: All humanity is now involved in a great controversy between Christ and Satan regarding the character of God, His law, and His sovereignty over the universe. This conflict originated in heaven when a created being, endowed with freedom of choice, in selfexaltation became Satan, God's adversary, and led into rebellion a portion of the angels. He introduced the spirit of rebellion into this world when he led Adam and Eve into sin. This human sin resulted in the distortion of the image of God in humanity, the disordering of the created world, and its eventual devastation at the time of the worldwide flood. Observed by the whole creation, this world became the arena of the universal conflict, out of which the God of love will ultimately be vindicated. To assist His people in this controversy, Christ sends the Holy Spirit and the loyal angels to guide, protect, and sustain them in the way of salvation.
9. *Life, Death, and Resurrection of Christ:* In Christ's life of perfect obedience to God's will, His suffering, death, and resurrection, God provided the only means of atonement for human sin, so that those who by faith accept this atonement may have eternal life, and the whole creation may better understand the infinite and holy love of the Creator. This perfect atonement vindicates the righteousness of God's law and the graciousness of His

character; for it both condemns our sin and provides for our forgiveness. The death of Christ is substitutionary and expiatory, reconciling and transforming. The resurrection of Christ proclaims God's triumph over the forces of evil, and for those who accept the atonement assures their final victory over sin and death. It declares the Lordship of Jesus Christ, before whom every knee in heaven and on earth will bow.

10. *Experience of Salvation:* In infinite love and mercy God made Christ, who knew no sin, to be sin for us, so that in Him we might be made the righteousness of God. Led by the Holy Spirit we sense our need, acknowledge our sinfulness, repent of our transgressions, and exercise faith in Jesus as Lord and Christ, as Substitute and Example. This faith which receives salvation comes through the divine power of the Word and is the gift of God's grace. Through Christ we are justified, adopted as God's sons and daughters, and delivered from the lordship of sin. Through the Spirit we are born again and sanctified; the Spirit renews our minds, writes God's law of love in our hearts, and we are given the power to live a holy life. Abiding in Him we become partakers of the divine nature and have the assurance of salvation now and in the judgment.

11. *Growing in Christ:* By His death on the cross Jesus triumphed over the forces of evil. He who subjugated the demonic spirits during His earthly ministry has broken their power and made certain their ultimate doom. Jesus' victory gives us victory over the evil forces that still seek to control us, as we walk with Him in peace, joy, and assurance of His love. Now the Holy Spirit dwells within us and empowers us. Continually committed to Jesus as our Saviour and Lord, we are set free from the burden of our past deeds. No longer do we live in the darkness, fear of evil powers, ignorance, and meaninglessness of our former way of life. In this new freedom in Jesus, we are called to grow into the likeness of His character, communing with Him daily in prayer,

feeding on His Word, meditating on it and on His providence, singing His praises, gathering together for worship, and participating in the mission of the Church. As we give ourselves in loving service to those around us and in witnessing to His salvation, His constant presence with us through the Spirit transforms every moment and every task into a spiritual experience.

12. *Church:* The church is the community of believers who confess Jesus Christ as Lord and Saviour. In continuity with the people of God in Old Testament times, we are called out from the world; and we join together for worship, for fellowship, for instruction in the Word, for the celebration of the Lord's Supper, for service to all mankind, and for the worldwide proclamation of the gospel. The church derives its authority from Christ, who is the incarnate Word, and from the Scriptures, which are the written Word. The church is God's family; adopted by Him as children, its members live on the basis of the new covenant. The church is the body of Christ, a community of faith of which Christ Himself is the Head. The church is the bride for whom Christ died that He might sanctify and cleanse her. At His return in triumph, He will present her to Himself a glorious church, the faithful of all the ages, the purchase of His blood, not having spot or wrinkle, but holy and without blemish.
13. *Remnant and its Mission:* The universal church is composed of all who truly believe in Christ, but in the last days, a time of widespread apostasy, a remnant has been called out to keep the commandments of God and the faith of Jesus. This remnant announces the arrival of the judgment hour, proclaims salvation through Christ, and heralds the approach of His second advent. This proclamation is symbolized by the three angels of Revelation 14; it coincides with the work of judgment in heaven and results in a work of repentance and reform on earth. Every believer is called to have a personal part in this worldwide witness.
14. *Unity in the Body of Christ:* The church is one body with many members, called from every nation, kindred, tongue,

and people. In Christ we are a new creation; distinctions of race, culture, learning, and nationality, and differences between high and low, rich and poor, male and female, must not be divisive among us. We are all equal in Christ, who by one Spirit has bonded us into one fellowship with Him and with one another; we are to serve and be served without partiality or reservation. Through the revelation of Jesus Christ in the Scriptures we share the same faith and hope, and reach out in one witness to all. This unity has its source in the oneness of the triune God, who has adopted us as His children.

15. *Baptism:* By baptism we confess our faith in the death and resurrection of Jesus Christ, and testify of our death to sin and of our purpose to walk in newness of life. Thus we acknowledge Christ as Lord and Saviour, become His people, and are received as members by His church. Baptism is a symbol of our union with Christ, the forgiveness of our sins, and our reception of the Holy Spirit. It is by immersion in water and is contingent on an affirmation of faith in Jesus and evidence of repentance of sin. It follows instruction in the Holy Scriptures and acceptance of their teachings.

16. *Lord's Supper:* The Lord's Supper is a participation in the emblems of the body and blood of Jesus as an expression of faith in Him, our Lord and Saviour. In this experience of communion Christ is present to meet and strengthen His people. As we partake, we joyfully proclaim the Lord's death until He comes again. Preparation for the Supper includes selfexamination, repentance, and confession. The Master ordained the service of foot washing to signify renewed cleansing, to express a willingness to serve one another in Christlike humility, and to unite our hearts in love. The communion service is open to all believing Christians.

17. *Spiritual Gifts and Ministries:* God bestows upon all members of His church in every age spiritual gifts which each member is to employ in loving ministry for the common good of the church and of humanity. Given by the agency

of the Holy Spirit, who apportions to each member as He wills, the gifts provide all abilities and ministries needed by the church to fulfill its divinely ordained functions. According to the Scriptures, these gifts include such ministries as faith, healing, prophecy, proclamation, teaching, administration, reconciliation, compassion, and selfsacrificing service and charity for the help and encouragement of people. Some members are called of God and endowed by the Spirit for functions recognized by the church in pastoral, evangelistic, apostolic, and teaching ministries particularly needed to equip the members for service, to build up the church to spiritual maturity, and to foster unity of the faith and knowledge of God. When members employ these spiritual gifts as faithful stewards of God's varied grace, the church is protected from the destructive influence of false doctrine, grows with a growth that is from God, and is built up in faith and love.

18. *The Gift of Prophecy:* One of the gifts of the Holy Spirit is prophecy. This gift is an identifying mark of the remnant church and was manifested in the ministry of Ellen. G. White. As the Lord's messenger, her writings are a continuing and authoritative source of truth which provide for the church comfort, guidance, instruction, and correction. They also make clear that the Bible is the standard by which all teaching and experience must be tested.

19. *Law of God:* The great principles of God's law are embodied in the Ten Commandments and exemplified in the life of Christ. They express God's love, will, and purposes concerning human conduct and relationships and are binding upon all people in every age. These precepts are the basis of God's covenant with His people and the standard in God's judgment. Through the agency of the Holy Spirit they point out sin and awaken a sense of need for a Saviour. Salvation is all of grace and not of works, but its fruitage is obedience to the Commandments. This obedience develops Christian

character and results in a sense of wellbeing. It is an evidence of our love for the Lord and our concern for our fellow men. The obedience of faith demonstrates the power of Christ to transform lives, and therefore strengthens Christian witness.

20. *Sabbath:* The beneficent Creator, after the six days of Creation, rested on the seventh day and instituted the Sabbath for all people as a memorial of Creation. The fourth commandment of God's unchangeable law requires the observance of this seventh-day Sabbath as the day of rest, worship, and ministry in harmony with the teaching and practice of Jesus, the Lord of the Sabbath. The Sabbath is a day of delightful communion with God and one another. It is a symbol of our redemption in Christ, a sign of our sanctification, a token of our allegiance, and a foretaste of our eternal future in God's kingdom. The Sabbath is God's perpetual sign of His eternal covenant between Him and His people. Joyful observance of this holy time from evening to evening, sunset to sunset, is a celebration of God's creative and redemptive acts.
21. *Stewardship:* We are God's stewards, entrusted by Him with time and opportunities, abilities and possessions, and the blessings of the earth and its resources. We are responsible to Him for their proper use. We acknowledge God's ownership by faithful service to Him and our fellow men, and by returning tithes and giving offerings for the proclamation of His gospel and the support and growth of His church. Stewardship is a privilege given to us by God for nurture in love and the victory over selfishness and covetousness. The steward rejoices in the blessings that come to others as a result of his faithfulness.
22. *Christian Behavior:* We are called to be a godly people who think, feel, and act in harmony with the principles of heaven. For the Spirit to recreate in us the character of our Lord we involve ourselves only in those things which will produce Christlike purity, health, and joy in

our lives. This means that our amusement and entertainment should meet the highest standards of Christian taste and beauty. While recognizing cultural differences, our dress is to be simple, modest, and neat, befitting those whose true beauty does not consist of outward adornment but in the imperishable ornament of a gentle and quiet spirit. It also means that because our bodies are the temples of the Holy Spirit, we are to care for them intelligently. Along with adequate exercise and rest, we are to adopt the most healthful diet possible and abstain from the unclean foods identified in the Scriptures. Since alcoholic beverages, tobacco, and the irresponsible use of drugs and narcotics are harmful to our bodies, we are to abstain from them as well. Instead, we are to engage in whatever brings our thoughts and bodies into the discipline of Christ, who desires our wholesomeness, joy, and goodness.

23. *Marriage and the Family:* Marriage was divinely established in Eden and affirmed by Jesus to be a lifelong union between a man and a woman in loving companionship. For the Christian a marriage commitment is to God as well as to the spouse, and should be entered into only between partners who share a common faith. Mutual love, honor, respect, and responsibility are the fabric of this relationship, which is to reflect the love, sanctity, closeness, and permanence of the relationship between Christ and His church. Regarding divorce, Jesus taught that the person who divorces a spouse, except for fornication, and marries another, commits adultery. Although some family relationships may fall short of the ideal, marriage partners who fully commit themselves to each other in Christ may achieve loving unity through the guidance of the Spirit and the nurture of the church. God blesses the family and intends that its members shall assist each other toward complete maturity. Parents are to bring up their children to love and obey the Lord. By their example and their words they are to teach them that Christ is a loving

disciplinarian, ever tender and caring, who wants them to become members of His body, the family of God. Increasing family closeness is one of the earmarks of the final gospel message.

24. *Christ's Ministry in the Heavenly Sanctuary:* There is a sanctuary in heaven, the true tabernacle which the Lord set up and not man. In it Christ ministers on our behalf, making available to believers the benefits of His atoning sacrifice offered once for all on the cross. He was inaugurated as our great High Priest and began His intercessory ministry at the time of His ascension. In 1844, at the end of the prophetic period of 2300 days, He entered the second and last phase of His atoning ministry. It is a work of investigative judgment which is part of the ultimate disposition of all sin, typified by the cleansing of the ancient Hebrew sanctuary on the Day of Atonement. In that typical service the sanctuary was cleansed with the blood of animal sacrifices, but the heavenly things are purified with the perfect sacrifice of the blood of Jesus. The investigative judgment reveals to heavenly intelligences who among the dead are asleep in Christ and therefore, in Him, are deemed worthy to have part in the first resurrection. It also makes manifest who among the living are abiding in Christ, keeping the commandments of God and the faith of Jesus, and in Him, therefore, are ready for translation into His everlasting kingdom. This judgment vindicates the justice of God in saving those who believe in Jesus. It declares that those who have remained loyal to God shall receive the kingdom. The completion of this ministry of Christ will mark the close of human probation before the Second Advent.
25. *Second Coming of Christ:* The second coming of Christ is the blessed hope of the church, the grand climax of the gospel. The Saviour's coming will be literal, personal, visible, and worldwide. When He returns, the righteous dead will be resurrected, and together with the righteous living will be glorified and taken to heaven, but the

unrighteous will die. The almost complete fulfillment of most lines of prophecy, together with the present condition of the world, indicates that Christ's coming is imminent. The time of that event has not been revealed, and we are therefore exhorted to be ready at all times.

26. *Death and Resurrection:* The wages of sin is death. But God, who alone is immortal, will grant eternal life to His redeemed. Until that day death is an unconscious state for all people. When Christ, who is our life, appears, the resurrected righteous and the living righteous will be glorified and caught up to meet their Lord. The second resurrection, the resurrection of the unrighteous, will take place a thousand years later.
27. *Millennium and the End of Sin:* The millennium is the thousand-year reign of Christ with His saints in heaven between the first and second resurrections. During this time the wicked dead will be judged; the earth will be utterly desolate, without living human inhabitants, but occupied by Satan and his angels. At its close Christ with His saints and the Holy City will descend from heaven to earth. The unrighteous dead will then be resurrected, and with Satan and his angels will surround the city; but fire from God will consume them and cleanse the earth. The universe will thus be freed of sin and sinners forever.
28. *New Earth:* On the new earth, in which righteousness dwells, God will provide an eternal home for the redeemed and a perfect environment for everlasting life, love, joy, and learning in His presence. For here God Himself will dwell with His people, and suffering and death will have passed away. The great controversy will be ended, and sin will be no more. All things, animate and inanimate, will declare that God is love; and He shall reign forever. Amen.

7

World Religion

Judaism and its Belief System

The Old Testament books of the Bible describe numerous struggles of the Jewish people. After their triumphant Exodus from Egyptian captivity following Moses, they wandered around in the desert for forty years before entering the Promised Land. They had many conflicts with neighboring societies, yet for several centuries were able to maintain a unified state centered in Jerusalem. This occupation of the Promised Land was not to last, however. In 722 BC, the northern part of the Hebrew state fell to Assyrian raiders. By 586 BC, Jerusalem was conquered by Babylonians. The land of Israel was successively ruled by Persians, Macedonians, Greeks, Syrians, and Romans in the time that followed. As a result of the Syrian King Antiochus IV Epiphanes' attempt to suppress the Jewish religion, a rebellion led by Judas Maccabaeus in 167 BC resulted in the independence of the Jewish nation. This is celebrated today by the festival Hanukkah.

In 70 AD, the Roman army destroyed Jerusalem, and the Jews were forced out of the area and settled in Mediterranean countries and in other areas in southwest Asia. This migration of the Jewish population is known as Diaspora. Many of these Jews settled in Europe and became victims of persecution and poverty. Ghettoes and slums became their homes and massacres were common. Because of these living conditions, many fled to the United States in the late 19th century. Migration to the States especially climbed during the aftermath of the Holocaust, the organized murder of Jews during and after World War II. Today the United States has the largest population of Jewish people with high concentration areas in New York, Los Angeles, Chicago, Boston, Miami, and Washington D.C.

In 1917, an attempt to reestablish Palestine as the Jewish homeland began. By 1948, the State of Israel became an independent country. They have regained their Hebrew language, which involved inventing words for modern inventions and concepts unheard of centuries ago and writing a Hebrew dictionary to unify the language.

Judaism is one of the world's four great monotheistic religions. It is identified as the religious culture of Jewish people and makes up the cultural system of Jewish law, tradition, and customs. It is also the smallest with a following of around 15 million people worldwide. Judaism is inextricably linked with a system of beliefs.

Origins of Judaism

Judaism originated in the Middle-East and has spread all over the world. It is considered that the Patriarchs of Abraham, Isaac and Jacob, are the founders of Judaism. They are also known as the physical and spiritual ancestors of Judaism. Jews derive their history from the written Torah, Talmud, Midrash and other sources. Judaism is considered the first religion to be based on ethical monotheism. It also influenced the early development of Christianity and Islam with a major impact on western civilization.

Central Beliefs

The most central belief is about the existence of one God who created the world and continues to rule it. It is also believed that God revealed himself to the Israelis at Mount

Sinai. The "Torah" is the content of the revelation. Another fundamental is the covenant between God and the Israeli. The Jews would obey and acknowledge God. God will also acknowledge the "Jewish people" as his chosen one. Jews believe Christ was just another prophet and God is yet to deliver them the promised "deliverer" of Humanity which will also deliver all people Justice and Peace in a messianic age.

Judaism in Practice

The "Torah" is considered the holy book of Jews. Studying the ' Torah ' is considered as an act of worship. On each sabbath and festivals, the 'Torah" is read religiously. In the Jewish year, major festivals include passover, Shabuoth, Sukkot, Rosh Hashanah, and Yom Kippur and two minor ones; Hanukkah and Purim. Synagogues or temples are a central institution of Jews since it is used for community prayer, studying and praying.

Synagogues may vary in style and design but have the same common components such as the everlasting flame burning only in front of the ark. Rabbis are the spiritual leaders of the Jewish community. A Rabbi is a formally educated teacher in Jewish Law (Halakhah). He instructs the community, settle disputes and answers questions regarding the Jewish law. He cannot perform rituals.

Judaism is one of the oldest religions still existing today. It began as the religion of the small nation of the Hebrews, and through thousands of years of suffering, persecution, dispersion, and occasional victory, has continued to be a profoundly influential religion and culture. Today, 14 million people identify themselves as Jews, and nearly 3.5 billion others follow belief systems directly influenced by Judaism (including Christianity, Islam, and the Bah'ai Faith). Modern Judaism is a complex phenomenon that incorporates both a nation and a religion, and often combines strict adherence to ritual laws with a more liberal attitude towards religious belief.

The central religious belief of Judaism is that there is only one God. Monotheism was uncommon at the time Judaism was born, but according to Jewish tradition, God himself revealed it to Abraham, the ancestor of the Jewish people. Beginning with Abraham, God has always taken special care of the Hebrews (who would later become the Jews). After rescuing them from slavery in Egypt, God revealed the Ten Commandments to Moses, and many more religious and ethical guidelines in the Torah ("the Law"). Many of the guidelines (*mitzvah*) emphasized ritual purity and the importance of remaining set apart from the surrounding polytheistic cultures.

Aside from its staunch monotheism, Judaism has few essential beliefs. Jewish identity arises primarily from belonging to an ancient people and upholding its traditions. Dogma, while important, is secondary. Although the medieval thinker Rabbi Maimonides once enumerated "13 Articles of Faith," many Jews do not accept all these, and Jewish beliefs vary widely on theological matters such as human nature and the afterlife.

Divisions within Judaism, known as "movements," have developed in modern times as varying responses to secularism and modernity. Orthodox Judaism is the most conservative group, retaining nearly all traditional rituals and practices. At the opposite end of the spectrum, Reform Jews retain their Jewish identity and some traditions but take a liberal approach to many Jewish beliefs and practices. Conservative Judaism lies in the middle of the spectrum, taking a moderate approach in its application of Judaism to the modern world.

Jews of all movement celebrate many special days throughout the year and throughout each person's life. Major religious holidays include Passover, Rosh Hashanah and Yom Kippur. Hanukkah, historically a minor holiday, has become more prominent in the last century for Jews who live in areas that celebrate Christmas. The Sabbath, a day of rest and worship at the synagogue, is observed each Saturday. In Judaism, all days begin at sunset, so all holidays begin at sundown and end at sundown.

To recognize the role of God and the Jewish community in each person's life, numerous life cycle events are observed with traditional rituals. At the first Sabbath after the birth of a child, the proud father is called forward in the synagogue to recite blessings for mother and child. Eight days after birth, baby boys are circumcised.

At the age of 13 (12 for girls), a boy becomes a Bar Mitzvah, or "Son of the Commandment" and a girl becomes a Bat Mitzvah, "Daughter of the Commandment." The occasion is marked by the youth's first public reading of the Torah in the synagogue (only boys may do this in Orthodox congregations), followed by a large and joyous celebration.

Jewish wedding ceremonies incorporate many ancient traditions and symbolic gestures (including the well-known breaking of glass), and divorces are obtained within the Jewish community. At death, a Jewish person's body is cared for by the *chevra kiddisha,* the "holy society," who washes the body and prepares it for burial. The deceased is treated with great respect and never left alone. After burial, the deceased's loved ones enter a formal period of mourning, which decreased gradually over the course of a year. The dead is then remembered and honored each year on the anniversary of death.

In addition to these special days and ceremonies, the Jewish life is marked by regular religious observance. Each Saturday, Sabbath is observed by ceasing work and spending the day in worships at the synagogue and at home with family. The study of Torah and other Jewish scriptures is considered very important, and many Jewish children attend Hebrew school so they can study it in its original language. In everyday life, traditional Jews observe the laws of *kashrut,* eating only foods that God has designated "kosher." Among non-kosher, or prohibited, foods are pork, any meat that has not been ritually slaughtered, shellfish, and any meal that combines dairy with meat.

Jewish Beliefs

Unlike Christianity and Islam, Judaism has no official creed or universal doctrinal requirements for membership. In general, a person can be considered "Jewish" whether he adheres to a complete system of beliefs about God and the afterlife, holds only a few simple beliefs that give meaning to ritual, or even (at least in liberal Judaism) does not believe in God at all.

This diversity in Jewish belief arises in part because actions (good deeds and the *mitzvot*), not beliefs, are the most important aspect of Jewish religious life. In addition, the term "Jewish" can be used to describe a race and a culture rather than a religion, so some who identify themselves as Jewish may have little interest in the beliefs and practices associated with the religion of Judaism.

Nevertheless, the Torah and Talmud have a great deal to say about God, humanity, and the meaning of life, and Jewish history has seen significant theological and mystical inquiry into religious concepts. These beliefs are of great significance not only for Judaism itself, but also for their direct influence on Christianity and Islam, currently the two largest religions in the world.

The Thirteen Articles of Faith

Many of the "Beliefs" sections on Religion Facts begin with an official list of essential beliefs agreed upon by all orthodox followers of the faith. But as noted in the introduction, Judaism has no such list.

However, the great 12th-century Rabbi Maimonides put together "13 Articles of Faith" that he believed every Jew ought to adhere to. These have been widely accepted as a proper expression of the Jewish faith and they still appear in Jewish prayer books today. So while it is not necessary to believe all of these articles to be Jewish (and in fact many Jews would likely question one or more of the articles) they serve as a good general summary of religious Judaism.

The 13 Articles of the Jewish Faith proposed by Maimonides are these:

1. God exists.

2. God is one and unique.
3. God is incorporeal.
4. God is eternal.
5. Prayer is to God only.
6. The prophets spoke truth.
7. Moses was the greatest of the prophets.
8. The Written and Oral Torah were given to Moses.
9. There will be no other Torah.
10. God knows the thoughts and deeds of men.
11. God will reward the good and punish the wicked.
12. The Messiah will come.
13. The dead will be resurrected.

Jewish Beliefs about God

In Judaism, ultimate reality is a single, all-powerful God. It is this belief that made the Jews unique among other ancient Semitic peoples and that became the legacy Judaism has passed on to the entire Western world. The sacred name of God, as revealed to Moses in the book of Exodus, is YHWH. Since ancient Hebrew was written without vowels, we do not know the original pronunciation of this word. The common pronunciation "Jehovah," however, is incorrect. It is derived from combining the vowels for Adonai ("Lord") with the four consonants of YHWH.

A more "correct" pronunciation, and that which is used among scholars, is "Yahweh." The discussion is irrelevant to observant Jews, however, as they do not pronounce this holiest of names. When the Torah is read aloud, Adonai ("Lord") is read in its place. This practice is reflected in most English translations, in which YHWH is rendered "LORD." Jews also refer to God as Hashem, "the Name." The word YHWH is sometimes referred to as the Tetragrammaton, from the Greek for "four-lettered."

It is also called The Forbidden Name or the Unutterable Name. The prohibition against pronouncing this name does not originate with the command to not take the Lord's name in vain, as is sometimes thought. Although traditionally this only applies to the Name in Hebrew, some modern Jews also refrain from writing the word "God," replacing it instead with "God." Opinions vary within Judaism as to the necessity of such a practice.

The Messiah in Judaism

Many of the world's religions have hope in a future heroic figure who will rescue the righteous, judge the wicked, and restore peace to the world (Krishna in Hinduism, Maitreya in Buddhism and the Second Coming in Christianity). In Judaism, this figure is the messiah. Christians believe the messiah has come in the form of Jesus of Nazareth; Jews emphatically do not.

Identity of the Messiah

The concept of the messiah seems to have developed in later Judaism. The Torah contains no specific reference to him, though some Jewish scholars have pointed out that it does speak of the "End of Days," which is the time of the messiah. The Tanakh gives several specifications as to who the messiah will be. He will be a descendent of King David (2 Samuel 7:12-13; Jeremiah 23:5), observant of Jewish law (Isaiah 11:2-5), a righteous judge (Jeremiah 33:15), and a great military leader.

Jews do not believe that the messiah will be divine. A fundamental difference between Judaism and Christianity is the Jewish conviction that God is so essentially different from and beyond humanity that he could never become a human. Moreover, Jews find no foundation in the scriptures for such a belief about the messiah. Passages viewed by Christians as indicating a divine messiah (such as the suffering servant of Isaiah 53) are viewed by Jews as speaking of the people of Israel. In general, only the following passages are accepted as referring to the messiah:

- Isaiah 2, 11, 42; 59:20
- Jeremiah 23, 30, 33; 48:47; 49:39
- Ezekiel 38:16

- Hosea 3:4-3:5
- Micah 4
- Zephaniah 3:9
- Zechariah 14:9
- Daniel 10:14

The "when" of the messiah's arrival is not made clear in the Tanach, and has been a source of much scholarly speculation. In general, attempts to predict the exact date are discouraged. Though millennial fervor has never been as strong in Judaism as it has been in Christian and Islamic movements, there have been those who either claimed to be the messiah or to know the date of the messiah's arrival. One notable example of the former is Shabbatai Tzvi, a 17th-century man who claimed to the messiah, then converted to Islam under threat of death.

A wide variety of opinions have been given by Jewish scholars as to the circumstances that will prompt the messiah's arrival. Some say the messiah will come when the world is especially good; others say when the world has become especially evil. The biblical clues that are offered suggest the messiah will come after a period of war and suffering (Ezekiel 38:16).

The Messianic Age

When the messiah does come, he will inaugurate the messianic age (sometimes called the Olam Ha-Ba, World to Come). The Tanakh employs the following descriptions about this period:

- Peace among all nations (Isaiah 2:4; Micah 4:3)
- Perfect harmony and abundance in nature (Isaiah 11:6-9) (but some interpret this as an allegory for peace and prosperity)
- All Jews return from exile to Israel (Isaiah 11:11-12; Jeremiah 23:8; 30:3; Hosea 3:4-5)
- Universal acceptance of the Jewish God and Jewish religion (Isaiah 2:3; 11:10; 66:23; Micah 4:2-3; Zechariah 14:9)

- No sin or evil; all Israel will obey the commandments (Zephaniah 3:13; Ezekiel 37:24)
- Reinstatement of the Temple (Ezekiel 37:26-27)

Ezekiel 37:24-28 sums up many of these requirements when it proclaims: And David my servant shall be king over them; and they shall all have one shepherd. They shall also follow my judgments and observe my statutes, and do them. And they shall dwell in the land that I have given to Yaakov my servant, in which your fathers have dwelt and they shall dwell there, they and their children, and their children's children forever; and my servant David shall be their prince forever.

Moreover, I will make a covenant of peace with them, it shall be an everlasting covenant with them, which I will give them; and I will multiply them and I will set my sanctuary in the midst of them forevermore. And my tabernacle shall be with them: and I will be their God and they will be my people. Then the nations shall know that I am the Lord who sanctifies Israel, when my sanctuary will be in the midst of them forevermore.

Jewish Beliefs about Human Nature

A fundamental Jewish belief about human beings is that they are created in the image of God. This does not mean that we look like God, for God is incorporeal. The general rabbinical interpretation of this concept is that humans have the ability to reason. When Genesis 2:7 says "God formed man," it uses the Hebrew word *vayyitzer* ("formed"). The Talmud finds special meaning in the unique spelling of the word in this context, with two *yods* instead of one. The two *yods,* the rabbis explain, stand for the two impulses found in humans: the *yetzer tov* and the *yetzer ra.*

According to this view, the *yetzer tov* is the moral conscience that reminds a person of God's law when one considers a specific action or choice. The *yetzer ra* is the impulse to satisfy one's own needs and desires. There is nothing intrinsically evil about the *yetzer ra,* as it was created by God and is, natural to humankind. It is also what drives us to good things such as eating, drinking, having a family, and making a living. However, it can easily lead to sin when not kept in check by the *yetzer tov*. The idea of human free will is fundamental to Judaism. The concept of original sin is rejected, and every person has the ability to choose good or evil.

The following rabbinical teaching is illustrative of the Jewish view of the soul:

This may be compared to the case of a king who had an orchard containing excellent early figs, and he placed there two watchmen, one lame and the other blind. He said to them: "Be careful with these fine early figs." After some days the lame man said to the blind one: "I see fine early figs in the orchard" said the blind man to him: "Come let us eat them." "Am I then able to walk?" said the lame man. "Can I then see?" retorted the blind man. The lame man got astride the blind man, and thus they ate the early figs and sat down again each in his place.

After some days the king came into that vineyard and said to them: "Where are the fine early figs?" The blind man replied: "My lord, the king, can I then see?" The lame man replied: "My lord the king, can I then walk?" What did the king, who was a man of insight, do with them? He placed the lame man astride the blind man, and they began to move about said the king to them: "Thus have you done, and eaten the early figs."

Even so will the Holy One, blessed be God, in the time to come, say to the soul: "Why have you sinned before Me?" and the soul will answer: O Master of the universe, it is not I that sinned, but the body it is that sinned. Why, since leaving it, I am like a clean bird flying through the air. As for me, how have I sinned?" God will also say to the body: "Why have you sinned before Me?" and the body will reply: "O Master of the universe, not I have sinned, the soul it is that has sinned. Why, since it left me, I am cast about like a stone thrown upon the ground. Have I then sinned before you?" What will the Holy One, blessed be God, do to them? God will bring the soul and force it into the body, and judge both as one.

Jewish Beliefs on the After Life

Jewish sacred texts and literature have little to say about what happens after death. This may seem surprising to non-Jews, since the sacred texts of Christianity and Islam (both of which have their foundations in Judaism) elaborate rather fully about the afterlife. But Judaism is much more focused on actions than beliefs, so it is actually to be expected that its prophets and sages have not spent as much time on speculations about the world to come as elaborations on the *mitzvot* to be performed in this life.

The Torah and Talmud alike focus on the purpose of earthly life, which is to fulfill one's duties to God and one's fellow man. Succeeding at this brings reward, failing at it brings punishment. Whether rewards and punishments continue after death, or whether anything at all happens after death, is not as important. Despite the subject's general exclusion from the Jewish sacred texts, however, Judaism does incorporate views on the afterlife. Yet unlike the other monotheistic religions, no one view has ever been officially agreed upon, and there is much room for speculation.

This section will begin with a look at biblical texts addressing the afterlife, and then explore various Jewish views on subjects such as the resurrection of the dead, judgment, heaven and hell, and the messianic age. The Hebrew word Olam Ha-Ba ("the world to come") is used for both the messianic age and the afterlife. The world to come is important and something to look forward to. A Mishnah passage says, "This world is like a lobby before the Olam Ha-Ba. Prepare yourself in the lobby so that you may enter the banquet hall." The tractate Moed Katan teaches, "This world is only like a hotel. The world to come is like a home."

Yet it is also emphasized that this world provides the ability and privilege of doing good works and performing the *mitzvot*: "Rabbi Yaakov also used to say, 'Better one hour in repentance and good deeds in this world than all the life in the world to come. And better one hour of tranquility of spirit in the world to come than all the life of this world.'" (Pirkei Avos, Chapters of the Fathers)

The After Life in the Torah

For the most part, the Torah describes the afterlife in vague terms, many of which may simply be figurative ways of speaking about death as it is observed by the living. An early common theme is that death means rejoining one's ancestors. Abraham, Isaac, Jacob, Moses, and other patriarchs are "gathered to their people" after death and in contrast, the wicked are "cut off (*kareit*) from their people". Other imagery emphasizes the finality of death: the dead are like dust returning to dust (Genesis; Ecc. 3:19-20) or water poured out on the ground (2 Samuel 14:14).

Another recurring biblical image of the afterlife is as a shadowy place called Sheol. It is a place of darkness (Psalm 88:13, Job 10:21, 22) and silence (Psalm 115:17), located in low places (Numbers 16:30, Ezekiel 31:14, Psalm 88:7, Lamentations 3:55; Jonah 2:7, Job 26:5). In 1 Samuel 2:6, God puts people in She'ol. In Isaiah 14:9-10, the departed in Sheol rise up to greet leaders who have now been brought low as they are. The author of Psalm 88 laments his impending death with these words:

I am sated with misfortune; I am at the brink of Sheol.

I am numbered with those who go down to the Pit;

I am a helpless man

Abandoned among the dead,

like bodies lying in the grave

of whom You are mindful no more,

and who are cut off from Your care.

You have put me at the bottom of the Pit,

in the darkest places, in the depths.

(Psalm 88:4-7)

Taken together, these early biblical descriptions of death seem to indicate that the soul continues to exist in some way after death, but not consciously. Later in the Torah, the concept of conscious life after death begins to develop. Daniel 12:2 declares, "And many of them that sleep in the dust of the earth shall awake, some to everlasting life and some to reproaches and everlasting abhorrence." Neh. 9:5.

Tehiyat Hameitim: Resurrection of the Dead

More developed concepts of the resurrection of the dead and afterlife seem to have entered Judaism under Hellenistic influence after the Torah was completed. It became one of the fundamental beliefs in rabbinic Judaism, the intellectual successors of the Pharisees. The Sadducees, familiar to New Testament readers as those who denied the resurrection, were an exception. As seen above, the resurrection of the dead is one of Maimonides' "13 Articles of Belief," and the frequently-recited Shemoneh Esrei prayer contains several references to the resurrection.

How this resurrection might occur has been a matter of speculation. Rabbi Hiyya ben Joseph suggested that "the dead will come up through the ground and rise up in Jerusalem... and the righteous will rise up fully clothed" (Babylonian Talmud, tractate Ketubot 111b). Saadia ben Yosef al-Fayyumi (892-942 C.E.), the head of the academy of Sura, offered this explanation:

Even fire, which causes things to be burned so quickly, merely effects the separation of the parts of a thing...,causing the dust part to return to ashes....It does not however, bring about the annihilation of anything. Nor is it conceivable that anyone should have the power to annihilate anything to the point where it would vanish completely except its Creator, who produced it out of nothing. Since then the matter can be thus explained, in view of the fact that none of the constituent parts of the human being who has been devoured could have been annihilated, they must all have been set aside, wheresoever they may have taken up, whether it be on land or sea, until such time as they are restored in their entirety.

Nor would such restoration be any more remarkable than their original creation.

Today, most traditional Jewish movements accept the concept of the resurrection of the dead. A notable exception is Reform Judaism, which official rejects the doctrine.

Judgment

Traditional Judaism includes belief in both heaven and hell. How is one's destination decided? The School of Shammai offered this description:

There will be three groups on the Day of Judgment: one of thoroughly righteous people, one of thoroughly wicked people and one of people in between. The first group will be immediately inscribed for everlasting life; the second group will be doomed in Gehinnom [Hell], as it says, "And many of them that sleep in the dust of the earth shall awake, some to everlasting life and some to reproaches and everlasting abhorrence" [Daniel 12:2], the third will go down to Gehinnom and squeal and rise again, as it says, "And I will bring the third part through the fire, and will refine them as silver is refined, and will try them as gold is tried. They shall call on My name and I will answer them" [Zechariah 13:9]... [Babylonian Talmud, tractate Rosh Hashanah 16b-17a]

The school of Hillel suggested a more merciful view, in which the middle group is sent directly to Gan Eden (Heaven) instead of Gehinnom after death. Rabbi Hanina added that all who go down to Gehinnom will go up again, except adulterers, those who put their fellows to shame in public, and those who call their fellows by an obnoxious name [Babylonian Talmud, tractate Baba Metzia 58b].

The Talmud teaches that all Israel will have a share in Olam Ha-Ba, but makes some notable exceptions:

All Israelites have a share in the world-to-come... [However], these are they that have no share in the world-to-come: one who says there is no resurrection of the dead prescribed in the Torah, and that the Torah is not from Heaven, and an Epicurean. (Sanhedrin 10:1)

General Jewish belief is that one need not be Jewish to enjoy Heaven. "Moses Maimonides, echoing the Tosefta to Sanhedrin, maintained that the pious of all the nations of the world have a portion in the world-to-come [Mishneh Torah, Repentance 3:5]."

Gan Eden: Heaven

In Judaism, the eternal destination for the righteous is Gan Eden (the Garden of Eden). It is generally described as a place of great joy and peace. Talmudic imagery includes: sitting at golden banquet tables (Babylonian Talmud, tractate Taanit 25a) or at stools of gold (Babylonian Talmud, tractate Ketubot 77b), enjoying lavish banquets (Babylonian Talmud, tractate Baba Batra 75a), or celebrating the Sabbath, enjoying sunshine and sexual intercourse (Babylonian Talmud, tractate Berachot 57b).

On the other hand, other sages have offered a more spiritual view of Gad Eden. Rav suggested that there will be neither eating nor drinking; no procreation of children or business transactions, no envy or hatred or rivalry; but sitting enthroned, their crowns on their heads, enjoying the Shechinah [Babylonian Talmud, tractate Berachot 17a (3rd century CE)]. Maimonides agreed, explaining:

In the world to come, there is nothing corporeal, and no material substance; there are only souls of the righteous without bodies — like the ministering angels... The righteous attain to a knowledge and realization of truth concerning God to which they had not attained while they were in the murky and lowly body. (Mishneh Torah, Repentance 8)

Gehinnom: Hell

The Jewish concept of the afterlife for the wicked is less developed. Known as Gehinnom (Gehenna in Yiddish) or Sheo'l, it has its foundations in the dark pit described in the Torah and an actual place where a pagan cult conducted rituals included burning children. Gehinnom is the postmortem destination of unrighteous Jews and Gentiles. In one reference, the souls in Gehinnom are punished for up to 12 months. After the appropriate period of purification, the righteous continue on to Gan Eden (Rabbi Akiba and Babylonian Talmud, tractate Eduyot 2:10). The wicked endure the full year of punishment then are either annihilated ("After 12 months, their body is consumed and their soul is burned and the wind scatters them under the soles of the feet of the righteous (Rosh Hashanah 17a)") or continue to be punished.

This belief is the basis for the Jewish practice of mourning and asking blessings on deceased loved ones for only 11 months (one would not wish to imply that the departed needed the full 12 months of purification).

The Messianic Age

The messianic age is a period in human history that will be initiated when the messiah comes. At that time the righteous dead will be resurrected, but the wicked will not. The messianic age will be a time of peace and the restoration of the land and organizations of Israel.

Founded a century and a half ago, the Bahá'í Faith is today among the fastest-growing of the world's religions. With more than five million followers, who reside in virtually every nation on earth, it is the second-most widespread faith, surpassing every religion but Christianity in its geographic reach. Bahá'ís reside in more than 100,000 localities around the world, an expansion that reflects their dedication to the ideal of world citizenship. The Bahá'í Faith's global scope is mirrored in the composition of its membership. Representing a cross section of humanity, Bahá'ís come from virtually every nation, ethnic group, culture, profession, and social or economic class. More than 2,100 different ethnic and tribal groups are represented.

Since it also forms a single community, free of schism or factions, the Bahá'í Faith comprises what is very likely the most diverse and widespread organized body of people on earth. People of virtually every background, in every nation, have become Bahá'ís. Many are members of the Aymara and Quechua indigenous groups.

The Faith's Founder was Bahá'u'lláh, a Persian nobleman from Tehran who, in the mid-nineteenth century, left a life of princely comfort and security and, in the face of intense persecution and deprivation, brought to humanity a stirring new message of peace and unity. Bahá'u'lláh claimed to be nothing less than a new and independent Messenger from God. His life, work, and influence parallel that of Abraham, Krishna, Moses, Zoroaster, Buddha, Christ, and Muhammad. Bahá'ís view Bahá'u'lláh as the most recent in this succession of divine Messengers.

The essential message of Bahá'u'lláh is that of unity. He taught that there is only one God, that there is only one human race, and that all the world's religions represent stages in the revelation of God's will and purpose for humanity. In this day, Bahá'u'lláh said, humanity has collectively come of age. As foretold in all of the world's scriptures, the time has arrived for the uniting of all peoples into a peaceful and integrated global society. "The earth is but one country and mankind its citizens," He wrote.

The youngest of the world's independent religions, the Faith founded by Bahá'u'lláh stands out from other religions in a number of ways. It has a unique system of global administration, with freely elected governing councils in nearly 10,000 localities. It takes a distinctive approach to contemporary social problems. The Faith's scriptures and the multifarious activities of its membership address virtually every important trend in the world today, from new thinking about cultural diversity and environmental conservation to the decentralization of decision making; from a renewed commitment to family life and moral values to the call for social and economic justice in a world that is rapidly becoming a global neighborhood.

The Faith's most distinctive accomplishment by far, however, is its unity. Unlike every other religion — not to mention most social and political movements — the Bahá'í community has successfully resisted the perennial impulse to divide into sects and subgroups. It has maintained its unity despite a history as turbulent as that of any religion of antiquity.

In the years since Bahá'u'lláh lived, the process of global unification for which He called has become well-advanced. Through historical processes, the traditional barriers of race, class, creed, and nation have steadily broken down. The forces at work, Bahá'u'lláh predicted, will eventually give birth to a universal civilization. The principal challenge facing the peoples of the earth is to accept the fact of their oneness and assist in the creation of this new world.

For a global society to flourish, Bahá'u'lláh said, it must be based on certain fundamental principles. They include the elimination of all forms of prejudice; full equality between the sexes; recognition of the essential oneness of the world's great religions; the elimination of extremes of poverty and wealth; universal education; the harmony of science and religion; a sustainable balance between nature and technology; and the establishment of a world federal system, based on collective security and the oneness of humanity.

Bahá'ís around the world express their commitment to these principles chiefly through individual and community transformation, including the large number of small-scale, grassroots-based social and economic development projects that Bahá'í communities have launched in recent years.

8

World Religions

Bahai's and its Belief System

Compatible with Christianity

The Baha'i faith incorporates many familiar Christian themes, words, and select scriptures into its beliefs; however, the Bible would have to be radically reinterpreted to fit Baha'i theology. Baha'is claim that the Bible has been misinterpreted and misunderstood by Christians for thousands of years, and therefore must be reinterpreted through Baha'i, which they believe is the true Christianity. Much like Mormonism, Islam and other religions founded by false prophets, Baha'i teaches that they have restored Christianity to its true form.

Unlike Mormonism and Islam, however, they claim that Baha'u'llah was not just a prophet but the actual Messiah and a fulfillment of the prophesied Second Coming. This belief alone reveals serious flaws in their interpretation of the Bible.

The prophecies of the Bible that are yet to be fulfilled before Christ returns are simply reinterpreted or ignored to support their belief that the Messiah has already returned. A look at other Baha'i beliefs further demonstrates the vast differences between the Baha'i faith and Biblical Christianity.

God is Unknowable

One goal of the Baha'i movement is to bring about an

all-inclusive global faith under a federalist world government. Their views on the nature of God reflect this desire to include all beliefs, gods, and religions neatly into their belief system. In Baha'i thought, people can never really know God personally.

They teach that God is so far beyond humans that no one can really know the essence of God. While Baha'i is clearly a monotheistic faith, an unknowable God means any god will fit the mold, whether it be Allah, Yahweh or Brahma. By ignoring what the Bible has to say about God, and putting him out of man's reach, they are free to worship anything and, in some cases, everything as God. By contrast, the Bible tells us that God reveals Himself to us (Hebrews 1:1-2), wants to be known (Isaiah 45:22-25; Hosea 11:1-11), and invites us into a relationship with Him (John 14:23; Revelation 3:20). He also makes false teachings about God evidence of a false prophet, and deserving of punishment (Deuteronomy 13:1-5).

Bahá'í Beliefs about God

Bahá'ís believe that there is only one God, the Creator of the universe. This one God has absolute control over His creation (omnipotence) as well as complete knowledge of it (omniscience). Bahá'u'lláh emphasized that God is entirely self-sufficient and independent of all His creation. He has no need of human worship or allegiance, so the obedience he asks of humankind is entirely for the benefit of individuals and motivated only by his love for them.

Bahá'ís teach that although we may have different concepts of God's nature and call Him by different names – Allah or Yahweh, God or Brahma – nevertheless, we are speaking about the same unique Being. According to the Bahá'í Faith, God is ultimately unknowable. Humans rightly describe God as the All-Powerful, the All-Loving, the Infinitely Just, but such terms are derived from a limited human experience of power, love, or justice. To remedy this, God has sent a series of divine Messengers to humanity.

Prophets and Messengers

Bah'ai believes that God is so beyond the limits of human understand that he is ultimately unknowable. To overcome this obstacle, God has made his nature and will known to humanity through means of a series of Messengers or Manifestations. Each of these Messengers – which include Abraham, Krishna, Zoroaster, Moses, Buddha, Jesus, and Muhammad – has founded a great religion. These Manifestations of God each revealed the attributes and will of God that was appropriate to the time.

In this way, God has gradually revealed more of himself and his desire for humanity over thousands of years. This idea - known as Progressive Revelation - is central to Bahá'í doctrine. The most recent Manifestation of God was Bahá'u'lláh, whose message of unity and social justice ushered in a new age of divine revelation. The previous prophets are no less valid or respected, but Bahá'u'lláh's revelation supercedes them in that it is the most recent and most relevant for our time. All the Messengers or Manifestations of God are highly exalted in the Bahá'í Faith, as they provide the most complete knowledge of God available to humanity.

Human Nature and the Soul

According to Bahá'í teachings, human nature is fundamentally spiritual and the essential identity of each person is defined by an invisible, rational, and everlasting soul. Although undetectable by physical instruments, the soul shows itself through the qualities of character that we associate with each person. The soul is the focal point for love and compassion, for faith and courage, and for other such "human" qualities that cannot be explained solely by thinking of a human being as an animal or as a sophisticated organic machine.

The soul animates the body and distinguishes human beings from the animals. It grows and develops only through the individual's relationship with God, as mediated by His Messengers. The relationship is fostered through prayer, knowledge of the scriptures revealed by these Teachers, love for God, moral self-discipline, and service to humanity. This process is what gives meaning to life.

Despite its emphasis on the soul, the Bahá'í Faith does not encourage a negative view of the body.

Sin, Satan and Evil

The Bahá'í Faith rejects the concept of "original sin" or any doctrine that teaches people are basically evil or have intrinsically evil elements in their nature. All the forces and faculties within us are God-given and thus potentially beneficial to our spiritual development. However, if a person, through his own God-given free will, turns away from this force or fails to make the necessary effort to develop his spiritual capacities, the result is imperfection. `Abdu'l-Bahá said that "evil is imperfection."

The Bahá'í Faith denies the existence of Satan, a devil, or an "evil force." Evil does not have independence existence, but is rather the absence of good, just as darkness is the absence of light and cold is the absence of heat. Just as the sun is the unique source of all life in a solar system, so ultimately is there only one force or power in the universe, the force we call God.

Bahá'u'lláh explained that references to Satan in the Scriptures of earlier religions are symbolic and should not be taken literally. Satan is the personification of man's lower nature which can destroy him if it is not brought into harmony with his spiritual nature. There is, in fact, a well-known philosophical problem concerning God's goodness and omnipotence and the possible existence of a Satan. This problem is discussed in some detail in both the writings of Bahá'u'lláh and 'Abdu'l-Bahá.

Sin and Salvation

According to Bahá'u'lláh, pride or self-centeredness is one of the greatest hindrances to spiritual progress. Pride represents an exaggerated sense of one's own importance in the universe and leads to an attitude of superiority over others.

The prideful person feels in absolute control of his life and the circumstances surrounding it and he seeks power and dominance over others because such power helps him maintain this illusion of superiority. Pride is such a hindrance to spiritual growth because it impels the prideful individual on an endless quest to fulfill the expectations of his vainly-conceived and illusory self-concept.

In the Bahá'í notion of spiritual progress, whatever is conducive to spiritual progress is good, and whatever tends to hinder spiritual progress is bad. This doctrine reminds one of the Buddhist perspectives. From the Bahá'í viewpoint, learning "right" from "wrong" means attaining a degree of self-knowledge that permits us to know when something is helpful to our spiritual growth and when it is not. And this knowledge can only be obtained through the teachings of the Manifestations (the prophets of the great religions).

Bahá'u'lláh repeatedly stressed that only revealed religion can save us from our imperfections. It is because God has sent his Manifestations to show us the path to spiritual development and to touch our hearts with the spirit of God's love that we are able to realize our true potential and make the effort to be united with God. This is the "salvation" that religion brings.

Bahai's do not think of salvation in terms of salvation from the stain of "original sin," nor does it protect us from some external evil force or devil. Rather, it delivers people from the captivity to their own lower nature, a captivity that breeds private despair and threatens social destruction. Salvation means drawing nearer to God and progressing on the path to a deep and satisfying happiness.

The After Life

Bahá'ís believe in an afterlife in which the soul is separated from the body. At death, according to the Bahá'í faith, the soul begins a spiritual journey towards God through many planes of existence.

Progress on this journey towards God is likened to the idea of "heaven." If the soul fails to develop, one remains distant from God. This condition of remoteness from God can in some sense be understood as "hell."

Thus Bahá'ís do not regard heaven and hell as literal places but as different states of being during one's spiritual journey toward or away from God.

Bahá'ís understand the spiritual world to be a timeless and placeless extension of our own universe—and not some physically remote or removed place.

But beyond this, the exact nature of the afterlife remains a mystery. Bahá'u'lláh wrote, "The nature of the soul after death can never be described."

Views of Other Religions

One of the fundamental doctrines of the Bahá'í Faith is the unity of the world's great religions. This does not mean that all religions are the same, but that there is only one true religion and all of the Messengers of God have progressively revealed its nature. The world's great religions are progressive expressions of a single unfolding Divine plan, "the changeless Faith of God, eternal in the past, eternal in the future."

Bahá'ís teach that the founders of the world's major religions, including Krishna, Buddha, Zoroaster, Abraham, Moses, Jesus Christ, and Muhammad, are divine Messengers sent by the one God to educate humanity through teachings and laws suited to its stage of development. The Bahá'í Faith recognizes two additional Teachers for this age: the Báb and Bahá'u'lláh. Bahá'ís believe that religious revelation will continue in the future to provide guidance to "an everadvancing civilization."

Bahá'ís do seek to spread their faith, believing it to be the most recent and beneficial revelation from God to humanity, but they strongly emphasize unity, harmony and respect between the world's existing religions.

Bibliography

A.H. Armstrong, ed., *Classical Mediterranean Spirituality*, World Spirituality 15, New York: Crossroad, 1989.

Abraham J. Heschel, *God in Search of Man: A Philosophy of Judaism* reprint of 1967 edition: Noonday Press, 1997.

Addae-Mensah, M., *Walking in the Power of God: Thrilling Testimonies about Supernatural Encounters with God*, Ontario, Canada: Guardian Books, 2000.

Ali, 'Abdullah Yusuf, *The meaning of the Holy Qur'an*, Amana: Beltsville, Maryland, 1989.

Ali, Ahmed, (trans.) *Islam: The Qur'an*, Princeton University Press, 1988.

Ali, Ahmed, (trans.) *Scared Writings, Islam: The Qur'an*, Princeton University Press, 1988.

Armstrong, Karen, *Muhammad: A Biography of the Prophet*, Victor Gollancz Ltd.: U.K. 1991.

Anderson, H. and E. Foley, *Mighty Stories, Dangerous Rituals*, San Francisco, CA: Jossey-Bass, 1997.

Angelika Malinar, *The Bhagavadgita: Doctrines and Contexts*, Cambridge: Cambridge University Press, 2008.

Annemarie Schimmel, *Mystical Dimensions of Islam*, Chapel Hill: University of North Carolina Press, 1975.

Armstrong, Karen. *Buddha*. New York: Viking Penguin, 2001.

Armstrong, Karen. *Islam: A Short History*. New York: Modern Library, 2000.

Babin, P., *The New Era in Religious Communication*, Minneapolis, MN: Fortress Press, 1991.

Barnstone, Willis (Ed.), *The Other Bible*, HarperSan Francisco, 1984.

Barrett, David V., *The New Believers: Sects, Cults and Alternative Religions*, Cassell & Co: London, 2001.

Blakney, R.B. (trans.), *The Way of Life Lao Tzu: Tao Te Ching: A New Translation*, New American Library: NY, 1955.

Bowker, John (ed.), *The Oxford Dictionary of World Religions*, Oxford University Press: Oxford, 1997.

Bavinck, J. H., *The Church between Temple and Mosque*, Grand Rapids: Eerdmans, 1966.

Bavinck, J. H., *The Impact of Christianity on the Non-Christian World*, Grand Rapids: Eerdmans, 1948.

Bell, C., *Ritual Thinking, Ritual Practice*, New York: Oxford University Press, 1992.

Binyamin Abrahamov, *Divine Love in Islamic Mysticism: The Teachings of al-Ghazali and al-Dabbagh*, New York: Routledge, 2002.

Bruce, S., *Religion in the Modern World: from Cathedrals to Cults*, Oxford: Oxford University Press, 1996.

Buddenbaum, J., *Reporting News about Religion: An Introduction for Journalists*, Ames, IA: Iowa State University Press, 1998.

Burnett, David, *World of the Spirits: A Christian Perspective on traditional and Folk Religions*, London: Monarch, 2000.

Chan, Wing-Tsit, trans. and ed. *A Source Book in Chinese Philosophy*. Princeton: Princeton University Press, 1963.

Chandra, Lokesh, *Iconography of the Thousand Buddhas*, International Academy of Indian Culture: New Delhi, 1996.

Conze, Edward (translator), *Buddhist Scriptures*, Penguin Books:New York, 1959 (1981).

Creel, H.G., *Chinese Thought: from Confucius to Mao Tse-tung*, University of Chicago Press, 1953.

Charles S. Prebish and Damien Keown, *Introducing Buddhism*, World Religion Series, New York: Routledge, 2006.

Daniel Chanan Matt, ed., *Zohar: The Book of Enlightenment*, Classics of Western Spirituality, New York: Paulist Press, 1988.

Dawood, N.J., (translated with revisions) *The Koran*, Penguin Books: NY, 1997.

De Bary, Wm. Theodore (ed.), *Sources of Indian Tradition*, Columbia University Press: NY, 1958.

Denise Cush, Catherine Robinson, and Michael York, eds., *Encyclopedia of Hinduism*, New York: Routledge, 2007.

Dominic Goodall, ed. *Hindu Scriptures with New Translations*, Berkeley: University of California Press, 1996.

Donald S. Lopez, Jr., ed., *Buddhism in Practice*, Princeton Readings in Religions, Princeton: Princeton University Press, 1995.

Donald S. Lopez, Jr., ed., *Religions of China in Practice*, Princeton Readings in Religion, Princeton: Princeton University Press, 1996.

Donald S. Lopez, Jr., ed., *Religions of India in Practice*, Princeton Readings in Religion, Princeton: Princeton University Press, 1995.

Eichhoefer, Gerald W. *Enduring Issues in Philosophy*. San Diego: Greenhaven Press, Inc., 1995.

Ginsburg, F. D., L. Abu-Lughod and B. Larkin (eds), *Media Worlds: Anthropology on New Terrain*, Berkeley, CA: University of California Press, 2002.

Gitlin, T., *The Whole World is Watching*, Berkeley, CA: University of California Press, 1980.

Hiebert, Paul G., *Understanding Folk Religion: A Christian Response to Popular Beliefs and Practices*, Grand Rapids: Baker, 1999.

Hiebert, R. E., Ungurait D. F. and T. W. Bohn, *Mass Media IV: An Introduction to Modern Communication*, New York and London: Longman, 1985.

Hillary Rodrigues, *Introducing Hinduism*, World Religion Series, New York: Routledge, 2006.

Holm, Jean and John Bowker, eds., *Human Nature and Destiny*, London: Printer Publishing, 1994.

Jacob Neusner, Judaism as Philosophy: The Method and Message of the Mishnah, Baltimore: Johns Hopkins, 1999.

James William Coleman, *The New Buddhism: The Western Transformation of an Ancient Tradition* (New York: Oxford University Press, 2001.

Jeffrey L. Rubenstein, ed., *Rabbinic Stories*, Classics of Western Spirituality, New York: Paulist Press, 2002.

John Esposito, Darrell Fasching and Todd Lewis, eds., *World Religions Today*, New York: Oxford University Press, 2001.

John L. Esposito, *The Oxford History of Islam*, New York: Oxford University Press, 2000.

John Renard, *Seven Doors to Islam: Spirituality and the Religious Life of Muslims*, Berkeley: University of California Press, 1996.

Johnston, R., *Reel Spirituality: Theology and Film in Dialogue*, Grand Rapids, MI: Baker Academic, 2000.

Joseph Dan, *Jewish Mysticism*, 4 vol., Northvale, NJ: Jason Aronson, 1998.

Kerrigan, Michael, Alan Lothian, and Piers Vitebsky, *Epics of Early Civilization: Myths of the Ancient Near East*, Duncan Baird Publishers: London, 1998.

Khan, Muhammad Zafrulla, (trans.) *The Qur'an*, Olive Branch Press: NY, 1997.

Krishna Sivaraman, ed., *Hindu Spirituality I: Vedas through Vedanta*, World Spirituality Series 6, New York: Crossroad, 1989.

Kurtz, Lester R., *Gods in the Global Village*, Thousand Oaks, CA: Sage, 2007.

Lyden, John. *Enduring Issues in Religion*. San Diego:

Greenhaven Press, Inc., 1995.

Malise Ruthven, *Islam: A Very Short Introduction*, New York: Oxford University Press, 2000.

Mark Juergensmeyer, *Global Religions: An Introduction*, New York: Oxford University Press, 2003.

McDannell, C., *Material Christianity: Religion and Popular Culture in America*, New Haven, CT: Yale University Press, 1995.

McManners, John (ed.), *The Oxford Illustrated History of Christianity*, Oxford University Press: Oxford, 1990.

Melton, J. Gordon, Martin Baumann, eds. *Religions of the World: A Comprehensive Encyclopedia of Beliefs and Practices.* Vols. 1-4. Santa Barbara: ABC-Clio, 2002.

Michael A. Sells, ed., *Early Islamic Mysticism: Sufi, Quran, Miraj, Poetic and Theological Writings*, Classics of Western Spirituality, New York: Paulist Press, 1996.

Michael Carrithers, *The Buddha: A Very Short Introduction*, New York: Oxford University Press, 2001.

Michael Cook, *The Koran: A Very Short Introduction*, New York: Oxford University Press, 2000.

Michael D. Coogan, ed., *The Illustrated Guide to World Religions*, New York: Oxford University Press, 2003.

Mircea Eliade, ed., *The Encyclopedia of Religion*, 16 vol., New York: Macmillan, 1987.

Ninian Smart, *Dimensions of the Sacred : An Anatomy of the World's Beliefs*, Berkeley: University of California Press, 1996.

Norman Solomon, *Judaism: A Very Short Introduction* (New York: Oxford University Press, 2000.

Nouwen, Henri J.M. *The Road to Daybreak: A Spiritual Journey*. New York: Doubleday, 1988.

O'Flaherty, Wendy Doniger (ed. and trans.), *The Rig Veda: An Anthology*. Penguin Books, NY, 1981.

Paul Williams, *Mahayana Buddhism: The Doctrinal Foundations*, New York: Routledge, 2008.

Peter H. Van Ness, ed., *Spirituality and the Secular Quest,* World Spirituality 22, New York: Crossroad, 1996.

Peter Harvey, *An Introduction to Buddhism,* New York: Cambridge University Press, 1990.

Peter Harvey, *An Introduction to Buddhism: Teachings, History, and Practices,* Cambridge: Cambridge University Press, 1990.

Pritchard, James B. (ed.), *The Harper Concise Atlas of the Bible,* HarperCollins: NY, 1991.

Radhakrishnan, Sarvepalli, and Charles A. Moore (eds.), *A Source Book in Indian Philosophy,* Princeton University Press: Princeton, NJ, 1957.

Renou, Louis, ed. *Hinduism*. New York: George Braziller, 1961.

Richard Valantasis, *Religions of Late Antiquity in Practice,* Princeton: Princeton University Press, 2000.

Rinpoche, Sogyal. *The Tibetan Book of Living and Dying*. New York: Harper Collins, 1993.

Seyyed Nasr Hossein, ed., *Islamic Spirituality I: Foundations,* World Spirituality 19 (New York: Crossroad, 1987.

Shakir, M. H., (trans.) The Holy Qur'an, Tahrike Tarsile Qur'an, Inc: NY, 1997.

Stephen J. Laumakis, *An Introduction to Buddhist Philosophy,* Cambridge: Cambridge University Press, 2008.

Steven Heine and Charles S. Prebish, eds., *Buddhism in the Modern World: Adaptations of an Ancient Tradition,* New York: Oxford University Press, 2003.

Sushil Mittal and Gene Thursby, eds., *The Hindu World,* New York: Routledge, 2004.

Tu Weiming and Mary Evelyn Tucker, eds., *Confucian Spirituality,* World Spirituality 11, New York: Herder & Herder, 2002.

Warms, Richard, James Garber and Jon McGee, eds., *Sacred Realms: Essays in Religion, Belief & Society,* New York: Oxford University Press, 2004.

Wilkins, W.J., *Hindu Mythology: Vedic and Puranic*, Rupa and Co.: Calcutta, 1986.

Wilson, Andrew (ed.) *World Scripture: A Comparative Anthology of Sacred Texts*, Paragon House: New York, 1991.

Weisheipl, James A., O.P. *Nature and Motion in the Middle Ages*. Washington, DC: Catholic University of America Press, 1985

William A. Graham, David Burrell & R.J. McCarthy, eds., *Al-Ghazali's Path to Sufism: His Deliverance from Error (al-Munqidh min al-Dalal) and Five Key Texts*, Louisville: Fons Vitae, 2000.

William C. Chittick, *Ibn Arabi*, Makers of the Muslim World, Oxford: Oneworld, 2005.

William C. Chittick, *Sufism: A Short Introduction*, Oxford: One World, 2000.

William C. Chittick, *The Sufi Path of Love: The Spiritual Teachings of Rumi*, New York: SUNY, 1983.

Wise, Michael, Martin Abegg, Jr., Edward Cook, *The Dead Sea Scrolls: A New Translation*, HarperCollins: NY, 1996.

Wuthnow, R., *Rediscovering the Sacred: Perspectives on Religion in Contemporary Society*, Grand Rapids, MI: Eerdmans, 1992.

Xinzhong Yao, *An Introduction to Confucianism*, Cambridge: Cambridge University Press, 2000.

Zaehner, R.C. (translation), *Hindu Scriptures*, J.M. Dent & Sons: London, 1966.

Index